Charles Chapman Grafton

Selected Writings

CLASSICS OF AMERICAN ANGLICANISM

Charles Chapman Grafton

SELECTED WRITINGS

ANNO DOMINI MMXXII
NASHOTAH HOUSE PRESS

EDITED BY
C.P. Collister

GENERAL EDITOR
B. J. LeTourneau

ISBN 978-0-9792243-9-3

AUTHOR: The Rt. Rev. Charles Graton.
EDITOR: Clinton Collister.
EXTERIOR: The Rev. Ben Jefferies.
INTERIOR: Brandon LeTourneau.

1st Printed Edition 2022.

Nashotah House Press
Nashotah, WI

nashotahhousepress.com

CONTENTS

O GOD, who didst endow thy bishop Charles Chapman Grafton with a burning zeal for souls and didst lead him to restore the chapel of this House: Grant that, following his example, we may ever live for the extension of thy kingdom, that thy glory may be the chief end of our lives; through Jesus Christ our Lord, who liveth and reigneth with thee and the Holy Spirit, one God for ever and ever. Amen.

—COLLECT FOR CHARLES C. GRAFTON
From the Nashotah House Customary

SERIES PREFACE

I WAS elated when I received the call from the Rev. Ben Jefferies asking if I would be interested in editing a series of American Theologians for Nashotah House. The unique voices belonging to the fertile shoots of our own branch of Christ's Church have been regrettably absent among American Anglicans for quite some time. This is unfortunate considering the recent scurrying among academics for Anglican *ressourcement*. Though I must say that I understand. It is unsurprising that throughout the formation of the Anglican Church in North America, the unification of the Continuing bodies, the resurgence of several competent theologians in the Episcopal Church, and the Anglican Realignment taking place in GAFCON, many are now looking to the English architects and expositors of our shared tradition. Even the Presbyterians are translating Hooker and Jewel! I am overjoyed to live in a moment in Church history where both Browne's *Exposition of the Articles of Religion* and Hall's *Dogmatic Theology* are available from more than a single publisher. There is no doubt in my mind that the present age will result in a renaissance of Anglican thinking and — Lord willing — *piety*. Still, there are many illustrious names who have been all too forgotten from these newly minted volumes. Many have read Dr. Pusey, but few Dr. DeKoven. Many are familiar with Forbes, Andrewes, and Laud, but few with Seabury, White, and Inglis. We celebrate the "Apostle to the English" but seldom the "Apostle of the Wilderness." It is quite unfair to our Fathers and Mothers of the *Ecclesia Americana* who have left to us the Church that we all cherish so highly. At best it is mere ignorance on our part, at worst it is ingratitude: "Forgive our disrespect — Forgive our selfishness towards thee, Forgive our great neglect!"[1]

This tragedy aside, however, there is another imperative particular to the student of theology: orthodoxy. Christian Religion — unlike other credos — is a matter of *continuity*; of handing over and joyfully receiving. St. Paul tells us that he has delivered what he himself had received.[2] "Contend," writes St. Jude, "for the faith that was

---

1. Helen Holcombe Denton, *An Apostle of the Wilderness*. This poem was read at the translation of the Rev. Dr. James Lloyd Breck's relics to Nashotah House.

2. 1 Corinthians 11:23

once for all delivered to the saints."[3] Thanks be to God that He has supplied us with the writings of myriads of faithful mothers and fathers to trace out the apostolic deposit handed down in succession to this very day; to our very churches. "One generation shall commend your works to another," O Lord, "and shall declare your mighty acts!"[4] We have much to be thankful for indeed! We say with Bishop Coxe:

> Oh! the duties and privileges which are ours in this ancient communion. In this Church of Bede and Alcuin, of Oswald and of Alfred; of the grand succession of bishops and presbyters who, with faithful laymen, laid the foundation of English and American freedom, and whose lives and characters were reproduced in our Colonial presbyters and laity; in our Washington and Jay, our White and Seabury, in our Hobart and Whittingham, our Ravenscroft and Doane and Atkinson, our Muhlenberg, Breck and Tucker.[5]

But of course it must be asked: how many are serious enough to read these figures? Very few I imagine. How many were ever given the opportunity to begin with? Fewer still. Yet, if we do not take the time to familiarize ourselves with the working of God the Holy Spirit in the lives of our predecessors, we prove ourselves to be liars. Monthly in the singing of the Psalms and thrice weekly in the praying of the Great Litany we declare: "O God, we have heard with our ears, and our forebears have declared to us, the noble works that you did in their days, and in the time before them."[6] Recounting the faithfulness of God in every generation is a Christian obligation. What's more, the righteous Job instructs us, "For inquire, please, of bygone ages, and consider what the fathers have searched out."[7] Have we done so? Perhaps we would not feel so much like a "Church without a theology" if we bothered to read what our forebears so carefully

---

3. Jude 1:3

4. Psalm 145:4

5. The Rt. Rev. A. Cleveland Coxe, *The Catholic Religion and the American People: A Sermon Preached Before the General Convention*, October 2nd, 1895.

6. Psalm 44:1

7. Job 8:8

recorded for *our* sakes.

Now continuity in dogma may be a fascinating exercise for the divinity student, but what about the rest of the faithful who fill our pews? In this regard, I would like to remind us all of our Evangelical duty. As Christians, the Gospel is our chief and most precious endeavor. The heavy responsibility to "stand by the door and wait," in the words of the Rev. Samuel Shoemaker, "for those who seek it"[8] is by no means limited to the clerical class and those who intend to join her ranks. It is the responsibility of every individual who has found safe haven within the Ark of the Church; we listen intently for cries for rescue amidst the confusing sound of the raging waters outside her walls. Therefore, the exhortation of our Most Reverend Father in God and North American *Protoepiscopus* Samuel Seabury applies to each and every one of us:

> As long as there are nations to be instructed in the principles of the gospel, or a church to be formed in any part of the inhabited world, the successors of the apostles are obliged, by the commission they hold, to contribute as far as they can, or may be required of them, to the propagation of these principles [of the Catholic Faith], and the formation of every church, upon the most pure and primitive model.[9]

For us, the Saints are our greatest allies in this work; they have converted us, and they will continue to convert others as well. If we reform our lives after their model, following them "as they follow Christ,"[10] receiving "with meekness the implanted word"[11] as they did, no doubt our lives will accomplish the very same. For instance, we know from history that when St. Anthony the Great set out to live the ascetical life, he first imitated the disciplines of an unnamed hermit from the village over. By following his good example we come to find that St. Anthony lived a life so faithful to the cross of Christ that St. Athanasius felt that he had to tell the world about it. After roughly one hundred years it was his account of *The Life of St.*

---

8. The Rev. Samuel Shoemaker, *I Stand at the Door.*

9. The Rt. Rev. Samuel Seabury, *A Discourse on 2 Timothy 3:16*, May 1777

10. 1 Corinthians 11:1

11. James 1:21

Anthony which cut St. Augustine to the heart and served as the cata-
lyst for his conversion. Fourteen hundred years or so later this work
was translated into English by the devout hands of our own Blessed
Dr. Pusey. Some two hundred years after *that*, St. Augustine's retell-
ing of this event was read in English by myself — a young Jewish
boy — in the back of my senior chemistry class. The *Confessions* had
me leave class red-eyed and embarrassed, but ready to follow this
Jesus who only made sense to me through the words of men who
knew Him a thousand years before I was born. The virtuous life of
an anonymous Egyptian hermit, mediated through the example of
St. Anthony, expressed and lauded by St. Athanasius, which infected
and converted St. Augustine, then translated and promulgated by
the Saintly Dr. Pusey for the English Church, is what Our Lord used
as the ordinary means to bring me to the waters of Baptism. In this
providential chain of events, I am just as indebted to Doctor Pusey
as I am the Doctor of Grace; I owe them both just as much. And my
story is by no means the exception! Blessed Dr. Breck's missionary
zeal and devout churchmanship can be traced to his having atten-
tively read Saintly Bishop William Ingraham Kip's *The Double Witness
of the Church.* How many souls have been saved because this young
man read a small volume during his school vacation! Were it not for
Bishop Kip's faithfulness there would be no Nashotah House. Without Nashotah House, you would not be reading this volume. Truly
the words of the Saints are not trifles; they continue to conquer "by
the blood of the Lamb and by the word of their testimony."[12]

    We all share a prestigious heritage. The Saints of the *Ecclesia
Americana* are jewels which have been handed down from mouth to
mouth and heart to heart. True, they may seem few, but all the more
precious! Now, by God's providence, it is our time to steward the
great deposit that we have received from our forefathers. They have
fought the good fight, they have run the great race, and now repose
in the hope of all those who share in the love of God that is in Christ
Jesus. Yet, we know that the eyes of the heavenly episcopate remain
fixed on us; on *you.* Their prayers continue to mingle with yours.
Even now the "great cloud of witnesses"[13] contend for your faith be-

---

12. Revelation 12:11
13. Hebrews 12:1

fore the "throne of God and of the lamb."[14] With St. Paul they pray: "may the Lord grant him to find mercy from the Lord on that day!"[15] It is in great indebtedness to these our heavenly friends, and with even greater joy and thankfulness to Almighty God, that we bring together the notable voices and insights of those come before us. For the salvation of souls, the strengthening of Holy Mother Kirk, and the glory of our Savior; may we — aided by God's unfailing grace — live up to the measure set by the lives of the Saints. *Amen.*

By all your saints still striving
For all your saints at rest,
Your holy name, O Jesus,
Forevermore be blest!

Brandon J. LeTourneau
Feast of St. Alban the Protomartyr
A.D. MMXXII

---

14. Revelation 22:3

15. 2 Timothy 1:18

Editor's Foreword

A RECENT revival of popular interest in the Church Fathers, Christian Platonism, and the great tradition of Orthodox Christian faith and practice parallels the Catholic revival of the Church of England and the American Episcopal Church in the Nineteenth Century in crucial respects. Increasingly aggressive liberalism and skepticism within and without the Church, in both contexts, left many people dissatisfied with regnant naturalistic ideologies and searching for the way, the truth, and the life. This search led Charles Chapman Grafton to give up a career as an affluent lawyer with bright prospects to serve Jesus Christ and press forward his Kingdom as an apologist, theologian, and bishop.

The leading proponent of the Oxford Movement in the United States, Grafton contributed to Christian letters as an influential historian, preacher, and theologian. Chapters in this book include selections from his classic works, such as the spiritual memoir, *The Journey Godward of a Servant of Jesus Christ*, the introduction to conciliar theology, *Christian and Catholic*, the sermons, "The Second Adam" and "Resurrection Lessons," and the letters, "An American Religious Community" and "To Candidates for Holy Orders." Together, his contributions to Christian spirituality, ascetic theology, sacramental theology, ecclesiology, and the Anglican tradition, — shown to be, at its best, a laudable expression of Catholic Christian Orthodoxy, — demonstrate the fruits of the Oxford Movement and the need for contemporary Christians to learn from one of its most able exponents.

I have chosen these selections from the eight-volume collected works with an eye for the unity of Grafton's life and thought and, I must confess, with hopes that the same stories and theological formulations that have stoked the fire of my own faith will also enliven other flames as we continue the pilgrimage Godward. Grafton's descriptions of the history of Christianity in England, the life of E.B. Pusey, and his own testimony will be of interest to scholars of the Oxford Movement, Anglo-Catholicism, and the American Episcopal Church. His interpretation of God's providence moving in England and America shows Anglicans, Evangelical and Catholic, how to understand their place in the communion of saints, and demonstrates how to honor their fathers and mothers in the faith. As a theologian, Grafton draws on the Scriptures, Fathers, and Scholastics to contend for Anglican Orthodoxy, developing a theology which owes much to Richard Hooker, John Pearson, and E.B. Pusey in its articulation of classical theism, sacramental realism, Chalcedonian Christology, and a conciliar ecclesiology. As Anglo-Catholics receive refugees from the wastelands searching for the narrow path, I trust that Grafton's theology, an Anglicanism which participates in the consensual teaching of the saints and divines, will prove a useful guide.

First of all, I would like to thank the Revd. Ben Jefferies for his work at Nashotah House Press, especially his commissioning of this book. Without his prodding and encouragement, I would still be debating which sermons to include. I am also indebted to Brandon LeTourneau, the series editor, who tracked down citations and added insightful footnotes. Most of all, I am grateful for my wife, Sarah Collister, and her patience and assistance as I edited this book. Her support, even reading *The Journey Godward* aloud as our priest drove us to a conference in Missouri, is matchless, as is her work as my first reader, always righting my wrongs.

Clinton P. Collister.
Feast of St. Bonaventure
A.D. MMXXII

I

CHANGES & CHANCES

For my own part, I felt that everyone needed, especially myself, in religious matters, a teacher, an example, a guide. If I recalled aright the old story, Socrates, meeting one day Alcibiades, on his way to the Temple, put to him, after his manner, many perplexing problems; and when Alcibiades in despair, said to his great teacher: "How then shall we know these things?" The great pagan philosopher replied, "Someone must come and teach us." Has He not, in Christ?

I was bidden by a friend to take up Comte's philosophy. I asked, "What sort of life did he lead?" "Well," was the reply, "he did not live with his wife." I did not think it worth while to try to do one thousand pages of stiff reading, along with my legal studies, and come out like the founder of this school. So my first great principle was to accept Christ as my teacher. When the world can produce somebody wiser or of a deeper spiritual insight, it will be time to reconsider this position. But I took the great Master as my master, and surrendering myself to Him, believed in Him and all He said, because He said it.

The other principle, and what made me a practical churchman, was this: If Christ was the special teacher sent from Heaven, He could not so imperfectly have taught His doctrine as that the larger number of His followers would be led into error.

I once, subsequently in my life, put this in the form of a dilemma to that sweet and lovely character, Professor Peabody. We were conversing on religious matters, and I said: "Here are two facts we must both admit to be facts: God sought to teach the world the religion that there was but one God, through the Hebrew nation. When the people fell into the sin of idolatry like the heathen, God severely punished them. When they came back from their Babylonish captivity, they became free from this sin. The world has been taught through the Jew. Man may give up a belief in God, but the world will not go back to the gods many, of the hills and plains. This great truth has been implanted in the race, that there is only one God, and to worship any other as God is a soul-destroying sin. The other fact is that four-fifths of all Christians have given divine honors to Christ

1

and worshipped Him. How then can Christ be a teacher sent from God, as in some degree Unitarians claim? We cannot suppose that God, having delivered mankind from the sin of idolatry, through revelation to the Jew, should send a teacher who should lead His followers into this sin. If Christ be not a divine person, to pay Him divine honors is idolatrous. Either He is what four-fifths of His disciples claim Him to be, or He is no teacher in whom we can trust as sent with a divine authority. The result and effect of His teaching shows what He intended to teach."

When I put this dilemma to dear Dr. Peabody, he said: "But if you believe all this, you must believe a great deal." "Certainly," I said, "the result of His teaching shows what He meant to teach, and I not only believe in His Deity, but in the Blessed Trinity, the Incarnation, the Real Presence of Christ in the Holy Eucharist."

It was at this time that I experienced a deeper religious conviction. (I had always believed in the Real Presence in the Blessed Sacrament, and I used to walk in from Cambridge and keep my fasting Communion, and what would now be called a rather strict Lent.) I had the question before me what I should do with my life, and I had a battle with myself whether I should give myself to politics or to religion. I was warned by a good Episcopal clergyman that the Church was stereotyped, and that it could not possibly be altered, and was in a deadly low condition. It was difficult to get much literature on the subject. We could not get Church books in Boston of a very decided Church character. I remember importing Dr. Pusey's devotional book, *Paradise of the Christian Soul,* to the curiosity of my English relatives in London, who wondered what a young man wanted with such a book. A few able Roman priests gave me Roman books to read Milner's *End of Religious Controversy,* Wiseman's *Lectures,* Moehler's *Symbolism,* Ives' *Trials of a Mind.* Bishop Southgate helped me to see that the true viewpoint of the Church was from Jerusalem. Jerusalem was the Mother Church. Rome, by its claim to supremacy, had made a rent in Christendom. It was not the source of unity, but the primal cause of schism. I realized also that our chief loyalty was to the one Catholic Church Christ had made, rather than to any one of the divisions the sins of man had made. When, years after, Newman put forth his *Apologia,* it seemed to me that he had never grasped the idea of the Catholic Church, and no wonder he fell away. He had been a low churchman, then a high churchman, and then invented a *via media* of his own, and, finally, tried to cover his secession by a doctrine of development, which many Romans rejected and which equally defended Protestantism.[1]

My studies led me to believe that the low church position in the Church did not do justice to the Prayer Book. For example, in the Baptismal Office it was declared of every child baptized that he was regenerated. The low churchman explained this as merely a hope based on the faith of the sponsor. But in the office for the Private Baptism of Infants, they were declared to be regenerated, and no sponsors were required. If our Lord's Presence in the Eucharist were not effected by the consecration of the elements, why were the Consecrated Elements which remained after the Communion ordered to be so reverently consumed? Why, if Episcopal ordination were not necessary, were we not schismatical in not admitting sectarian ministers to officiate at our altars? I became fully convinced of the validity of our orders and sacraments, and that our Church was indeed a true branch of the Catholic Church. It had also under its English ornaments-rubric a right to the ancient vestments, lights, and altar ritual. I realized the Catholicity of our position and our sacramental gifts, and the sin involved in leaving the Church for Rome. I remember subsequently passing a night in Trinity Church in New York in devotion, and sincerely praying God that I might be taken away during the coming year, even by railroad accident, rather than live on and proclaim, as I felt it my duty to do, the Catholicity of our Church, if it were not true.

There were few, if any, Catholic churchmen. I remember asking Father Prescott, at this time, in the early fifties, whether he supposed there were any other Tractarians than ourselves in America. Bishop Ives had gone over to Rome as had some others in Maryland, and

---

1. Bishop Grafton consistently stresses historical objectivity, emphasizing the continuity of doctrine. Either *dissent* from this continuity of doctrine or *addition* to it by the "development of doctrine," equally disqualifies the claims of both Rome and Radical Protestantism. In a future chapter titled *The Rule of Faith* (*Chapter IX*), he writes: "If it is a fatal objection to the Protestant theory of 'the Bible and Bible only,' that the Bible was not in the hands of the people till the fifteenth century, it is equally a fatal objection to the present Roman rule that its element of the papal infallibility was not certified to the Church till the nineteenth century. Rome, in this respect, is three hundred years more modern than Protestantism."

it looked as if few were left.[2] I believed in the Church and I said: "Though I shall not see her recover her heritage of doctrine and ritual in my day, it is well for a man to give up his life in an endeavor to bring a revival of the Church to pass. It is a greater work to free the Church than it is even to free the slave. For my own poor part, I will throw my hat into the ring and do what I can in the fight."

It was at this time that, under the grace of God, I determined to give myself up wholly to Christ and His service. In the presence of so great a fact as God's becoming Incarnate, I felt there was nothing that I could hold back from Him. I therefore determined to live for Him, and for Him alone; to forgo marriage and family; to consecrate whatever I might have of means or ability to His service; and to live upon such an amount as alone would be necessary to cover the expenses of food, raiment, and shelter. However imperfectly I may have fulfilled my consecration, I have never regretted it.

At that time the anti-slavery question was strongly in evidence, and Mrs. Stowe's book was written. A study of the law problems involved led me, from a legal point of view, to believe that the slave's relation, as established by law as a "thing," was inconsistent with his duty as "a man" to his Creator. I wrote a pamphlet on the subject, which Wendell Phillips, who had taken an interest in me, thought worthy of publishing. I was not originally an Abolitionist, but I became, by the legal study of the slave question, much drawn to Phillips. The nobleness and self-sacrifice of his character much interested me. But I began to feel, and eventually felt, that I could do more good for humanity by going into the Church than into politics. I felt, however, that I could never write a sermon. I knew what speaking from a brief was, but the sermons I heard were full of words I did not understand. I did not feel that I had the literary ability to write them. Then my clergyman, the Rev. Father Prescott, told me that if God intended me to be a third-rate clergyman, rather than a first-class lawyer, my

---

2 The Rt. Rev. Levi Silliman Ives was the Episcopal bishop of North Carolina, consecrated on September 22nd, 1831, by The Most Rev. William White. On December 26th, 1852, he was received into the Roman Communion by Pope Pius IX. He was — according to the 1860 July edition of the *American Quarterly Review* — one of only two Protestant Bishops (the other being The Rt. Rev. Dr. John Gordon, Bishop of Galloway, in 1668) to join the Roman Communion since the Reformation, while fourteen Roman Bishops had left for our Branch of the Catholic Church.

duty was to enter the ministry rather than to seek the other profession. One must seek first to know one's vocation, and then trust God and follow it. It was thus, partly under his influence, that I had the courage to offer myself to Bishop Whittingham,[3] of Maryland, as a candidate for Holy Orders.

Bishop Whittingham received me very kindly, but made a strict examination as to my motives in seeking Holy Orders. He gave me a homily on the poverty which might ensue if I entered the ministry. If I had to starve, I was not to blame him.

I remember an amusing incident at this time. I was a young man in society life in Boston, and though I had never indulged much in the habit of smoking, I took out a cigar and offered it to the Bishop. I never forgot his answer and look. "I can't imagine," he said, "an Apostle smoking." I thought at the time the logic was imperfect, as I could not imagine an Apostle doing many things we are obliged to do now. Nevertheless, the words, and the injunction from that saintly man, settled in my heart, and I soon concluded that it would be better for me as a priest, if I were to do priestly work for God, to give up such a habit.

I was much beset by relatives and friends not to take Holy Orders. They made very large offers of worldly success and emolument and fortune if I would not do so. But I felt that the Church needed lives of sacrifice, and that man could never give more to God than God could give to him.

I remained in Maryland under Bishop Whittingham for about ten years. I began during the slavery times. I remember my first six months were spent in a deserted rectory, where I practically camped out, and had twenty-six dollars for my first six months' stipend. The arrangement of the church, which was not uncommon, was after this fashion: there was a door from the vestry at the east end, through which one passed to the desk from which the service was said and the sermon preached. Below it was the Communion table. The two were surrounded by a semi-circular rail. It was anything but Churchly. I was curate to a very saintly man, Dr. Rich. I had often to walk miles to one of our missions. We did not have overmuch in

---

3. The Rt. Rev. William Rollinson Whittingham was the fourth Episcopal Bishop of Maryland, consecrated September 17th, 1840 by The Most Rev. Alexander Viets Griswold.

the way of food, and we used to warm over what was sent in for our Sunday meals.

I was asked by a clerical friend who had gained the approval of the Bishop, to take up settlement work in a poor district in Baltimore. This, I believe, was the first settlement work ever done in our Church in America. We lived amongst the poor and opened our house to them. We had a chapel, a co-operative store, and various other appliances for city missionary work. I had charge also of a small colored mission. Here I remained with the Bishop's approval, as I was then a Deacon, and I looked up to him as Newman looked up to his Bishop. I never rang his doorbell without saying a prayer, and never left his presence without kneeling down and asking his blessing. He directed my studies and was very kind to me. But he was always on his guard, after the troubles he had been through with some Romanizers, against ritual. We didn't have much, to be sure; but on one occasion I remember his coming to the mission when I had given up my surplice to a visiting clergyman, who, I believe, was afterwards Bishop Doane, and the one I wore was a little short. It came down to about the ankles. The good Bishop called me aside after the service and requested that I would wear longer surplices. I did not state the circumstances, but I told him I would do so. He did not object to our having a black cross at the end of our stoles, but did object to a fringe on them.

There are two incidents in connection with Bishop Whittingham that I remember so well and which will serve, perhaps, to reveal his own holy life. On one occasion I said to him: "Is it proper for one who is a priest to do menial work, as I think in religious orders one must do?" "Dear Grafton," he said, "I've always reserved to myself the duty of blacking my own boots. I want to do some menial work." In reference to the same subject I remember getting into a stage-coach, when we were going to travel some twenty-eight miles over a rough and hilly road, and I said, "Dear Bishop, you have taken the worst seat in the coach." Well, Grafton," replied he, somebody must take it." I constantly learned lessons of denial and self-sacrifice from him.

About this time I was called to the founding of a mission of the Epiphany at Washington under Dr. Pine. This had a great many social and other attractions. I told the Bishop that if he wished me to go there, I would do so. But I shrank as a young man from the dan-

gers or attractions of the social life in Washington, and the difficulty
I felt about establishing the system of free sittings, which I believed
in, and a weekly Eucharist. It was by his permission that I declined
the offer. Subsequently I was called to be an assistant at St. Paul's
Church, Baltimore. Again I went to my Bishop about it. He said to
me: "It is the heart of the diocese; I can't ask you to go to it, but if
you will go, you can save it. I will give you my blessing." So I went.
This church was the mother church of the city, and was under the
charge of the venerable rector, Dr. Wyatt, who had been its rector
for nigh fifty years. His clerical life went back to the early part of
the nineteenth century, and he was intimately conversant with all
its history. He was for a number of years president of the House
of Deputies. He had been a prominent candidate for the Bishopric
of Maryland. One can never forget his gentlemanly and scholarly
bearing. It was his custom in his early days to come to church in
small clothes and silk stockings. He told me it was considered bad
etiquette to go into the pulpit in boots. He wore a silk gown through
the streets. His manner was extremely dignified, and his sermons
were couched in Addisonian English. He wore gloves in the pulpit,
with one finger cut so as to turn the pages over. He felt it unclerical
and undignified to speak extemporaneously. He was most courteous
in his bearing and reverent in his performances. By contact with him
I learned much of the foundation and the history of our Church in
America. I shall always be grateful for the way in which he treated
me for the five years I was with him, as his dear son; and he hoped I
would succeed him. He was a pattern of punctuality in regard to the
Church service. "If," he said, "you are only a minute late and there
are sixty persons on a week day present, you have lost for them an
hour's time."

One day I was complaining as to the treatment he was receiving
from some of his parishioners, and he checked me, saying, "Charles,
God bears with us and we must bear with our people."

He always reserved a large portion of the precious Blood of the
Holy Sacrament, He did this in a most reverent manner. He said
he had reasons for doing this in the prevention of irreverence in its
consumption. He placed it in a large glass receptacle, which was
silver mounted and locked. This was always placed in an ambry, or
small closet, locked, in the wall of the vestry. Of course, as a curate,
I conformed to my rector's custom. I was told that this was a custom

of Dr. Craik, at Louisville, who was a high churchman. But having a question about it, I conferred with a friend of mine, the Rev. Dr. Hawkes, who, I knew, was a canonist and a low churchman; and Dr. Hawkes gave me opinion that the rector was quite right and was following out a received custom of our Church in doing so.

I remained at St. Paul's Church for about five years, and during the prolonged illness of Dr. Wyatt, about one and a half years, had charge of it. It was a never forgotten period of my life. The congregation was trained in the principles of the Prayer Book and the influence of daily prayer, and weekly or more often Communion, and I have never known a holier body of instructed churchmen.

During my stay at St. Paul's I was called to the rectorship of St. Peter's, Philadelphia; made vacant by the election of Dr. Odenheimer to the Bishopric of New Jersey. He was a very warm friend and persistently urged me to accept St. Peter's. The committee offered me what was then a large salary, three thousand dollars, and possible preferment. It was a very attractive offer to a young man. But I felt that God had called me to the work at St. Paul's, and that without very decided reasons I ought not to leave it. The rector was an old man and confined to his bed, and the parish was not in such a good financial condition as formerly. I gave up a considerable portion of my own stipend, in order that the old rector should be comfortable.

This was a most trying political time. I had felt it my duty as a clergyman of the church to read the pastorals which Bishop Whittingham, who was a most decided Unionist, put forth. They were couched in very trenchant language, and with quotations from the homilies on the sin and wickedness of rebellion. During the illness of the rector, when I was forced to read them, I can well remember the way the pew doors were slammed and the people left during their delivery. A number of Confederate Church people loved me for my ministrations, but when a vacancy occurred in the rectorship the people naturally chose a Southerner to succeed Dr. Wyatt.

For some length of time I had felt a drawing towards the religious life. The Roman Church had these orders, and if our priesthood and sacraments were valid, why should they not produce the same fruits? The lives of the saints and of the founders of religious orders grew upon me. I began, wisely or not, a life of more strictness and devotion to our Lord. Dear Dr. Wyatt asked me if I would not like a Communion in the week, and I gained from him the establishment of one at St. Paul's. I began to confer with persons who, I felt, were drawn to a higher and more devotional life. A few began to say that if I would start such an order they would join me. I placed the whole matter before Bishop Whittingham. He was one with me in the desirability of having such a religious order in our Church. We had a number of conferences on the subject. After dear Dr. Wyatt had passed away, I again went to my Bishop. "Am I not free now," I said, "to give myself up to the religious life?" He said: "I would gladly give up all the surroundings here in my house thus to live with God." He felt, as I did, that this alone would be the salvation of our Church. He gave me his blessing and told me he agreed with me that, as I was now free to give myself up to the religious life, the best thing would be for me to go to England to study up the subject.

Before going to England, along with Father Prescott, I determined to keep a retreat. As we expected to deal with the poor, we had partly in view the idea of finding out upon how small a sum it was possible to live. Chiefly, I wanted to keep a few weeks in the way of preparation for the religious life. We found an empty old shack of a building on the southern coast of Fire Island, Long Island, near the lighthouse, which we hired for the purpose. It was in December and quite cold weather. We went over in a small boat from the mainland, taking a mattress and some bedding and some few provisions for food. These were of the simplest kind. We took some meal, molasses, potatoes, ham, and a few other things. We had a good sized room to live in, with a large open fireplace. When it was cold we had to surround it with a wall of matting to keep the warmth in. We cut up our own wood and did our own work. Father Prescott was the cook. We had a rule for our offices, and got up for the night offices at 2 A.M. There was a small spring nearby of fresh water. We spent the morning in study and prayer, and I made the Meditations out of *Manresa*. We translated out of the *Sarum Portiforium* the services for St. Thomas' Day and kept it as a festival.

We were getting along very well when one day a United States cutter anchored opposite our house, and presently a large number of marines and sailors surrounded our dwelling. The commanding officer told us we were suspected of being Confederates, and that he had come to arrest us. It seems our night lamps and our visits to the lighthouse had been noticed and had been reported to Washington, and it was supposed that we were in league with a Confederate boat, which was to land and destroy the lighthouse. Being a Unionist, I was rather glad to see the vigilance of the Government, but Father Prescott, who sympathized with the Confederates, did not take it so kindly. Our trunks and all we had were examined, but as I gave references to Dr. Dix and others in New York, the officer departed, leaving us in possession.

But as it drew near Christmas our connection with the mainland was cut off by the ice, and I feared our water supply would fail us; so we concluded we would, at the end of these weeks, finish our retreat and go home for Christmas. There was no way of getting to the mainland except by walking the whole length of Fire Island, along its sandy beach and stormy shore. But we heard that a number of miles away there was a bridge, by which we could make connection with the mainland. So after packing up our things and leaving them, we started on our walk.

During the early part of the day it was a very grand sight to see the great ocean waves breaking in on the shore, but as nightfall drew on we could see no bridge, and the peril of our situation began to dawn upon us. We knew that if we did not make some shelter we probably would not live through the night, so greatly exhausted by cold and fatigue had we become. So we held a council of war to consider what was to be done. The first thing for us was to say Compline. After doing so, hardly had we taken a few steps when we saw before us an opening in the sand hills, and I proposed going to the other side of this strip of land. No sooner had we turned in thither than we came to a fisherman's hut. It was the only habitation within miles east or west, one way or the other. You may imagine how surprised was the woman who came to the door on seeing us. Her husband, a fisherman and hunter, was away for the day, but she recognized our distress and took us in. I felt anew that it was God's Providence that had saved my life.

The next morning we tried to cross the bay over the ice, but it broke once or twice and we were unable to do so, so there was nothing to do but resume our journey on foot; and this we did. We could not believe that the bridge could be very far distant. But we walked and walked and walked, until the sun began to go down. Now I was indeed in great apprehension. But just as my heart was fainting we espied a little rail of what turned out to be the bridge, half hidden in the show and ice. We wended our way through it, and finally reached the mainland. There, from a neighboring farmhouse, we obtained a wagon and drove a few miles to a country hotel. Oh how good and reviving was that cheerful open fire, and how grateful the look of a comfortable bed to sleep on, instead of the cold sand on which I had expected to lie down.

Father Prescott soon prepared to retire. As he was getting into bed I said: "Father, aren't you going to say Compline with me?" "Oh," he said, with a laugh, " I said my Compline coming over in the wagon." Tired as I was, however, I felt I must say it, if all alone, for this second great act of God's mercy and deliverance. The next morning we got a train and went back to New York in time for Christmas.

In 1865, on my arrival in England, I was received and entertained by Dr. Pusey. He and the late Bishop of Brechin[4] were much impressed with the fact of this American's call to the religious life. He called together, along with the Bishop, a meeting of about ten of the leading Catholics at All Saints', Margaret Street, to consider the matter. The Rev. Upton Richards took much interest in the effort. I had visited Brother Ignatius at Norwich, who had begun a Benedictine Monastery there, but was not drawn to unite with him. I got to know the Rev. S. W. O'Neil, a curate at Wantage, who had been thinking of the religious life, and some others. Among them was the Hon. Chas. Wood, now Lord Halifax. He honestly desired to unite with us. The question of his vocation and duty was submitted to the Bishop of Oxford and one other, who decided that for the good of the Church he ought to remain in the world. How wise this was, how well and nobly he has labored for the Catholic cause, the Church well knows. At this time some one asked O'Neil and myself if we knew the Rev. R. M. Benson. He was a student of Christ Church, Oxford, of high academical degree, of cultured scholarship and marked ability. We were led to go to him and ask if he would lead the enterprise of founding a religious order. He said he would if I would remain with him for some years in England. This hindered my plan of returning to America, but believing it was the providential drawing of God, I threw my lot in with the learned and saintly man. Bishop Wilberforce gave us his sympathy and co-operation.

---

4. The Rt. Rev. Alexander Forbes or Brechin, the first Tractarian Bishop.

II

REMAIN AT YOUR POST

THE Romans were very busy in their proselytizing. Manning was a past master as an ecclesiastical politician. His Life, as given by Purcell, is not so very edifying. He and his confreres were very skillful in insinuating doubts in the minds of devout Anglicans. "You cannot be saved," I know one of them to have said to a devout Anglican, "unless you have the true faith, and you have not true faith unless you believe what you do on the authority of the Church." She seemed to be much distressed in mind. I asked her if she then thought the Martyr Laud, or Bishop Andrewes, or saintly Keble were lost. She laughed, and this broke the spell.

Dr. Manning knew whom he could, by his personality, affect and whom it was best to leave alone. He was observed escorting the Rev. Mother Superior of Clewer, the Hon. Mrs. Monsell,[1] through a Roman institution, and a former Anglican remarked to the Mother: "You and the Archbishop seem to be on very good terms." "Yes," she replied; "it is because he knows I am not a convertible article."

Lady Herbert was also a prominent figure in this work of making proselytes to Rome. She brought her social position to bear upon those in a lower society position than her own. She gained some influence in a branch house of St. Margaret's at Hackney, where I used to visit. The Mother Superior had formerly been a Roman Catholic, and the Chaplain had become Romanized, but by God's grace I was enabled so to put their duty before the sisters that about half of them determined to remain loyal to the Church. Among these was Sister Louisa Mary, who afterwards came to Boston and for many years was the Superior of St. Margaret's there. Another, Mother Kate, established a noble work in the East End. The Bishop of London sent his blessing to the loyal sisters and personally thanked me. Father Mackonochie was asked to be the new chaplain, but he hesitated about taking it without the Bishop of London's assent, as the Blessed Sacrament was reserved in the chapel. It is a

---

1. Mother Harriet Monsell founded the Community of St. John Baptist, an order of Augustinian nuns in the Church of England. She is commemorated the 26th of March.

testimony to the loyalty of Mackonochie, and to the true breadth
and liberality of the Bishop, that Mackonochie submitted his case
to the Bishop, and the Bishop allowed him to accept the chaplaincy.

By God's grace, when in England, I kept many from falling away
to Rome. I got to know the arts by which Roman proselytes sought
to inject doubts into pious souls.

It was my privilege to help some of the clergy, among them Father O'Neil, to be delivered from their attack of Romanism. Father
O'Neil had settled the matter and announced his intention of going
to Rome, and had gone to be with the Jesuit Fathers. I did not feel
equal to meeting him intellectually. He was a Cambridge honor man,
remarkable for his mathematical accuracy and logic. All I could do
was to pray. I spent a whole night in prayer for him.[2] Afterwards he
wrote that he wanted to come here to get some things he had left
behind at Oxford. He came and stayed on for about a week, prob-
ing me, during this time, with all sorts of questions and problems. I
seemed to have made no impression. At last, at the end of the week,
he turned to me and said: What, then, would you advise me to do?"
I said: "Remain at your post where God has put you." He settled the
question then. We went down to the Jesuit House, near Windsor, together, and he took leave of the Father. We then went over to Clewer,
and he saw Father Carter and made his confession. I remember well
that Sunday, for the Gospel told of the resurrection of the young
man from death. O'Neil became a noble missionary and laid down
life for God in India.[3]

---

2. A similar event took place when Bishop Forbes of Brechin contemplated joining the Roman Communion. We are told that Keble and Dr. Pusey kept vigil for
him, after which — through their prayers no doubt — Bishop Forbes remained a
convinced Churchman.

3. Fr. Benson writes regrading Fr. O'Neil's death: "I hope that the grave at Indore
will put forth living branches, but there may be a time of stillness first. If others
carry on the work which we cannot, we must be thankful that God permitted one
of us to start it. I am sure that Fr. O'Neil's death will not be fruitless, whether its
results be found immediately on the spot or elsewhere." (*Letter to Fr. Page, Feast of
St. Michael, 1882.*)

III

CAN THESE DRY BONES LIVE?

I F we may look for hidden and little beginnings, of God's great purposes, we may find one in the connection of our Church with the saintly work of the house at Little Gidding. The holy Nicholas Ferrar was a member of the London Society that set forth the enterprise of the Virginia colonization, and we recognize as one of its objects the establishment of the Church there and the conversion of the Indians.

The Church at this time in England, however, was in a low spiritual condition, and this may be the cause of the subsequent difference in churchmanship between Virginia and New England. The Virginians were conservative and held on to the Church as they had received it. In New England the Church had to maintain itself against the fierce prejudices of the Puritans, and, this forced it to a fuller grasp of Church principles and its life.

After the Revolution a great effort was made to obtain the Episcopate. The colonists up to that time had been under the jurisdiction of the Bishop of London, who never visited them. The clergy, especially those of Connecticut, New Jersey, and New York, desired Bishops as essential to the preservation of the Church. The scheme was violently attacked by sectarians and some in the Church, as likely to bring in the English system of Episcopal rule over the clergy, and tithes imposed upon the laity.

It was, however, contended that the Episcopate was to have no connection with the civil government whatever. The Bishops were not to be appointed, but elected by clergy and laity. The Bishop was to govern along with a council of advice, elected by the Diocesan Convention. The establishment of the American Church has been regarded as the greatest of all reformation. Up to that time, from the days of Constantine, State and Church had been united, sometimes to the detriment of both parties. But now the American Church was to be free, and the responsibility of growth rested on herself.

The Episcopate was at last obtained.[1] First, by Dr. Seabury, from

---

1. In his 1901 *Address to the Annual Convention in the Diocese of Fond du Lac*, Bishop Grafton Writes: "As we study the history of our Church in England, we can but

the Scottish Bishops on the fourteenth of November, 1784, at Aberdeen. It was a wonderfully providential event, as it brought, through Seabury, our Church under the influence of the Scotch Liturgy. The Scotch Liturgy differed from the English, showing signs of a more Eastern origin, and in its recognition of the great Eucharistic Sacrifice.

Seabury, it is said, was willing that changes might be made in the offices of Morning and Evening Prayer, if he might direct those relating to the Eucharist. It was this that gave the American Church the more full and Catholic recognition of the Holy Eucharist as the great Christian Sacrifice. Seabury said that he left it to men of another generation who were to come after him, to restore the losses in the offices. The *Magnificat* and *Nunc Dimittis* had been left out, the *Benedictus* had been abbreviated. The Nicene Creed was practically bracketed, and the recitation of the clause in the Apostles' Creed, "He descended into hell," was made optional.[2] All of these blemishes have now been done away. Seabury's words have become true, and our grand canon in our Communion service will ever be a monument to his wisdom and piety.

Early in the nineteenth century the Church's doctrines were tended by the administration of the great Bishop Hobart, who boldly declared that he was a high churchman. He founded a society for the distribution of the Book of Common Prayer. He was greatly attacked by the existing Bible Society for doing this, but he declared

---

regret the numbers which formed themselves into sects, and went out from her. The evils of which they complained, have in the American Church been done away with. In our American Church government the Bishop is no lordly Prelate appointed by a Prime Minister, but is elected by the Clergy and the people. Her Bishops govern not autocratically but with the advice of counselors chosen by Clergy and Laity. Here the Priests, by virtue of their office, sit in Council along with the Bishop, and the Laity have their own recognized place in Conventions and Vestries. The American Catholic Church thus combines the advantages of the Episcopal, Presbyterian, and Congregational systems."

2. The North American *Protoepiscopus* complained to his clergy in 1786: "How others are depressing the Offices, corrupting the Government, and degrading the Priesthood of Christ's Church —on the one side,— his divinity denied on the other ,—Two of the old Creeds, the guards of the true faith against Arianism and Socinianism, thrown out— The descent of Christ into Hell, the invisible place of departed souls, by which his perfect humanity, and our perfect redemption, of soul, as well as of body, are ascertained, rejected from the Apostles' Creed —Baptism reduced to a mere ceremony, by excluding from it the idea of regeneration..." (*Second Charge*)

that he held that the Bible and the Prayer Book ought to be side by side in every house.[3] His motto was, evidently, that the Church teaches, while the Bible proves.

It is thus interesting to note how the great Church revival of the nineteenth century began quite independently in America. Before Keble had preached his great Assize Sermon in 1833, which is usually given as the date of the beginning of the Tractarian Movement, Seabury, Hobart, and others had laid, here in America, its foundations. But, as is well known, the Church revival met in England with fierce opposition. The low church, or Evangelical, party had lost much of its early fervor, and gained large political influence. The Bishops appointed were mostly from this school. They regarded the *Tracts for the Times* as full of dangerous errors, and violently denounced them. The theological system, which taught that grace was given through the Sacraments, was taken to be in opposition to the received doctrine that man was justified by faith or, simply, trust in Christ's merits. The two ideas, rightly understood, were not really contradictory, but supplementary of each other. Christianity has its objective and its subjective side. While the sacraments are means through which Christ acts and bestows His gifts, faith and repentance are the subjective and necessary conditions for their profitable reception.

The controversy in England and America began to be very fierce. Each party appealed to the Scriptures, the Prayer Book, and the Articles. The contest at first raged about the doctrine of the Apostolic Succession, and the remission of sins in Baptism.

In the American edition of the Prayer Book the doctrine of the Apostolic Succession was clearly stated in its Collect in the Institution office. It declared that God had "promised to be with the Ministers of Apostolic Succession to the end of the world."

The doctrine of baptismal regeneration was also clearly stated, for after every baptism the Minister gives thanks to God that "this per-

---

3. Bishop Hobart writes in 1815: "I comply with this request the more readily, from a wish to call the attention of the Church people generally, to the importance of establishing Bible and Common Prayer Book Societies, and of aiding these institutions by their contributions... Let me recommend the institution of new societies in districts where the number of Clergy and congregations in a vicinity render this practicable; and where this cannot be done, in individual parishes and congregations." (*Pastoral Letter to the Laity of New York*)

son is regenerate." The Articles were shown by the Tractarians, and really by *Tract 90*, to be patient, in their true literal and historical meaning, of a Catholic interpretation.

In Holy Scripture, in the sixth chapter of St. John, fairly interpret-ed, there could be little doubt as to the Real Presence of Christ in the Eucharist; and the new birth from above was ever associated, in Holy Scripture, with the one act of water and the Spirit.

There was connected with these teachings a slight improvement in the arrangement of our churches and some details of our worship. The ordinary arrangement, as is now seen in some survivals of the old church, was to have a high pulpit, beneath it a desk for the cler-gyman, sometimes a lower one for the clerk who made the responses, and beneath this the three-decker arrangement there was a plain table for the Communion. The prayers were said by the minister in a surplice, though this was never adopted in Virginia by some of the clergy. The minister went out at the end of the prayers and changed it for a black academical gown to preach in. Any innovation of this order was visited by riots in England, and the denunciation of the Bishops.

Bishop Eastburn of Massachusetts, an earnest but narrow Cal-vinist, would not go to the Advent because there was a cross on the wall over the altar, flowers were at times placed on the altar, and the prayers were said stall-wise. Good old Dr. Edson of Lowell told me that when he began to say the prayers in that way, Dr. Eastburn being present, the Bishop rose up, came to him, took him by the shoulders, and forced him to turn around with his face to the people. The great Bishop McIlvaine of Ohio forbade any altar with a solid or closed front.[4] It must be, he said, an honest table, with four legs. But a growing knowledge of architecture led to some improvement in the Church's appointments, and chancels took the place of the old three-decker arrangement.

The low church opposition took, next, the form of attack, and the ordination of young Carey, a student at the General Theological Seminary, who held Catholic views, was publicly protested against. Attacks were made on Bishop Onderdonk of New York, and Bishop

---

4. The Rt. Rev. Charles Pettit McIlvaine was bishop of Ohio and twice Chaplain of the United States Senate. He was consecrated October 31st, 1832, by the Most Rev. William White. See his 1846 *Reasons for Refusing to Consecrate a Church having an Altar.*

Doane of New Jersey, which were instigated by the low church party spirit. One proof of this is seen in the fact that in the judgment of the court in Onderdonk's case, the low churchmen voted for condemnation and high churchmen for acquittal.

These contests so full of human bigotry and uncharitableness, greatly checked the growth of the Church. The Church herself, by her internal strife, has been her own greatest enemy.

In 1844 the Convention was stirred up to take action, and endeavor to deal with the Tractarian Movement. But you could as little check its onward career by resolution, as you could, by addressing a series of them to an advancing locomotive, to stop its progress. In spite of the desertion of Newman of England and of Bishop Ives of North Carolina, the work continued to grow. It was of God and could not be stopped. It was a promulgation of the truths in the Prayer Book. It was an assertion of the Church's right to her ancient heritage of worship.

Early in the fifties Bishop Eastburn, urged on by the low element, brought the Rev. Oliver S. Prescott, an assistant at the Advent, to trial. The writer, who was at that time a law student at Harvard, attended the three trials to which he was subjected, and took notes. The Hon. Richard H. Dana, a noted lawyer and staunch churchman, was Father Prescott's counsel. It was proved that Father Prescott had offered to hear confessions privately, and to give absolution. He had also, in a sermon, spoken of the Blessed Virgin Mary as the sinless mother of a sinless Child. The trials lasted some years, the first having failed for want of particularity concerning time and place in the indictment. At length a conclusion was reached. It was evident that the phrase "a sinless mother of a sinless Child" might be differently construed, and did not necessarily involve the doctrine of the Immaculate Conception. But in respect to confession the judgment was different. It was that "though the charge was not proven" as to Father Prescott's having heard confessions privately, nevertheless he must "agree that he would not preach it, and until he so agreed he should be suspended from the ministry."

So far as the Church at large was concerned, the brave stand taken, and the fullness of the Anglican authority cited in favor of sacramental confession were such, that a new impulse was given to the Church's doctrine and principles. The effect on the Church at large was contrary to what low churchmen supposed it would be. Dr.

Whittingham, the great and learned Bishop of Maryland, wrote Father Prescott and invited him into his diocese. He said what a Bishop could do a Bishop could undo, and he released Father Prescott from any obligation to obey the decision of the Court in his diocese.

One of the most significant events in our Church history was the founding of Nashotah House. James Lloyd Breck, with two others, came out from the East to found a mission. They lived in community, they had some rule of life. They had not to avow poverty; poverty was upon them. Their lives were very hard and heroic.[5] They thought nothing of walking ninety miles or more, through the forest, in order to reach a little consecrated church, for their ordination. Of course there were men then, and Bishops who said, "It will come to naught," advised against it, and tried to keep men from joining it. But a work was planted which passing through many vicissitudes, nevertheless has given hundreds of clergy to the Church. It is one of the greatest lessons the Church has had of faith. We would like to dwell upon the noble work done by Bishop Kemper and Philander Chase[6] and others, but we only mention this to show how the great struggle was going on, and though opposed, the Church was slowly responding to the Holy Spirit's guidance.

It was but natural after this that in England, as well as in America, contests arose over the doctrine of the Real Presence. Mr. Bennett said he taught that there was "in the Sacrament an actual presence of the true Body and Blood of our Lord." It was there by virtue of the consecration, and extended to the communicant, and separately from the act of reception. He held that the Communion table was also an altar of sacrifice, and that adoration was due to Christ in the Sacrament, on the ground that under the veil of bread and wine was our Lord. The Privy Council declared this not to be contrary to

---

5. The Rev. Dr. James Lloyd Breck was a missionary priest affectionately known as the "Apostle of the Wilderness" for his valiant efforts to spread the Church's teaching Westward during the early years of the United States. Together with William Adams and John Henry Hobart, Jr., he founded the *Nashotah Mission*, now known as *Nashotah House Theological Seminary*, where his relics were later translated and re-interred. His feast is kept April 2nd.

6. The Rt. Rev. Jackson Kemper, known as "An Apostle of the Western Church," was the first Missionary Bishop of the *Ecclesia Americana*. He was consecrated September 25th, 1835, by the Most Rev. William White. His feast is kept May 24th. The Rt. Rev. Philander Chase was consecrated February 11th, 1819, by the Most Rev. William White, and was likewise a pioneer missionary. His feast is kept September 22nd.

the Church's allowed teaching. Though the Privy Council is not a Church court, nevertheless the decision of these lawyers at this time gave much encouragement to churchmen.

The same doctrine was taught in America. In a note to a famous sermon preached in 1836 by Dr. Samuel F. Jarvis[7] before the Board of Missions, he wrote: "We have no right to banish from our communion those whose notions of the Real Presence of Christ in the Sacrament rise to a mysterious change by which the very elements themselves, though they retain their original properties, are corporally united with or transformed into Christ."

But at this time the Holy Communion was celebrated very rarely; in a number of cases not once a month. A very devout woman, Miss Seton,[8] who subsequently left our Church for Rome and founded an order for Sisters of Charity, went to the rector of Trinity Church, New York, and asked for more frequent Communions. But as she was refused, she turned elsewhere to find that fuller satisfaction of communion with her Lord.

It was in 1844 or 1848 that Dr. Muhlenberg, Dr. Croswell, and others met in New York to consider the question, whether it was possible in the Episcopal Church to have a weekly Eucharist. Not long after, a Sunday celebration began in a few churches, one of which was the Advent in Boston.

Attention was now especially drawn to the doctrine of the Eucharist. Bishop Whittingham had taught me that "one ought to go to the death for the doctrine of the Real Presence."

Later on a great controversy arose between Dr. Craik of Kentucky and Dr. DeKoven.[9] The latter contended that, while in Baptism

---

7. Born in 1786 in Middletown, Connecticut, Samuel Farmar Jarvis was the first historiographer of the Protestant Episcopal Church.

8. Elizabeth Ann Seton founded the Sisters of Charity and the Roman Catholic Parochial School System in the United States. She would later go on to be the first American to be Canonized in the Roman Communion.

9. The Rev. Dr. James DeKoven was a priest and educator at both Nashotah House and Racine College where he is buried. Though labeled a "ritualist" in his day, he famously remarked "I never was in any church in connection with the Protestant Episcopal Church at a time when incense was used." (*Canon on Ritual & The Holy Eucharist*) He was elected Bishop of Illinois in 1875 but was rejected by the standing committee due to misunderstanding of his doctrine of the Holy Communion. This led to his clarifying his position which has become perhaps the most precise — and careful — teachings on the "Real Presence" that our

there were but two parts of the sacrament mentioned, in the Catechism three statements were made respecting the Blessed Sacrament. There was, in the latter, the outward sign of the element, and the inward part or thing, the Body and Blood of Christ, and the grace of the Sacrament, which those received who communicated worthily. He denied the old doctrine of Transubstantiation of pre-Reformation times, which taught the destruction of the elements. He did not hold to the Lutheran Consubstantiation theory, that the two parts were in some way mingled together.[10] The union was caused by the act of consecration and the power of the Holy Ghost, but it was a sacramental union, and a mystery. He asserted the fact of the Real Presence, but would not define the how. It was thought by most that he gained the victory in the controversy. The great transaction is one which takes place, not in a natural order governed by natural laws, but in the spiritual organism which is the Body of Christ. It is the non-recognition of this fact that has led to such unwise controversy.

But to return. The advances, which were being made in the Church, became more and more distasteful to the extreme low churchmen. They saw, however, at last, and admitted, that the high church doctrines had support in the Book of Common Prayer. They said it contained "Roman germs." They admitted that it taught Baptismal Regeneration. One of their leaders explained how he came to this conclusion. He had always held that it was in consequence of the faith of the sponsors, that the hope of regeneration was expressed, but on the occasion of his administering baptism privately, he saw that no sponsors were required, and the Church in her prayers stated the same truth, that the person was regenerate. His theory thus fell to the ground.

Another one, who subsequently became a Bishop in the Reformed Episcopal body, said: "Father Grafton, you are right in holding that the Prayer Book teaches the doctrine of the Real Presence. I don't believe in that doctrine, and therefore I have left the Church."[11]

Church has ever produced. His feast is kept March 22nd.

10. With all due respect to Bishop Grafton, this is by no means the Lutheran view. DeKoven's Eucharistic Theology falls in line with many of the early Protestant Reformers and their expositors who clearly speak of the same "sacramental union."

11. Fortunately the Reformed Episcopal Church (REC) has once more returned to Church principles and has clarified this initial rejection of the "Real Presence"

So the low church party tried to get the Prayer Book changed. The Church in General Convention refused to do this. Presently a number, led by Dr. Cummins, Assistant Bishop of Kentucky, left the Church and began the formation of a new sect.

It is quite clear that the Reformed Episcopalians have no valid Orders. One reason is, they had no intention, when their first Bishop was set apart, to make him a Bishop in the old sense of the word. It was thus different from the case of the consecration of Archbishop Matthew Parker. There all the four Bishops who were consecrators were the official agents of the Church and used her own Ordinal. In that Ordinal the intention of the Church was explicitly stated, that its object was that the ancient orders should be "continued." As the consecrators acted as agents of the Church, they could not, by any private opinions or belief, alter the intention. It was different in the case of Dr. Cummins. He was founding a sect. His own expressed intention was the intention that governed his act. As he proclaimed at the time that he did not believe in the ancient doctrine of the Church concerning episcopacy and priesthood, he did not make a Bishop. It was something like this: Suppose a man should define that by the term "bishop" he meant one who opened the church, made the fires, swept and took care of it; in other words, defined the office and work of a sexton. If he laid his hands on one and prayed that he might be a bishop, since he defined the term "bishop" to be only a sexton, only a sexton would be made.[12] The exodus, thus, of these low churchmen, was in the nature of a demonstration of the Catholicity of the Prayer Book.

As the century went on, a new school of theology arose. It came to be called the Broad Church. The discoveries of science, the new doctrine of evolution, the different methods of historical research

---

in the statement titled *Understanding the Declaration of Principles in the 21st Century*, published in 2018.

12. Once more we may dismiss this declaration of the Saintly Bishop. The Apostolic lines of the REC have been preserved and accepted by the wider Anglican Tradition. Though perhaps imperfect, Bishop Cummins' intention was assuredly to "do that which the Church does," and there is no doubt that this *intention* was one of *continuity*. At the inauguration of the REC, Bishop Cummins stated: "We have not met to destroy, but to restore…We claim an unbroken historical connection, through the Church of England, with the Church of Christ from the earliest Christian era." (*Memoir*, p. 435f.)

led some to seek a reconciliation between the old Church teaching
and the spirit of the age. It was marked also by a growing spirit of
philanthropy and an enthusiasm for humanity. It had, thus, its good
side. But each school of the Church has its weak side. The high
churchman, emphasizing the institutional form of the Church and
the need of authority, tends, if not balanced, gradually towards a
papacy. The low churchman, with his subjective view of religion,
weakens his realization of the objective side in Church and Sacraments. The extreme of the broad or rationalistic school tends to
break with tradition and authority and with the facts stated in the
Creeds. Just as the low church negations were checked, so it has
come about with the rationalizing broad school. The Church's discipline is like the movement of a great glacier, which gradually throws
out from itself substances foreign to it. And so it came to pass that
Bishop Colenso in Africa, MacQueary and Dr. Crapsey in America,
ceased to be teachers in the Church.

The Catholic Movement, which had been largely academic in the
sixties, greatly developed its scope and effectiveness by increased
ceremonial. Then again another series of attacks began. The low
church party raised a large sum of money and formed a society
for the purpose of crushing out Ritualism. It appealed in England,
eventually, to the highest civil court, that of the Privy Council. There
were decisions pro and con and some things were allowed and some
not. But the Privy Council was not regarded as an Ecclesiastical
Court, and rather than obey it priests went to prison. It was the beginning of what began to be called the Victorian persecution. Her
Majesty, it is said, was very much displeased that such a stain as a
religious persecution should be placed on her reign.

In time the convicted priests were released. They had nobly suffered, and taught the English nation a great lesson. The Church
also came to realize better her own spiritual character and her independence of the State. A desire for disestablishment, or at least
for a readjustment of the relations of the two, began to be popular.
Convocation, which had been silenced for one hundred and fifty
years, had resumed its sittings. A Lay House was added to help give
expression to the mind of the laity. In 1867 the first great mission
in London, organized by the Cowley Fathers, was given, and one
hundred and forty-six churches united in the effort, and some sixty
thousand persons were in daily attendance. An heroic missionary

spirit was developed, and mission houses were established in London, India, Africa, and elsewhere. Clergy houses, where priests lived in community life, were established. The clergy began to go to the yearly retreats, and those given by Carter, Randall, and Benson were remarkable for their deep spirituality.

The cathedrals became centers again of missionary effort; St. Paul's especially, under the ministration of Dean Church and Canons Gregory and Liddon. I remember praying, in Dean Milman's days, as I saw the cathedral dome out of my little garret window, that the daily Eucharist might be re-established there, and I used to send penitents down to St. Paul's to pray for this. At last it came.

What is called the Ritualistic Movement made steady progress. In America the ornaments-rubric had been omitted from the Prayer Book, and the result was that it gave freer scope to the development of ritual and ceremonial. However, it met, as every forward step is met, with fierce opposition. The Church was roused by partisan efforts into a fury and panic. The opposition said it meant to crush out Catholicity. If they could not get the Prayer Book altered, they would forbid all acts of worship offered to Christ in the Eucharist. But, as Dr. DeKoven said, you may pass what law you please, you cannot prevent the inward worship of the heart and adoration to our blessed Lord.[13] The canon that was passed proved to be futile. It

---

13. DeKoven writes: "You may take away from us, if you will, every external ceremony; you may take away altars, and super-altars, and lights, and incense, and vestments; you may take away, if you will, the eastward position; you may take away every possible ceremony; and you may command us to celebrate at the altar without any external symbolism whatsoever; you may give us the most barren of all observances, and we will submit to you. If this Church commands us to have no ceremonies, we will obey. But, gentlemen, the very moment any one says we shall not adore our Lord present in the Eucharist, then from a thousand hearts will come the answer, as of those bidden to go into exile, 'Let me die in my own country and be buried by the grave of my father and my mother!' to adore Christ's person in His Sacrament, is the inalienable privilege of every Christian and Catholic heart. How we do it, the way we do it, the ceremonies which we do it, are utterly, utterly indifferent; the thing itself is what we plead for, and I know I should not plead to unkind or unfeeling hearts."

It is important to understand that the saintly Dr. DeKoven is speaking in the vein of Keble, and is not approving of the use of the monstrance or other Roman devotions. In the same place he gives six forms of adoration and does not approve of half of them. He says: "It is quite possible that in Mexico and the States of South America, and possibly in Southern Europe, where the Host is carried

was held, even by those who opposed ritual, to be unconstitutional. The Church's Prayer Book could not be altered, nor the Church's worship regulated, by canon.

As an evidence of the marked way in which God protected the Faith, it was not noticed that the canon itself was fatally defective in respect to the object sought. For while it forbade all acts of worship in any form to be paid to the elements — no one denies that — it did not forbid worship to the *consecrated* elements. A great jurist and ecclesiastical lawyer said that no one could be condemned under such a canon. But at the last revision this canon was repeated. How wonderfully God has protected the Faith of our Church.

We are, of course, opposed by a body of skillful legislators, whose effort is to undermine the whole movement under the specious plea for unity. Our Lord prayed for both unity and union, and the desire of it must be agreeable to His will. But it must be sought in a right way and on right principles, or more harm than good will be done. During the last century the Holy Spirit has been striving with our communion, leading it to the recovery of its Catholic heritage, and the Church has been responding to this leading. The Holy Spirit has also been pleading with the Roman Church, calling it back to primitive doctrine and true Catholicity, and it has rejected the Spirit's guidance and become more papal. Union with Rome is therefore an absolute impossibility. Her term of union is simply submission to monarchical papacy. The Eastern Church asks, not for submission, but whether we are of the same faith, and if so, we are brethren. That which stands in the way is the clause in our Creed which we inherited from Rome, speaking of the procession of the Holy Ghost from the Father "and the Son." For one, I should be willing to have these unauthorized words omitted from the Creed.[14]

---

about the streets — a practice which I believe to be a terrible evil — it is possible that the ignorant may adore the outward elements; but I never heard or knew of anybody in our Church or in the Church of England who held to any such erroneous or false doctrine." Rather, "in the Book of Common Prayer there is but one Rubrical direction of this sort. It is all I want. We are directed to kneel, and I do not want any other posture whatsoever to express my feelings of adoration to Christ." (*The Canon on Ritual & the Holy Eucharist*)

14. The Lambeth Conference of 1978, Resolution 35, "requests that all member Churches of the Anglican Communion should consider omitting the *Filioque* from the Nicene Creed." The 1994 General Convention of the Episcopal

Looking back, what great things hath God wrought! It is said that Newman placed beneath a picture of Oxford hung in his room the words, "Can these dry bones live?" The answer is, *Circumspiceri!* His melancholy and despairing farewell came from a broken heart. His subtle intellect could cleverly defend any theory that, at the time, presented itself to his imagination. Pusey was so different. His dominant principle was submission to the authority of the Church. His great mind was filled with vast stores of learning, and his humility was that of a little child. John Mason Neale was a far better prophet than Newman. What Neale saw in a vision has come to pass:

"Again shall long processions sweep through Lincoln's minster pile:
Again shall banner, cross, and cope gleam thro' the incensed aisle;
& the faithful dead shall claim their part in the Church's thankful prayer,
And the daily sacrifice to God be duly offered there;
And Tierce, and Nones, and Matins, shall have each their holy lay;
And the Angelus at Compline shall sweetly close the day
England of Saints, the peace will dawn but not without the fight;
So, come the contest when it may and God defend the right."[15]

Church resolved to delete the *filioque* from the Nicene Creed in its next edition of the Prayer Book. Likewise, the Anglican Church in North America's (ACNA) *2019 Book of Common Prayer* has placed the clause in brackets in compliance with Lambeth 1978. It ought to be pointed out that the ommission of the clause "and the Son" from the Nicene Creed does not necessarily remove the belief in the double procession of the Holy Spirit from Anglican Theology, it only recognizes that it was not added by ecumenical concensus to the Creed. The ACNA's Prayer Book, for example, states that the *Filioque* may still be used "in worship and for elucidation of doctrine." (*2019 BCP* 769) Yet, both the Episcopal and ACNA catechisms are silent on the double procession. See also the Rev. Dr. Pusey's letter to the Rev. Dr. Liddon titled *On the Clause "AND THE SON"* for a robust and thorough defense of the Anglican use of the *filioque.*

15. The Rev. Dr. John Mason Neale, *The Good Old Times of England.*

IV

ATLAS OF THE HOLY TRINITY

IN HIS INTERIOR NATURE. {
Simplicity in Essence.
Quality of Internal Operations.
Trinity of Persons.

IN THE SIMPLICITY OF HIS ESSENCE GOD ALONE POSSESSES {

Substantial being, by virtue of which He is {

one, uncompounded, pure spirit, existing without parts;

necessary, because without Him the contingent could not exist ;

eternal, because He is that which has always existed, having neither beginning nor ending;

infinite, because nothing can limit Him;

omnipotent, by virtue of which He can execute all He desires ;

omnipresent, because all that is lies in His own thought and is sustained by the presence of His Power.

profound and inexhuastible source { of all truth; of all goodness; of all justice; of all perfection.

Infinite Intelligence which implies {

His omniscience and knowledge of all things { past, present, future, & all protentialities.

infallibility, because He knows all; veracity, because He is the Truth itself;

wisdom, because He never acts from motives unworthy of Himself, or without purpose.

An infinitely perfect will, from which follows {

Holiness, which is essentially identical with His other attributes, and God is Holiness just as He is Love.

Justice, which demands a recognition of His sovereignty, obedience to the moral law and which renders to every one according to his work.

Goodness, that leads Him to seek the good of all His creatures; here by gifts and discipline, and hereafter by a perfected union with Himself.

Love, which He is Himself. He is Love. His love towards His creatures is a Benevolent love, being His own Love directed towards them; a Gratuitous love, being freely given; a Wise and Holy love that punishes to save; an Intimate love that unites man to Itself and gives a participation of its own beatitude. In its relation to fallen humanity, it is mercy and salvation. In its relation to sinners, it is long-suffering and freely offered.

His Beauty, Blessedness, and Joy, as complete and self-satisfying in His own life.

GOD IS ESSENTIALLY { *Infinite Intelligence.*

Perfect Will and Infinite Love.

DUALITY OF INTERNAL OPER- ATIONS.

Two operations are essentially active in God, and God is Himself the first and essential object of their action. They are God s acts of know ing and loving.

Con- cerning the two opera- tions,

the one of the Intelligence whose property is to conceive and produce the Thought;

the other of the Will, whose property is to aspire and unite itself by Love, to the Thought, so conceived and produced.

An infinite intelli- gence.

God is eternally and essentially thinking by an act, pure and always effective.

He is necessarily Himself the essential object of His Eternal Thought.

This Eternal Thought is the faithful, complete, and eternal reproduction of Himself.

By the same, the thought is eternally and essentially living and subsisting in Him.

This Thought, eternally living and subsisting in God, is then the Product, or the Son eternally conceived and begotten. It is the Word, the Wisdom of the Eternal Father. The Wisdom knowing itself to be the Wisdom is possessed of personality.

Hence two primary relations exist in God : Fatherhood and Sonship.

As perfect will & un- bounded love.

By an act pure and simple, and always effective of His Infinite Will, God aspires and unites Himself , forever and essentially by Love, to the Word that He eternally conceives and begets in Himself.

The Word is then the Eternal Object of His aspira- tions and of His love.

On His side, this Word of God, this Eternal Son, being essentially living and subsisting in Him, aspires and unites Himself forever and essentially by love to the Father, who conceives and begets Him and who is Him self the Eternal Object of the aspirations and love of His Son.

The result of this mutual aspiration is mutually essen- tial Love, always living and subsisting in God, of the Father Eternal, for the Son, and of this Eternal Son for the Father, that conceives and begets Him.

Hence it comes that this Love, breathed forth and pro ceeding, is called the Holy Spirit, and knowing Itself to be, is a Person.

There is in this Trinity

The Father or the Source, who is neither made nor created nor begotten; but who beggets ever & eternally His Son like to Himself in all things, save in the act of begetting.

The Son or the Word of the Father, neither made nor created, but eternally and ever being begotten of the Substance of the Father.

The Holy Spirit or the Love of the Father & of the Son neither made nor created nor begotten, but ever proceeding eternally from the Father and through the Son, by way of breath or spiration.

& in this Trinity there is unity, cpnsubstantiality, perfect equality as to essence ; distinction without division or confusion of personality.

TRINITY OF PERSONS

Was imperfectly known before Jesus Christ, being taught in an enigmatical manner in the Old Testament ; positively for mulated & taught by Our Lord Jesus Christ in the formula given for Holy Baptism.

Has always been believed since then as the fundamental mystery of Christian and Catholic faith.

Offers nothing in its annunciation which is contrary to reason, because { the Unity is affirmed of the nature of the Divine Essence; the Trinity of the personality only.

Although relating to the same object, this double affirmation does not treat of it in the same way, & this accounts for there being no contradiction of terms.

Moreover this adorable Mystery

Is nevertheless above the powers of reason, which cannot give completely to itself an account of all these relations. It cannot therefore be comprehended by reason, though it may be apprehended by it.

Can always be explained to a certain point, by the similitudes taken from the triple nature of man, consisting of body, soul, & spirit; of the three faculties of the human soul, the memory, understanding, & will; from the triple oneness of light, & from other operations of nature, where one sees constantly multiplicity summing itself up in unity.

Is in perfect accord with what we know of the nature of God, who cannot be conceived of as without being, intelligence, & will, & whose nature is of such mysterious character that these three, i.e., being, intelligence, & will, may readily be conceived as being eternally distinct centres of self-consciousness, i.e., persons.

Because, if there were not three persons in the Godhead, but only one, God would be condemned thereby to an eternal solitude, & so would be the most miserable of beings. Thus the Unitarian hypothesis is seen to be an irrational one.

Hence, the mystery satisfies the reason of him who apprehends that God must be the most blissful, perfect, & beautiful of beings, & which without this Divine Companionship He could not be.

EXTERNAL OPERATIONS
- *of the Father*
- *of the Son*
- *of the Holy Spirit.*

Creation, what it is

It is the act by which God gives existence to all that which is not Himself and draws not from His Own Substance, but creates from no pre-existing matter, the angels in the heavens, and everything from the grain of sand to man, on the earth.

It is the glorious manifestation of the Divine Power.

Opposing theories

Materialism leaves the structure of the Universe to chance, which is irrational.

Pantheism, or the theory which holds that "All is God," makes God the author of, and responsible for, all evil.

The dual theory: "No God without a universe and no universe without a God," either makes two Gods or confounds God and matter.

OF THE FATHER THE 1ST PERSON

The continuous energy of God in Creation

by which He maintains in the world order { physical and mortal.

assigns to each being
- the ends to which it ought to tend, all means for attaining these ends,
- all that is necessary for { nutrition, preservation, propogation.

concurs "physically" in all the actions and operations of created things and persons.

It is the glorious manifestation of the intelligent and sustain ing energy of God.

Although the act of creation by the doctrine of "appropria" may be "economically" attributed to the Father, yet all the external works of creation are common to the Three Persons of the Blessed Trinity.

The common action of the Godhead in it.

Thus in the Holy Scriptures it is said

that the Blessed Trinity act together, "Let us make man."

the Father shares in the operations of the Son.

of the Son, that all has been made by Him, and with out Him was not anything made that was made.

of the Holy Spirit, that He brooded over the face of the waters and breathed into man the breath of life.

The Son and the Holy Spirit thus participate equally in the cre ative action and in the government of the world.

It is the glorious manifestation of the oneness of the Divine Will.

EXTERNAL OPERATIONS

of the Son, or the 2nd Person.

The Incarnation by which

- the creative activity is consummated in the Incarnation.

- the Word, the Son of God, sent by the Father, by the operation of the Holy Spirit takes of the Blessed Virgin a Body and a Soul, like ours, sin only excepted, and becomes man, uniting together in His one Divine Person { the divine and human natures.

- in order that there should be but one personality uniting the two natures, it was ordained that by birth from a single human parent, a second or human personality should be avoided.

- it is the divine personality which is the bond of union between the two natures.

- Christ s humanity was impersonal, not having a personality before its union with His divinity. God took on Him not the nature of a man but of man.in the Incarnation, nothing of the divine nature, save its glory, was laid aside.

- in consequence of the inseparability of the two natures and the oneness of the person, Christ's acts and words are the acts and words of God.

- The Incarnation is the glorious manifestation of the Divine Wisdom.

He becomes the 2nd Adam

- Being born of one of our race, Christ becomes not one like us, but one of us. As such He is capable of being the Representative of the race, with which and with whose fortunes He identifies Himself.

- By His obedience unto death, in which humanity was involved by sin, He reconciles God and humanity. By His victories over sin, Satan and death, He reverses Man s defeat.

- In consequence He becomes as the second Adam, the head of a new and redeemed race.

- The Incarnation is the glorious manifestation of the Divine Goodness.

of the Holy Spirit or the 3rd Person

The Holy Spirit Cooperates.

- in inspiring the prophets and evangelists who pro claimed Christ;

- in making fruitful the Blessed Virgin in bringing Him into the world;

- in indwelling, without measure, perpetually in Him;

- in consecrating Him to His Mission as the Messiah on the day of His Baptism;

- in descending finally on the Church at Pentecost;

- in preparing the world for the propagation and reception of the Gospel;

- in abiding in the Church, and making the preaching of the Word and the ministration of the Sacraments efficacious.

- The Incarnation is the glorious manifestation of the Divine Love.

V

HEAVEN'S AMBASSADOR

THE revelation of Himself which God primarily makes in nature and man, He has given more fully to the race through philosophers, poets, seers, in all lands and times, unfolding more and more His divine purpose, man's destiny and His Love. Soaring above their fellows like great mountain tops, these chiefs among men first caught the rays of the coming day.

It has been a gradual and progressive revelation adapted to the race's childhood, maturity, needs. God gave to different nations their separate work in the progress of humanity. He overruled their antagonisms and their successions in power. He gave to each a special mission. He made Israel the world's religious lighthouse. He made the Hebrew prophets the organs of the revelation of His Oneness. There were not, as pagans held, gods of the rivers and of the mountains and of the plains. The Olympian deities of man's creation had no existence. "The Lord thy God is one God."[1] This was Israel's message. It was something more. The childish idea of God is a God of power, a God Almighty. In apprehension the quantitative precedes the qualitative. The earlier man-created deities were thus gods of force. They hurled vast mountains together, forged fatal armour, ruled the bellowing clouds, and on bent shoulders upheld the world. But Israel's God was not only the Almighty One. He was the God of Truth and Righteousness. The Indian Law of Karma, the Greek Nemesis, issued from his judgment seat. He punished the guilty. He watched over the oppressed. But He ordered all to ends beyond any individual's rights or needs, for He was for all and over all. He was the God for all time and of all people. The mark of limitation, showing its transitory character, rested on all pagan worship. It was so bound up with certain nationalities that it could never have a universal application. But the revelation of Israel not only declared the Oneness of Gold but foretold its own development. It enshrined the great prophecy of a Teacher to whom all nations would come. A light was to break forth as the sun from the clouds and illumine the world. With man's advancing preparation, the daylight gradual-

---

1. Deuteronomy 6:4

ly increased, and at last that fuller light came in the person of Jesus Christ.

Before, however, considering Him we must recognise the fact that religion, being an element of our nature, presents itself in several forms besides that of Christianity.

We can but pause here to remark how its revelation of God, man's destiny, and the aids it brings, denotes its superiority. It has elevated and enriched mankind more than any other religion. It has been an invigorating force in man's progressive elevation. Under its benign influence slavery has been abolished, the horrors of war have been mitigated, woman has risen in position and dignified companionship. Multiform philanthropies have extended their alleviating blessings into every byway of human misery. It has enriched man's intellect and been the mother of art. It has left an ennobling impress on the character of every Christian nation in Europe. It has tended to the unity of the human family, and made man more considerate of the rights of his brother man. In its principles are to be found the only solution for the destructive contests between labour and capital. Christ was not, as some modern socialists have declared, a failure. He was not a mere ideal philanthropist preaching an impractical religion. He set in motion an agency for the benefit of mankind which has achieved a permanent success, and is extending itself with a self-productive energy. He has revealed and made possible an elevation of man in a final union with God beyond aught that any other religion has conceived. Christianity offers an end to man, beyond that of any scheme of human progress, an end worthy of God and most ennobling to man.

It presents us with the noblest conception of God, as not only an Almighty and Omnipresent Being, but as Wisdom, Goodness, Love, Beauty itself. It represents Him not as a merely ever-existing Ancient of Days, but as Eternal Youth. It condemns Him not to the misery of an eternal solitude, but reveals Him as having, in the self-consciousness of each of His necessary eternal activities, of Being, Knowing, Loving, a triple personality, so that He has ever an adequate object and return to His own Infinite Love. It solves best the purpose of creation by the revelation of its destined progress to the evolution of a new heaven and earth from which all evil and sin shall be forever banished. It explains best the permission of temptation with its consequent evils in this preparatory stage, as necessary to the development of the character of a nature endowed with free will. It offers the highest conceivable end to man in the attainment of such a further union with God, as, without destroying his personality, will secure him in permanent righteousness and consequently everlasting bliss. It comes to him with a free offer of pardon for all his errors and sins, a blotting out of the guilty past, an elevation and transformation of his nature, fitting it for eternal glory. It sets all this before him, in and through union with Christ.

And so we come to a question it behooves us to seriously consider. It was a question once put to the great Master Himself. "What think ye of Christ?"[2] If you think at all favourably about Christianity, what do you think of its Founder? Nothing is more certain than that Jesus Christ lived in Palestine and was publicly put to death there by the Roman governor. It is as certain as the life and death of any recorded in history, as that of Socrates or Julian Cæsar or Abraham Lincoln. "Not to be interested in the life of Jesus Christ is to be," said Liddon, "I do not say irreligious, but unintelligent. It is to be insensible to the nature and claim of the most powerful force that has ever moulded the thought and swayed the destinies of civilized man."[3] Listening, at Saint Helena, to the bells that called to church attendance on Sunday, Napoleon said he recognized in Christ a power greater than he or any of the world's conquerors possessed. A modern French orator, speaking of the motive forces of late centuries, how liberty had been the watchword of the eighteenth century and progress that of the nineteenth, exclaimed, "But, gentlemen, Jesus Christ is Progress." By the acclaim which all nations have accorded Him, He stands as a religious teacher, matchless and supreme. If we accept this in any fair degree, we may well ask ourselves, what has given Him this pre-eminence, and what are His credentials for it?

The first characteristic concerning Him, and that differentiates Him from all other of the world's renowned religious teachers, is that He came as the fulfillment of prophecy. In this He is unique. Modern critical research may show us how the Bible grew into its present shape. It may show us how many were its writers or redactors. How, as it intimates, in its composition they used ancient myths and legends. How they made selections from various sources. How

---

2. Matthew 22:42

3. The Rev. H.P. Liddon, *Some Elements of Religion*, Lecture VI §1

they rewrote history. The Bible ends in a revelation of the wonderful mystery of grace and glory, just as it begins with an inspired allegory which sets forth the mystery of Creation. But all the way through there is from the beginning to the end of the Old Testament the promise of a Messiah who shall enlighten and redeem Mankind.

In the light of that wonderful revelation wherein we first learn of man's relation to His Maker and the dire results of separating himself from God, we read also of man's promised Deliverer. One would come who should "bruise the serpent's head."[4] God put man outside of the garden where he had access to the Tree of Life, to teach him that sin separates from God. Separation indeed from God's power man cannot accomplish, for that were to annihilate himself; and annihilation would be an act of omnipotence equal to creation itself. Man can, however, separate himself from the Grace of God, and to do this is to bring upon himself spiritual death. Of this God lovingly forewarned him. "In the day thou eatest thereof thou shalt surely die."[5] Given the possibility, to pass after trial into a state of secured sinlessness and so bliss, man lost the special grace by which alone that supernatural end could be secured. This grace being a super-added gift to his nature, when forfeited, man could not regain the prize he had lost. A supernatural end cannot be attained by natural effort. The flaming Cherubim of Righteousness and Justice stood guard over the sacred way. But a Deliverer came for man and as man, could retrieve man's defeat, and for human nature, win its re-entrance into paradise and its renewed union with God.

"O loving wisdom of our God!
    When all was sin and shame
A second Adam to the fight
    And to the rescue came.
O Wisest love! That flesh and blood
    Which did in Adam fail
Should strive afresh against the foe,
    Should strive and should prevail."[6]

The promise that a Deliverer should come is next narrowed by

---

4. Genesis 3:15

5. Genesis 2:17

6. John Henry Newman, *O Loving Wisdom of Our God.*

promise that he shall be of a particular race. He shall be of the seed of Abraham. "In thy seed shall all the nations of the earth be blessed."[7] This Saint Peter quoted on the day of Pentecost as applicable to Christ, whom Saint Matthew tells us was descended from Abraham. The same promise was renewed to Jacob, who by like authority is recorded as the ancestor of Christ. Subsequently it was further narrowed to a tribe. He was to come of the tribe of Judah. Then as God in guarded wisdom revealed His purpose, a special family was designated. The Messiah was to be a rod out of the stem of Jesse. The Lord also declared to David that He would "establish his throne for ever;"[8] and this promise the Angel Gabriel quoted to the Blessed Virgin concerning her offspring, saying, "The Lord God shall give unto Him the Throne of His father David: and of His Kingdom there shall be no end."[9]

His threefold offices also were prophetically set forth; slowly God drew the portrait of the coming One. He was to be a prophet like unto Moses, the great leader of Israel out of bondage: "The Lord thy God will raise up unto thee a prophet like unto me, unto whom ye shall hearken."[10] Of this special prophet, unlike all others and for whom the nation looked, the Pharisees made inquiry of John Baptist, "Was he that prophet?"[11] To this promise Saint Peter and Saint Stephen both appealed, and claimed that Jesus was that prophet that should come into the world. He was no mere teacher revealing truths, but a mighty leader like unto Moses. So He came to the Jewish sheepfold and led His people out from Judaism into the broader Christian pastures and from the brighter day.

It was also prophesied that the Great Deliverer should wear the vestment and character of a priest. He should be a high priest forever after the order of Melchizedek. The order of Melchizedek was a priesthood unlike that of Aaron, in that it had an assigned supernatural descent. The person of Melchizedek appears as a mysterious figure upon the stage of history. He was as if a supernatural being without father, without mother. The writer of Genesis omits, per-

---

7. Genesis 12:3

8. 2 Samuel 7:16, Psalm 89:29

9. Luke 1:32

10. Deuteronomy 18:15, Acts 3:22

11. John 1:21

haps by ignorance or forgetfulness, his genealogy. It is an interesting
and instructive instance of how God makes use even of the ignorance and imperfection of His creatures to declare His message. He
was to come not only after the order of Aaron and offer a bloody
sacrifice, but like Melchizedek to bring forth an offering of Bread
and Wine. In the upper chamber Christ fulfilled this type. On the
Cross and at the Institution we recognise Christ as our High Priest.

He was also to be a King. The Jewish heart beat wild with delight
as they dwelt on this element of the promised Deliverer. He was to
occupy the throne of His father David, and of His kingdom there
was to be no end. The Kingdom he founded was indeed unlike the
worldly one they expected; nevertheless it was a Kingdom. It was
so heralded, and the gospel He preached was "the gospel of the
Kingdom."[12] Asked by Pilate if He was a King, He declared He was,
Thou sayest it — *that* I am — a King.

He was to be certified to the world by a special herald. A special
messenger, a second Elijah, was to precede Him. "I will send my
messenger and he shall prepare the way before me." "I will send
you Elijah the prophet before the day of the Lord."[13] Speaking of
John Baptist, Christ said this is Elias which was for to come. Moreover, the place was designated where he was to be born. He was to
be born in Bethlehem of Judea. To this the priests and scribes bear
witness, quoting the prophecy, "and thou, Bethlehem,"[14] etc. He was
to come, so Isaiah foretold, preaching good tidings, healing the broken-hearted, bringing deliverance to captives, recovering of sight to
the blind. This He claimed to have done, and to it every account
of His life bears witness. His manner and His method were pre-an-
nounced and so also was His rejection. The incidents of the final
tragedy are by different prophets most minutely foretold. We could
gather its history from the prophets alone. They give a connected
story from His entry into Jerusalem, "Behold my King cometh unto
thee,"[15] to the "My God, my God, why hast thou forsaken me?"[16] He
will be betrayed by a friend and for thirty pieces of silver, and aban-

---

12. Mark 1:14-15, Matthew 4:23, 9:25, 24:14

13. Malachi 3:1, 4:5

14. Micah 5:2

15. Zechariah 9:9, Matthew 21:5

16. Psalm 22:1, Matthew 27:45–50

doned by His disciples. "Smite the shepherd and the sheep shall be scattered."[17] He is to be treated as a criminal, "numbered with the transgressors,"[18] and He is to be despised and rejected of men. False witnesses are to rise up against Him and He is to be oppressed and afflicted, yet opens not His mouth. He will be grievously insulted and scourged. He will not hide His face from shame and spitting, and He will give His back to the smiters. He shall be put to a most cruel death of crucifixion. "They pierced my hands and my feet,"[19] and "They shall look on Him whom they have pierced."[20] The scene on Calvary is minutely described. "They part my garments among them and cast lots upon my vesture."[21] "They shall stand jeering upon me." "They gave me gall to eat, and when I was thirsty they gave me vinegar to drink."[22] These and other details are given by the prophets. Daniel declares that the expected "Monarch shall be cast off."[23] Isaiah sees Him as One who was wounded for our transgressions. "He was bruised for our iniquities. He was oppressed and afflicted. He was cast off out of the land of the living, and He made His grave with the wicked and with the rich in His death."[24]

Nor by these alone, but by a series of connected types, and by the whole Jewish ceremonial law, its worship and sacrifices, was the coming Deliverer and His offices and work proclaimed. We may not accept the application of all these many and sometimes mystical references to Christ, but a Mind other than the writer's evidently moved them, age after age, to depict with increasing particularity the Person of Christ, His advent, character, life, and death. The critical spirit of our day in its rigid demand for proof rejects the spiritual exegetical methods of the fathers. But enough and more than enough remains, in a broad view of Jewish history, to justify the contention, that Israel looked forward to a great Deliverer. He was to be anointed from on high, and God's purpose to bless mankind

---

17. Zechariah 13:7, Matthew 26:31

18. Isaiah 53:12, Mark 15:28

19. Psalm 22:16

20. Zechariah 12, John 19:37

21. Psalm 22:18, Matthew 27:35, John 19:24

22. Psalm 69:21,

23. See Daniel 9

24. Isaiah 53:5–10

through Israel was to find its fulfillment through Him. Any reasonable view of the life of our Lord so conforms to these multiform predictions to show that Christ was He.

And not alone did Hebrew prophets proclaim His advent, but aided by that divine light that lighteth every man that cometh into the world, heathen poets and philosophers saw, in their better moments of inspiration and through their tears over the falling fortunes of mankind, the coming of One who should restore its lost nobility and usher in a brighter day. So through the haze of hopes and fears Plato and Virgil and others, kindling with aspirations for humanity's betterment, discerned a shadowy outline of a heaven-sent Ideal and to the pagan world foretold of Christ. Ancient prophecy thus becomes focused on Him. As has been well said, "Prophecy takes off its crown and lays it at the feet of One who is to be."[25] Thus Christ stands out on the luminous background of prophecy, peerless and supreme, among the world's religious teachers. He alone comes authenticated by the cumulative evidence of a series of converging lines of prophecy. It is then a fair and reasonable conclusion, believing that there is a God, that Christ is a Teacher sent by Him. Not merely like those not so authenticated, but with the transcendent authority of One, specially certificated to be the Prophet and Light of the world.

---

25. Possibly quoted from Bishop Gore's collection of essays *Lux Mundi*, Chapter IV: *Preparation in History for Christ*, written by Bishop Talbot.

VI

THE GREAT CREDENTIAL

THE Divinity of Christ may be proved by argument, but He can only be known by submission and prayer. When the soul accepts Him for its Master and Guide, it is willing to believe what He says because He says it, and to do what He wills because He wills it.

Now Our Lord gave one great credential of Himself. Men asked Him to give them a sign for the authority He claimed to possess. "Destroy this temple," and He spake of the temple of His Body, "and in three days I will raise it up."[1] Likewise on several occasions He foretold His resurrection to His disciples. "The Son of Man shall be betrayed into the hands of men. And they shall kill Him, and the third day He shall be raised again."[2] It is clear that He speaks not in a metaphorical sense of His resurrection. For just as He foretold that His crucifixion was to be a literal one, so, His words imply, was to be His resurrection. If one was literal so was the other. He reiterated this promise again and again. He pledged Himself to it. Believing in Christ we rest securely on His Word. We know He rose from the dead, because He said He would. This is enough for a Christian. There is no higher authority or more secure proof.

We may ask, however, what corroborative evidence is there that He did so rise?

We will not pause to argue with those who believe that no evidence can be sufficient, because the resurrection involves the violation of the natural order. Any idea of law which makes a miracle impossible is inconsistent with an intelligent belief in the existence of God. A miracle is only an unusual manifestation of power, but it does not necessarily involve an infraction of law. If man can work marvels, which are miracles to the unlearned, by combinations of nature's laws, more so can the Almighty, who knows them intimately and thoroughly as His own thoughts. God does not contradict Himself when He works a miracle, but uses modes unknown to us. The so-called laws of nature are but as a keyboard upon which the Almighty Hand doth play.

---

1. John 2:19
2. Matthew 16:23, 17:23, Mark 9:31, 10:34
40

The first corroborative proof that Christ kept His word is to be found in a fact of which we all are cognizant. For the Master did not leave the evidence of Himself, as many seem to think, to the risk of manuscripts, liable as they are to destruction and interpolation. He established a much more sure and certain witness. Men were not forced to rely on manuscripts, but were to have a living witness of His resurrection. Christianity extends throughout the world. However separated, it is solidly in accord in one matter. Throughout the world on the first day of the week all Christians assemble to worship. They have done so from the beginning. "Upon the first day of the week the disciples came together to break bread."[3] And now everywhere on the first day we hear the church bells calling men to worship. How are we to account for this fact? Christianity rose out of Judaism. The Jew with the strictest observance sacredly guarded the seventh day of the week. God Himself had bidden him so to keep it, and its obligation had the awful sanction of Sinai. The Christian Church began keeping another day which in time superseded the Jewish Sabbath. What right had it so to do? Something as tremendous as the proclamation of the law on Sinai could alone be its warrant. We know the reason. On the third day Christ rose from the dead. Christians kept, therefore, the first day of the week and called it "the Lord's Day."[4] It stands as a witness of the resurrection. It declares that such was the universal belief from the beginning, and that it was on the third day Christ rose.

In examining the proofs of the resurrection, we find it gains credibility from the attacks unbelievers and hostile critics have made upon it. It has been said, for instance, that Christ did not really die. He swooned and became numb, and in that condition was placed in the tomb. The coolness of the stony chamber stayed the hemorrhage, the aromatic odor of the spices with which He was embalmed restored animation. Somehow, the manner not explained, He got out of the tomb after some days, and rejoined the disciples. The disciples deceived themselves into calling it a resurrection, and He Who was the Truth itself let them cultivate this delusion. Then He, to help on the fraud, went away and hid Himself in some obscure place where, unattended and uncared for by His former devoted friends, He died.

---

3. Acts 20:7

4. Revelation 1:10

Now it has a bearing on His resurrection that by the ordering of Divine Providence our Lord met His death in a most public manner. It was also a matter of great concern to a large number of persons that He should be put to death. These persons were of the highest rank in the Church and State. His death was a great public event upon which the attention of the nation was concentrated. It was at the time of the great feast, when Jerusalem was crowded, and the many thousand pilgrims were encamped on her hills. He was tried before the High Priest and the Ecclesiastical tribunal and examined by Herod and Pilate. He was condemned, publicly executed, and the Roman centurion made an official report of His death. To make His death doubly sure, His side was pierced and the spear-thrust touched the heart. The water and the blood flowed out. If He had been in a swoon, the piercing would have extinguished life, while the outflowing water, modern science tells us, indicated that life was already extinct. There is no question, then, but that Christ died on the cross. As to the theory of His recovering, Strauss contemptuously shattered it. "Would," he said, "a man half dead, dragging himself from the mortuary cell, so weak as to require medical treatment and an infinity of care, who finally, in spite of all, succumbs to his sufferings, would he have produced on the Apostles the impression that He was the Prince of Life, the Vanquisher of the Tomb?"[5]

Another criticism which has been made from the time of Celsus asks why did not Christ show Himself to Pilate, Herod, and the chief priests? This objection is also a helpful one, for its answer will reveal the character and purpose of the resurrection. But first let us say there was no more obligation on our Lord's part to appear to them than to doubters of any succeeding age or to us. But there were moral considerations why Christ should not appear to His enemies. There is no reason to believe that our Lord's appearance would have done them any good. They were prepared to reject every kind of proof. Their state of mind is shown by their words. "That deceiver said while He was yet alive, after three days I will rise again."[6] They were prepared for Him. Had our Lord appeared they would have either denied His identity, or said, as they had before, it was the work of Beelzebub. They would have again seized upon Him

---

5. David Strauss, *A New Life of Jesus for the German People.*

6. Matthew 27:63

and endeavored to subject Him to further indignity. It was better for them that Christ should not appear before them. It gave to any in whom was aught of good a chance of restoration by an act of faith. But in respect of ourselves, so far as evidence is concerned, their testimony would have been of little value. They were not competent witnesses to His identity. They had seen Him but little. They did not know, as the Apostles did, His look, movement, gait, manner, voice. It required previous and intimate acquaintance with these in order to identify the Risen Lord with the Christ of Calvary. But these are not the real reasons why Christ showed not Himself to Pilate and the high priests.

The reason was He had finished His work with the world. With Him creation advances into a new stage of development. He is the new Fact and the Beginner of the new elevation in the evolutionary process. His public life was divided into three periods, viz.: His prophetical life, His priestly and suffering life, and his risen and royal life. When He had attained to the latter, He could no more go back into those that preceded it than the world having attained one geological period could return to a former period. His prophetical ministry to the world was closed and He could not return to it.

Moreover, it is well to remember that Christ's resurrection was not a return to His former life. By His own will He had separated His soul from His body. "I have power," He said, "to lay down My life and power to take it again."[7] It was not by the crucifixion that His natural life was taken, but the soul was separated from His body by His own will. Yet though separated from each other, neither was separated from His Divinity. For, as we have seen, He was Divine. His body and soul hung on His Divinity as the sword and sheath to the warrior's belt. As the drawing of the sword from its scabbard separates neither from the soldier, so the human soul and body of Christ when separated from each other were not separated from His Divine Person. His body is in the tomb, but it cannot see corruption. It was dead only in the sense that the soul was separated from it, but was not dead as our bodies are said to be dead. For it was living with an indestructible life in that it was united to the Divine Nature. When that soul returned and re-entered the body, then it rose. He did not, as in the cases of Jairus' daughter or of Lazarus, come back

---

7. John 10:18

to the old conditions of life. He had passed through death and, so to speak, come out on the other side. So in the days of His resurrection He gathers about Him those only who were His, and to His disciples only He appears.

Let us turn to other corroborative confirmation of Christ's words. It has been so ordered that the resurrection of Christ should be evidenced both by His enemies and His friends.

Let us consider first the proofs offered by the former.

They are five in number. First, if Christ did not rise from the dead, His enemies were bound to prove He did not by producing the body. All the accounts agree in this, that Christ's Body having been taken down from the cross was laid in a new tomb which had been hewn out in the rock and "wherein was never man yet laid."[8] The Jews went to Pilate, saying, "Sir, we remember that that deceiver said, After three days I will rise again. Command, therefore, that the sepulcher be made sure until the third day." "Pilate said, ye have a watch: go your way, make it as sure as ye can. So they went, and made the sepulcher sure, sealing the stone, and setting a watch."[9] Now it is admitted that shortly after the Apostles in Jerusalem preached publicly that Christ had risen. His body had been taken charge of by the Jews. They were responsible for it. They were therefore bound to produce it, or give some reasonable explanation of its disappearance.

The explanation given furnishes us with another proof. The story told of the disciples coming by night while the soldiers slept and taking the body is on the face of it a lie. It is incredible that the Roman guard would all have been asleep; and if so, how could they have known who were the perpetrators of the deed. This lie is effective evidence of the truth of the account it seeks to disparage.

Again, the act assigned to the Apostles is without any adequate motive. Why should they wish to disturb the tomb? Either they believed Christ would rise and in that case they would do nothing, or they were in a state of doubt, and still less would they take any action; or they had lost all hope in Christ as the Messiah, then surely they would not have risked their lives for a man or a cause in which they had lost all faith. Terrified, heart-broken, crushed, an effort to recover the body is the last thing that would have entered their minds.

---

8. John 19:41

9. Matthew 27:63–66

One of the latest efforts at explanation is to say that the Jews took away the body themselves. This theory clears the Apostles but is open to an easy refutation. Within a few weeks of the resurrection the Apostles were arraigned before Annas, the high priest, and Caiaphas and John and Alexander, and the rulers and elders and scribes, for curing the impotent man, and they boldly proclaimed that it was by the power of Jesus Christ whom God raised from the dead. It is inconceivable if the Jews themselves had the body of Christ secreted in some place, that they should not, by producing it, have crushed and annihilated the hated Christian sect.

We offer as another proof the fact that Christ's enemies admitted the truth of the resurrection. When the Apostles were brought before them they did not dispute their story. If the tomb was still sealed they would have pointed it out. If they had removed the body they would have produced it. They did not venture on what they knew was a lie, and accuse the Apostles of having taken it. All they did was to forbid the Apostles to speak in the name of Jesus. Their inability to meet the testimony of the Apostles is an admission of its truth.

But finally, many of Christ's enemies changed their minds and believed. Upon the preaching of the resurrection of Christ by S. Peter about three thousand converts were made; shortly after, we read, "Many of them which heard the Word believed; and the number of men was about five thousand."[10] We learn also that "a great company of the priests were obedient to the faith."[11] There was thus a very large number, eight thousand or more, who believed the Apostles' witness. Undoubtedly, living in Jerusalem they made for themselves every investigation. The tomb would be visited by every tentative believer. Every person connected with the event would be obliged to tell his story again and again to untired listeners. The intelligent and critical inquirers would be sure to examine and cross-examine every detail. It is said that the critical faculty was not so developed as in our day. This is true "if we apply it to certain departments of literary evidence, like the authorship of a book or the value of a local tradition."[12] But there is no truth in it as applied to a public

---

10. Acts 4:4

11. Acts 6:7

12. The Rev. H.P. Liddon, *Easter in St. Paul's: Sermons bearing chiefly on the resurrection of our Lord*, Sermon X

fact, like that of the resurrection. The common-sense methods of finding out whether a fact of this kind is true are unvarying, and were possessed equally as well by the Jews of that day as by ourselves. Starting out as unbelievers, this large jury of eight thousand persons became convinced. The evidence must have been irrefutable to have converted so many.

One thing, moreover, is sure, that had the Apostles merely related their Galilean experience, they would not have made their converts in Jerusalem. If they had merely declared that after the third day, when, as they alleged, Christ rose, they had gone away into Galilee and there He had been seen by them, their story could have received little credence. If, it would be said, He rose on the third day, why did He not appear to some one or some persons on that day? Why, if He rose here, out of a tomb in Jerusalem, did He not appear here in Jerusalem? Why wait for days and then appear in distant Galilee where we cannot go and examine the conditions of His apparition? If He desired that we here in Jerusalem should believe, by all these reasons He was bound to appear here. It is foolish to suppose that the report of S. Peter's sermons are a whole account of what was said and done by the Eleven. It was because the Apostles, dealing with individuals, could appeal to all the facts relating to His entombment, the empty tomb, the failure of the Jewish rulers to produce the body, and could give their own witness to His appearances at Jerusalem, that they carried conviction. Thus Christ's enemies by their conversion testify to the truth of His resurrection.

Let us now turn to the other side of the case. Here the evidence divides itself into two sections. What can be known apart from the narratives in the four Gospels, and what is assured us by them?

In the first category we are struck first with the remarkable change of conduct found in the Apostles after the alleged resurrection.

The death of Christ had confounded the Apostles and crushed their hopes. All through the bright days of His ministry, when the sick had crowded about Him for healing and the common people had heard Him gladly, they had looked eagerly forward to the restoration of the Kingdom. The glories which had filled the visions of the prophets were upon the eve of their accomplishment. With what buoyant expectation had they awaited the glorious triumph. Suddenly all was at an end. A most dire calamity had taken place. Christ had succumbed to His enemies. He had been unable to extricate

Himself. No intervention had taken place from heaven. The Father
with whom He had associated Himself had not come to His assistance. Like a miserable criminal He had been nailed to the cross of
shame, and He was dead. They would never see Him again or hear
His voice. He was completely vanquished, and there was an end of
all their hopes. They were shocked, completely cowed, and in a state
of physical as well as moral collapse. They are found either wandering away or huddled together in a room, with locked doors, in fear.

In what vivid contrast is their appearance after the resurrection.
They are not in hiding, they are publicly in the Temple, and elsewhere, preaching Christ Risen. They are standing before the great
Ecclesiastical Court, and do not hesitate to tell Annas and Caiaphas
and all the assembled dignitaries that they had crucified the Christ.
They declared that He was risen from the dead. No threats, no punishments can make them cease their testimony. No one of them falters from his great truth-proclaiming mission. They go everywhere,
throughout the world proclaiming it. They manifest the sincerity
of their own belief by laying down their lives for its truth. We ask,
What wrought this change? Whence had they the sustaining energy of their conviction? The only satisfactory answer is to be found
in the fact of the resurrection. No interior reminiscence, no shadowy or imaginary vision could have kept them united. Nothing but
hard facts could have enabled them to bear necessarily oft-recurring
questioning and mental strain. It was because Christ had risen that
they, resting on that adamantine fact, became transformed from
desponding cowards, to transcendent heroes and martyrs. Another corroboration may be found in those two sacraments which are
called by us on account of their universal application, "Sacraments
of the Gospel." Christ, as we have said, left not His revelation to be
evidenced by manuscripts alone. Christianity came into the world
as an institution. This institution is a living organism, in which the
Holy Spirit dwells and through which He acts and speaks. This organism has from the first declared that on the third day Christ rose
from the dead. It does this to-day, not only by her creeds, but by her
sacraments.

Go into what Christian Church you will, and infants and adults
are all baptized by the same formula, viz.: "In the Name of the Father, and of the Son, and of the Holy Ghost." Now, at the beginning
of each dispensation we find God's character and nature revealed

by a new Name. This is the mark upon the Patriarchal and Mosaic developments. The Christian is, in like manner, marked by the new and wonderful revelation of the Name of the Triune God. It lies at the basis of the Christian dispensation, and upholds it. But where and when was this great revelation made by Christ? Not during His life, anterior to the resurrection. There is nothing said about it in His public teaching. It was made after His resurrection, consequently the resurrection was not a myth nor an apparition alone, but a reality. Every baptism is a continuous witness that Christ rose from the dead. For it teaches, moreover, that Christians are buried with Christ and risen in Him. This, it is obvious, would be an unmeaning metaphor or symbolism, if Christ rose not from the dead.

The Holy Eucharist bears the same witness to the resurrection. It commemorates, as we all know, the death of Christ. But why should the Church do it, if Christ rose not from the dead? Why celebrate the tragedy in which Christ closed His life, which, if He rose not according to His promise, was only a tragic failure? If He rose not, the words and action of the Eucharist are a meaningless sham and a horrible falsification. For in that Holy Service are necessarily said the words, "This is My Body which is given for you," and "This Cup is the new covenant in My Blood." The words give the lie to the theory that our Lord did not resume His body and does not now wear it. For if His body saw corruption and disappeared, then the words, "The bread which we break is it not a participation of the Body of Christ,"[13] would not be true. For there would be no body in existence, spiritually or otherwise, of which we could be partakers. There could be no communion of body and blood that had ceased to exist. The Holy Eucharist thus bears witness to the death and resurrection of Christ. The two witnesses stand before the Temple doors, and proclaim that Christ has risen. Again, apart from the Gospels, we have an independent witness in S. Paul. His testimony is recorded in the fifteenth chapter of the first epistle to the Corinthians. This epistle, written about A. D. 57, is accepted by all critics as authentic. There he writes, "I delivered unto you first of all, that which I also received, how that Christ died for our sins according to the scriptures; and that He was buried, and that He rose again the third day according to the scriptures; and that He was seen of

---

13. 1 Corinthians 10:16

Cephas, then of the twelve: after that, He was seen of above five hundred brethren at once; of whom the greater part remain unto this present, but some are fallen asleep. After that, He was seen of James; then of all the Apostles. And last of all He was seen of me also, as of one born out of due time."[14] S. Paul had, so we learn from himself, received his information directly from S. Peter and S. James, whom he had visited in Jerusalem; we have thus the record of their testimony apart from the Gospel narrative. S. Paul adds also his own. He knew the difference between an internal spiritual revelation, a vision, and an external bodily appearance of Christ. The Lord had appeared to him bodily in the Damascus roadway, and the glory of His ascended body, like as when S. John beheld it, had blinded him. It has been asked, why does not S. Paul say aught concerning the visit of the holy women and the walk to Emmaus. His omission does not show he did not know them. He omits them because he is not giving an account of the resurrection, but is telling the Corinthians what as Christians they were bound to believe. He therefore states the fact of the resurrection and cites the authority of S. Peter and the Apostles as being by Christ authorized witnesses to it. It was on their authority and witness that the resurrection on the third day had become an article in the Creed, which existed before the Gospels were written. S. Paul adds his own testimony, and cites the fact of which he most well assured himself, that five hundred persons could testify to the resurrection.

Let us now examine the Gospel narrative.

Each evangelist gives an account, and with such differences as show there was no prearrangement. These differences, then, are a proof of their credibility. Moreover, under the guidance of the Holy Spirit, they were intended to set forth different aspects of Christ. One emphasizes His kingship, another His priesthood; one dwells on His humanity, another on His divinity. These different characteristics run through each Gospel from the beginning to the end. They consequently differ in their account of the resurrection. S. Matthew, who depicts in his Gospel Christ as the king and His kingdom, makes the chief event in the resurrection the assembly at Galilee and the royal mandate of Jesus: "All power is given unto me in heaven and on earth. Go ye therefore and make disciples of all nations, baptiz-

---

14. 1 Corinthians 15:3–8

ing them in the name of the Father, and of the Son, and of the Holy
Ghost, and lo, I am with you alway, even unto the end of the world."[15]
S. Luke, who brings out the priesthood of Christ, has nothing to say
of Galilee, but dwells upon the recovery and appearance to S. Peter,
and the wandering disciples, and the making Himself known in the
breaking of bread, and the command that repentance and remission
of sins should be preached to all nations; and ends with lifting up
His hands and blessing them; and their continually abiding in the
temple. S. John, the evangelist of the Incarnation, and who especially sets forth the divinity of Christ, gives the apparition of our Lord
both at Jerusalem and in Galilee. He dwells upon the divine side of
His resurrection, on the evidence of the empty tomb and the grave
clothes, which first flashed belief into his soul, on the interview with
Mary Magdalene, wherein our Lord revealed His gracious humanity, and the divine sanctity of His nature. "Touch me not; for I am not
yet ascended to my Father."[16] "I ascend," not unto our Father, but to
"my Father and your Father and to my God and your God." S. John
alone records the mysterious gift of peace and the solemn breathing
on the Apostles, their wonderful empowering, "Receive ye the Holy
Ghost Whose soever sins ye remit, they are remitted unto them; and
whose soever sins ye retain, they are retained."[17] It is in this Gospel
of the divinity that we have recorded the confession of St. Thomas,
"My Lord and my God."[18] This closes the manifestation in Jerusalem. In Galilee we have the last miraculous draft of fishes. S. John,
true to the spirit of his evangel, is the only one who records this, the
only miracle wrought in the days of the resurrection. It is the only
miracle, save the greater one of mercy, by which, on his threefold
protestation, Christ restores Peter to his apostleship and the Gospel closes with the promise of the Divine Lord that He will come
again. S. Mark is the delineator of Christ as the prophet and Son
of Man. His Gospel is shorter than the others, but is fuller of detail
and human incident. It is questioned by critics where the original
of S. Mark's Gospel closes. If it ends at the sixteenth chapter, ninth
verse, we have the empty tomb, an angel announcing to the women

---

15. Matthew 28:18–20

16. John 20:17

17. John 20:23

18. John 20:28

the resurrection. If it ends later, there is a brief confirmation of the Emmaus incident, and a description of our Lord appearing to the eleven as they sat at meat, quite characteristic of S. Mark, and with the command to go into all the world and preach.

We thus see why the evangelists do not give the same identical accounts of the resurrection. One dwells, like S. Matthew, on the Galilean manifestation, with its kingly command; one, like S. Luke, on that at Jerusalem, with its remission of sins and benediction. S. Mark brings out the human side; S. John, the divine. We may not be able to harmonize all the details. We are not bound "to demand identical accounts from historians who were unequally informed, who had no intention of recounting everything, and who, moved to write by different motives, distributed the events in different order."[19] The accounts given, however, do not, necessarily, contradict each other. The differences fit in with, and are consistent with, the characteristics of the separate Gospel. The Gospel narratives thus are credible and bear witness to the resurrection of Christ.

Let us now look at some details. All the evangelists tell us of the visit of the band of women to the tomb. They came bringing the spices they had prepared. They find the stone rolled away and the tomb empty. They seem to have met at some appointed rendezvous. They set off together, when we may suppose that either Mary Magdalene goes ahead as an advance guard, for they were in much fear, to see that the way was clear, or that the others lingered for some one of the party to join them, or went back for something which may have been forgotten. This accounts for the Magdalene arriving alone and first at the tomb. Finding it empty she immediately goes by some other way to find Peter and John, who were probably staying together. Meanwhile, the other women arrive and are addressed by an angel, who tells them Christ is risen. They depart with fear and great joy. And as they went to tell His disciples, behold Jesus met them, saying, "All hail. And they came, and held Him by the feet, and worshipped Him."[20]

Meanwhile, Peter and John arrive and examine the condition of the tomb and depart. Then Mary Magdalene, who has followed, sees the two angels sitting, the one at the head and the other at the

---

19. Vincent Rose, OP, *Studies on the Gospels*, VIII § 3

20. Matthew 28:9

feet, where the body of Jesus had lain. They address her, "Woman, why weepest thou?" Her memorable reply need not be repeated. The question and answer show it was not in a vision. As she was not expecting the resurrection, there was no suggestive motive which would predispose her to imagine one. With loving slowness so as not to overpower or suddenly shock her, Jesus discloses Himself. During all the resurrection time we discern Christ's majestic calmness and dignity coupled with personal consideration and tenderness. It is the same Christ who delivered the Sermon on the Mount, testified before Pontius Pilate, stooped with loving-kindness to the fallen, who calls His faithless disciples by the endearing name of "children," and who consoles Mary. "Jesus saith unto her, Woman, why weepest thou? whom seekest thou?"[21] And she, supposing the speaker to have been the gardener, saith, "Sir, if thou have borne Him hence, tell me where thou hast laid Him and I will take Him away. Jesus saith unto her, Mary. She turned herself, and saith unto Him, Rabboni; which is to say, Master. And she came and told the disciples she had seen the Lord."[22]

Not less interesting and confirmatory is the visit of the two Apostles to the sepulcher. They run both together. Naturally S. John, who gives us the account, being the younger, outruns Peter and comes first to the tomb. With his meditative, contemplative manner he stoops down and looks, then pauses, but does not go in. S. Peter, following, with his eager, impulsive nature, enters at once, gazes about and retires. "Then went in also that other disciple which came first to the sepulcher and he saw and believed."[23] The interesting question that arises here is, what did he see that made him believe? The answer is to be found in the Eastern manner in which the body was wrapped and bandaged for interment. A hundred pounds of spices had been used and the body then tightly wound in linen, made fast by long strips which were wound under and over the body and crossed behind and before. The head was treated after the anointing in the same way and the headgear resembled a sort of covering or helmet. Now what was it S. John saw? He saw the linen clothes. This might suggest to him the fact that the body had not been surrepti-

21. John 20:15
22. John 20:15—16
23. John 20:8

tiously removed. Had the Jews, or had any one, taken the body they would have removed it just as it was. The myrrh would have caused the linen clothes to adhere closely to the body, and it would be a long as well as useless task to remove them. The body could not, therefore, have been stolen. But this would not account for the conviction that flashed into S. John's mind that Christ was risen. What he observed was that the grave clothes in which the body had been wrapped were not, as is given in the authorized version, "Laid by themselves," but, as in the Revised Version, simply "lying." Lying, as we read in S. Luke, lying alone, i. e., lying empty. The clothes had caved in and were lying down flat. The napkin which had been upon His head was rolled up in a place by itself. It had been bound and bandaged about the head, and had retained its helmet-like form. It was not rolled up like a ball, but held the twisted shape it had received and now stood by itself in the place where the head had been. It is not unlikely, as it retained some marks of the countenance of our Lord, that this was the origin of the ancient legend of S. Veronica. When S. John saw this arrangement of the grave clothes there was only one deduction to be drawn. No body could have been taken out of those clothes, with the bandages lying as they were, nor could any one have got out of them without disturbing them. When Christ rose, He passed through them, even as He did through the tomb, and as His body subsequently came through the closed doors. So John saw and believed.

It is but fair to state the last opposing theory of German criticism. It is that there are two accounts or two sets of appearances, one at Jerusalem and the other in Galilee. The latter is found in S. Matthew and S. Mark. They say nothing about the Jerusalem manifestations, if the last nine verses of Mark are omitted. S. Luke and S. John give the Judean appearances, and say nothing of Galilee, if we may omit the last chapter of John. Now these two accounts present great difficulties in the way of harmonizing them. We must therefore give up one or the other. The Galilean one is the simpler and more methodical, is in S. Mark and should therefore be adopted. In confirmation of this theory we have the testimony of S. Paul who does not mention the Jerusalem incidents. He says Christ rose on the third day, and that He appeared to Peter. But that is not saying He appeared to Peter on the third day. The disciples had fled terrified to Galilee.

There Peter imagined he saw Christ. The spirit of seeing visions became contagious, so the Apostles thought they saw Him. They came back to Jerusalem, kept quiet, settled down, and gradually belief in the resurrection grew.

We have, however, seen why the Gospel narratives are not identical. It is therefore difficult to harmonize them. Our Lord most fittingly, however, appears both in Judea and in Galilee. S. Paul gives not a full account of the resurrection but adduces the authorized proof of it. He learned from S. Peter himself the fact of our Lord's appearance to him. S. Luke, who wrote under S. Paul's oversight, is the only one who records the fact, and it takes place not in Galilee but in Jerusalem. The Apostles told their story publicly and at once, and were arrested for it. The eight thousand at Jerusalem would never have been converted by such a Galilean tale. The questions concerning the body, where it was if Christ had not risen, would remain unanswered. This theory does not hold well together. It leaves the credibility of the Gospel narrative unshaken.

Let us, then, draw our conclusion. It is of record that S. Peter preached at Pentecost that Christ had risen, and so it is clear that the story was not a myth. For myths grow, but this account did not. It was stated from the beginning.

The Apostles declared they had seen the Lord. It was not then a spectral illusion, could not have been a ghost For they knew the voice, touched the body, put their hands into His side, they walked with Him, they ate with Him. He said, "Handle me, and see; for a spirit hath not flesh and bones, as ye see me have."[24]

As it was not a ghost, neither was it a reminiscence which took delusive shape in their minds. They would have soon got tired of announcing as a fact what in sober moments they would know was but a mental illusion. It could not have been a reminiscence for the further reason that Christ went on with His teaching. He opened their minds to the understanding of the scriptures. He revealed the new name of God, which they knew not before. He gave them the royal power of administering absolution. He established the sacrament of Holy Baptism.

He rose from the dead and was with the Apostles off and on during forty days. Rising in triumph over death, it was but natural, as the

---

24. See Luke 24:39

benefit was for all the world, He should appear in Judea and in Galilee of the Gentiles.

The Apostles saw Him in the house, by the lake, in the evening, at daybreak, at all times, and listened to His instruction and received His gifts which were embodied in institutions.

Then He led them out to Bethany, and according to His promise that He would ascend into heaven, openly, in broad daylight, He ascended till the cloud received Him out of their sight. Not only did He promise it, but one whole Book of the New Testament, which might be called the Gospel of the Ascension, bears witness to it. Thus He the divinely sent and commissioned Teacher, whose words and life prove His divinity, rose from the dead and ascended to the Right Hand of Power.

What a light this Great Credential throws upon His whole life. He was, as St. John declares, the Word Incarnate. God had wrapped round His divine nature our humanity, that through it He might set forth the Divine Life.

We need not be staggered by the consideration that this planet is a small one. God loves little things. He loves to hide Himself. He comes to the little nation. He is born in the little town. So He comes to the small planet. Yet as He comes into the world for all men, He comes into creation for the benefit of the whole of it. The universe is a unit and God enters it that He might unite all things in Heaven and earth in Himself.

He has thus given us proof of His divine nature by His resurrection. No wonder that one who had so supernatural an exit from this world should have an equally supernatural entrance. As our first parents could not have been derived from a preceding pair, but must have been singly produced, so when Creation advances to a new stage, the new Head and Type is produced in like unique manner. Christ Himself bore testimony to His own pre-existence. Blessed S. Joseph declares he is not His earthly father. The sanctity of the ever Blessed Virgin bears witness to the testimony S. Luke has recorded. God the Word became Flesh.

What wonder, then, that when He was born all creation was present at His birth to honour it. The stars, created it may be for the very purpose, shone at His birth. One especially formed or angel-borne guided the Magi from their Eastern home. The angel hosts and chorus from off the great rood screen of the skies, jeweled and lit with its many thousand lamps, chanted the glad gospel of peace and of good-will to man. All nations were represented by Jew and Gentile; the shepherds and the kings came to do Him homage. The high and low, the rich and poor, man and woman, surround His cradle throne. There, too, are the kneeling or waiting cattle, and the sheep of the flock, and the produce of the earth, the straw of the manger, and the mineral gifts of the kings. When the Lord of creation entered it, most fittingly all creation was representatively present. Most naturally, too, when He entered on His work, all creation acknowledged Him as its Lord. The winds and waves obey His command. He controls the law of gravitation by a greater law, and walks on the sea. He is Master of the law of the extension of matter, and multiplies the loaves. The fishes obey His behests and gather in crowds into the net. The fig tree withers away at His condemnation. The Roman soldiers go back and fall to the ground at His simple word. Sickness and disease flee before Him who is the life itself. The blind regain their sight, the lame walk, the lepers are healed, death gives up its prey and the dead are raised.

did not frustrate the scheme of God. It is wrong to speak as if He devised a scheme as a remedy for the consequences of the fall. Christ was before all things, and by Him all things consist. In Him He created man, and His incarnation, though it came later than the fall, was really in God's purpose before it."[3]

Christ came to unite creation to God by a new tie, by uniting man to God in Himself, and, since man was alienated from God by sin and his nature marred, to reconcile him to God and restore his nature. It was by the Cross this work was to be effected. A late French critic maintains that Christ did not expect to die. He considered Himself safe at the Passover feast, because the rulers would not dare then to arrest Him. He intended at its close to go immediately into Galilee where He could meet His disciples. Judas, learning of this project, forced the hand of the high priests to arrest Christ during the feast or else He would escape them. This precipitated the tragedy. But Christ had not intended to die, and it was the peculiar genius of S. Paul, filled with his Jewish ideas of sacrifice, that originated the idea of a redemption through Christ's death.

But this theory breaks down before two facts. The prophets had foretold the suffering death of the Messiah. They had pictured almost every incident of it and had assigned to it a redemptive value. "He was wounded for our transgressions, He was bruised for our iniquities: the chastisement of our peace was upon Him; and with His stripes we are healed. All we like sheep have gone astray; and the Lord hath laid on Him the iniquity of us all."[4] The other fact is that Christ foretold His crucifixion long before it occurred. "If I be lifted up, I will draw all men unto me."[5] He taught the disciples that the Son of Man would be "delivered into the hands of men, and they shall kill Him."[6] He earnestly desired it. He said, "I have a baptism to be baptized with and how am I straitened till it is accomplished."[7] He asked S. John and S. James, who sought to sit on His right hand and left, whether they could be baptized with the baptism He was baptized with? He clearly declared to them the redemptive charac-

---

3. Frederick Denison Maurice, *Life* I, 375-576

4. Isaiah 53:5–6

5. John 12:32

6. Mark 9:31

7. Luke 12:50

ter of His death. The Son of Man came "to minister and to give His life a ransom for many."[8] No question can be raised here concerning the word Christ uses. He came to be a "ransom."

So likewise at the institution of the Last Supper, He said, "Take ye, this is my body." "This is my blood of the new covenant which is poured out for many." We cite from S. Mark's Gospel where we have the shortest form of the institution.[9] But it is sufficient for our purpose and the others agree with it. Our Lord is contrasting His blood with the blood of the victims under the old covenant. He implies thereby that He also is a victim and His blood is shed in sacrifice. As the blood of the old sacrifice, sprinkled upon the people, established them in a covenanted relation with God, so His blood would be shed for the benefit of many. As S. Matthew records it, "This is my blood of the new covenant which is shed for many for the remission of sins."[10] Christ came therefore to die, not as a martyr, or to give an inspiring example of stoic endurance, or to deliver us mortals from the fear of death, but "to give Himself a ransom," "being made sin," i. e., the sin-victim, for us, that we might have "redemption through His blood, even the forgiveness of sins."[11]

Without attempting, what is beyond us, an exhaustive theological analysis of Christ's ransom work on Calvary, yet we may be helped to a practical consideration of this mystery, by noticing the threefold effects of sin which were by the cross removed.

First, sin separates man from God. Secondly, man becomes the servant of him whom he obeys. Thirdly, by sin man mars his own nature. It was to rectify these three evils that Christ endured the cross.

I

The whole work of man's redemption has its source in the love of the ever Blessed Trinity. It was a conception of Milton, erroneous as audacious, that imagined a divergence between the Father and the Son. God the Father, God the Son, God the Holy Ghost loved the creature He had made and came to rescue him from his evil and turn the evil into good.

---

8. Matthew 20:28, Mark 10:45

9. See Mark 14:12–26

10. Matthew 26:28

11. Ephesians 1:7

Another truth helps us. God deals with us as individuals, but also in our collective capacity. He deals with us as families, as nations, and as a race. There is great love and wisdom in God's doing this. As a race, we are possessed of a common human nature. In this we are unlike the angels. They are created by God's fiat, in all their beauty, one by one. God created human nature differently. He created a nature and gave to it a law by which it extends itself. All individuals share in that human nature and are members of it. It accounts for that sympathy which like a hidden force binds humanity together. Now this nature abused its glorious prerogative, and, becoming disobedient, separated itself from the grace of God.

How was it to be restored to God's favor? Did God's anger need to be appeased? God, we venture to think, needed nothing done to make Him love His child. He had made him. He knew the temptations to which he would be exposed. He knew whereof we were made, He remembered we were but dust. His child's misery only called into exercise the love of His mercy. Sin or lawlessness is repellent to His nature. But He loved His child, perhaps like some earthly father, all the more for the wrong he did to himself by his fall.

But if God loved His creature, did not His justice or righteousness require that some penalty should be undergone on the part of man, or his representative, before a reconciliation should take place? This has been pressed in modern times by some, to the extent of a mercantile theory. According to it, for every transgression, satisfaction must be made by a determined amount of pain. We need not say we do not hold this theory. But in one sense (there may be others), we can see why the justice and righteousness of God demanded that a reparation should be made. God, with an infinite love, loved His child, grieved over his childlike folly and sins and falls and wickedness. In spite of all his errors God's great heart loved him beyond what earthly love can compass or express. But while His child remained in a rebellious attitude, God could not for His child's sake, or in justice to Himself, treat him as He otherwise would. The rebellion of the child hindered the free action of God's love to him. For sin had created a barrier between man and God. It was this barrier Christ did away. Having taken upon Himself our human nature, He became its representative. And acting for the race, He became its representative penitent. Beneath the olive trees He wept, on the cross He endured sin's penalty. He culminated a life-long obedience by an obedience unto death. It was a great price to pay, but so He paid it. Human nature, on the cross, turned in obedient love to God. The handwriting that was against us was done away. The restraint upon the action of God's love was removed. God and man were reconciled.

II

Again, man by his lawlessness brings himself under the control of sin. Sin winds its cords about him by ever-tightening habits. They seem at first light as gossamer, but become as steel. The flippant, cynical reason holds in prison the spiritual nature.

The proud, rebellious will easily rules the unbelieving heart. Unseen, yet not without power, stand close to us evil spirits who tempt us, as well as angels who guard. He who knew, as we do not, the unseen world, has revealed to us Satan's malefic power. Serving evil spirits, men have so far come under their control as to be in a degree possessed by them. Sin, too, brings its own punishment. Sin, when it is finished, bringeth forth death. Christ, for those who are united to Him, changes death into a gate of life. For others it is only a prelude to that separation from God which is death eternal.

Now Christ by His cross delivered us from our foes — sin, Satan, and death. The cross rises between earth and heaven, for by it God and man are reconciled. It stretches laterally, and on its transverse beam the blessed hands were nailed. The cross was not only Christ's altar whereon He as our high priest pleaded for our ransom; it was also a throne from which as the king He exercised His sovereign power of forgiveness, His pulpit from which He preached. It was a battle-field where He fought with Satan, and all the powers of darkness, and with death, and conquered. He delivered human nature from the dominion of their powers. Death had no dominion over Him nor those members who are His. He delivered us from these our foes at a great cost. As soldiers are said to have redeemed their country, taking it out of the enemy's hand at the cost of their lives, so Christ, our Redeemer, redeemed us, and paid this great ransom. By Christ man was set free, in Him men may be freed.

III

The third thing Christ did by the cross was to restore and elevate man's nature.

And here we may notice the significant fact that there are two distinct sheddings of the precious blood. It flows down from His bleeding head, His blessed hands and pierced feet. Through His long agony it flowed from the wounds of His holy body. But when this was over, and the " It is finished" was said, there came another outpouring from His pierced side. The soldier's lance that pierced to the heart and caused the water and the blood to flow added nothing save an indignity to Christ's work of redemption. That work was over with the dismissal of His Spirit into His Father's hands, the offering unto death was then made. The merits, infinite by reason of the infinite dignity of His person, were all accumulated. Why then did the divine economy provide for this second and independent blood-shedding? Because human nature had not only to be reconciled and redeemed, but restored.

Man needed four great aids to achieve his proper greatness. He needed greater light concerning himself and destiny than nature alone could give. But if this was his only need, God could have satisfied it by sending angels who week by week might teach us our duty and our destiny. But man wants something more than light. Angels might bring it to us. But moral truth in abstract form would little profit us. Angels with more than human eloquence might present it to us, but we should reply, you have not a nature like our own and you cannot understand us. What man cries out for, is truth and life embodied in an example. It must be in a form that we can see. It is one who goes before us, that says, step where I step, take my hand, lean on my arm.

This is what we know Christ came to do. He is our great exemplar. But if this was all we needed, why should He not have come as the first Adam is believed to have come? Why did He not take on Himself the nature of man, formed from the dust, or in some other way? Why did He humble Himself to be born of a virgin? Why did He not appear, as we find Him in His public life, and so set us an example of the ideal man? If we only needed a great exemplar He might have done so. But what we also needed was to be delivered from the pangs of conscience, the burden of sin, and to be reconciled to God. Man had sinned and needed forgiveness. And so, that He might deliver the race, God entered into the race. He made Himself one with it. He took our nature on Him in the womb of the Blessed Virgin. He did not become like one of us, but one of us. And so, as our representative, effected the At-one-ment for the race and opened the way for man's pardon.

But if the work stopped with our reconciliation and pardon, why, when our Lord had effected it, did He not lay aside the nature He had assumed? Why should He not only rise from the tomb with it, but carry it into heaven? Why wear it now and for all eternity? Yet this is a fundamental Christian truth. The reason is, because man needs not only acceptance and pardon, but restoration. "No remission of penalty," said S. Athanasius, "or equivalent compensation, no *fiat* of God's will would have sufficed; there was needed a change in man himself." "It is not only the penalty for sin, but sin itself, from which man must be freed. The condition of deadness within him must be quickened into life."[12]

Of the forgiveness of sin and deliverance from its effects nature knows nothing. "Each of us," said Bishop Alexander, of Derry, "is set down in the perilous game of life to contend with a player who is perfectly fair but absolutely remorseless. Play but one pawn ill, and you must abide the consequences. You cannot take back a single move. You have to do with the passionless majesty of an order that can never be broken, with the pitiless sequence of an unforgiving necessity."[13] You are in the grasp of a tyrant who says

"Fool! All that is at all
    Lasts ever. Past recall."[14]

But what nature cannot do, Christ can.

As symbolizing this and proclaiming the means, Christ's side is opened and the water and the blood stream out. This mystery of the precious blood declares to us that as Eve was formed out of the side of Adam, so the Church, the second Eve, should be formed from out the side of the second Adam, the head of the new race. We can thus better understand the text, "As in Adam all die, even so in Christ shall all be made alive."[15] We do not die in Adam by believing in him, or by any mental connection with him. We die in Adam

---

12. Quoted from J.F. Bethune-Baker's *An introduction to the early history of Christian doctrine: to the time of the Council of Chalcedon*, 347.

13. This is a paraphrase taken from the Rt. Rev. William Alexander's Sermon *The Efficacy and Joy of Repentance* — Preached in Westminster Abbey, Third Sunday after Trinity, 1885.

14. Robert Browning's *Rabbi Ben Ezra*.

15. 1 Corinthians 15:22.

because we are connected with him by an actual and real contact of natures, through descent. Even so in Christ we are to be made alive; not by any act of faith or trust or repentance merely, but by union of our natures with His. And the only way ordained by which this can be secured is by the sacraments. For human nature needed not only light, an exemplar, pardon, but healing of its wounds, restoration, the invigoration by a new, divinely given energy. So the water and the blood are extended to us through the divinely ordered channels of grace. We are by them incorporated into Christ, are inoculated with His life, made partakers of His victory over sin and death, are crucified to self and the world through union with His crucifixion, are buried and risen with Him in newness of life, and so pass through the living Door and Way, which is Himself, to a joyful resurrection.

And here we may answer some questions we have often heard.

If it is true that we are restored, not merely by acts of faith but by an incorporation into the triumphant nature of Christ, how are the heathen and the faithful Jews who lived before Christ to be saved? Concerning the faithful dead who lived before Christ, we know they did not go to heaven. One very satisfactory reason is that for man heaven did not exist. Heaven is not only a place but a state in which man enjoys the beatific vision of God. The human nature of Christ was the first that possessed this vision and it is as members of Christ and in Him that we shall. The fathers of the Old Testament were in a state of waiting and preparation. When our Lord descended into Hades, He preached to them. He delivered to them by word the same graces He gives us, who are in the flesh, through the sacraments. They had been justified by faith. They were just men, justified by faith. But when Christ communicated to them the grace of His humanity, they became "the spirits of just men made perfect."[16] Thus our Lord provided for all the elect who had preceded Him. The heathen, we are told, are a law unto themselves. But as the only way to eternal life is in and through Christ, we may believe, as He provided for the faithful Jews in that waiting world of "many stations," so in some way He may reach them.

But then it is sometimes asked, why should God have required all this process of Redemption: His incarnation, redemption, suffering,

---

16. Hebrews 12:23.

machinery of Church and sacraments? Why should not the Almighty Father by a word of His power have restored man and removed all evils from him? Granting that He could have done so, a difficulty would yet remain. You complain that the scheme of redemption does not look simple. You look at it askance as being theological. Although there is nothing very simple in this world, yet you want a very simple solution of a matter the most intricate and mysterious. Why, you ask, should not God have determined the whole matter by a word of forgiveness and restoration? But this difficulty would remain. How many times would you ask Him to go on doing so? No forgiveness nor restoration by an external word of power would secure man in a sinless condition. As S. Athanasius said, man would then be worse off than he was in his original state because he would have learned to sin. Moreover, if restored in such wise he would be more likely, restoration being found so easy, to sin again. So God would have to go on eternally, and man would not be delivered from the power of sin, and evil would continue in God's universe.

And this brings us to the final cause of the Redeemer's work. He sought not only to provide a way for man's forgiveness, deliverance, and restoration, but to drive out sin and all evils from His universe. He would complete creation, by so establishing it that righteousness should reign forever.

If God's purposes are tending to so glorious a consummation our hearts should be filled with hope and joy. Men, straining their eyes into the future, prophesy great things for their country or for the race. But "civilization is a self-limited elevator of men."[17] It rests on the law of inequality in men's mental equipment and an unequal distribution of wealth. It brings temptation as well as amelioration. It has no specific remedy for the source of all evil, sin. We know, too, how earthly kingdoms rise and fall, and how the planet itself must run its course and die. But the end of creation, revealed by Christ, gives us the vision of a permanent kingdom that can never dissolve and of a glory that will never pass away. It secures forever the happiness of man and reveals a purpose and an end of creation worthy of God.

Do we in childish wonder ask, why did not God begin by so making the universe? One reason is because, in His great love, He desires

---

17. Unattributed.

us to work with Him in the making of it. This is the greatest privilege of man that he is allowed to be a co-worker with God. If, for a short time and in a preparatory stage, God allows sin and evil, it is that we, by a victory over temptation, may be fitted for that further state. God indeed might have so created us that, like the plants and trees, we should have mechanically obeyed His laws. But He has shown His omnipotence not merely in making things, but in so making, that with a free-will endowment His intelligent creatures might, with His aid, rising to a higher degree of union with God, make themselves.

But how is it that this condition of life and being is to be eternally secured?

To understand this we must know that there are three degrees of union with God. First, man is united to God by His power. We live and move and have our being in Him. Next, as Christians we are united to Christ, the God-Man, by grace. We are in Him and He in us. Then there remains a third union which is to come. Union with God in glory. In Christ we may attain to the beatific vision and be upheld, in a new way, in union with God's holiness and bliss.

This final union with God is called the gift of eternal life. "The gift of God is eternal life in Jesus Christ our Lord."[18] It is a gift, an added blessing, not something that inherently belongs to our nature. It is different from immortality. Immortality belongs to us by the terms of our nature. The greatest of earth's philosophic thinkers have believed this. What is so universal a desire in man's nature must have its satisfaction. But there is a vast difference between natural immortality and the gift of eternal life. Immortality only assures us a future, it says nothing more. It tells us nothing of the character of that future. It secures us nothing in it. We merely know that we shall hereafter exist

If, believing that we shall pass finally into some fair heaven, pray ask yourself the question, what is to secure your state or residence there? The angels fell from heaven. Adam sinned in Paradise. You may be sheltered there from many temptations, but you will have yourself still to contend with. One sin lost the angels their heavenly estate. One sin forfeited for Adam Paradise. Any one spiritual sin would shut out the brightness and joy of heaven from the soul. It would fall like Lucifer. If then we are merely elevated to a condition

---

18. Romans 6:23

or place where our position is only secure on our perfect obedience, is this immortality to be desired? Is the warfare never to cease? Is the struggle with self and temptation never to be over? If this is so, take back, Mr. Philosopher, your arguments about immortality. Under this agonizing condition we don't want it. A heaven in which we are not eternally secure is not desirable and is no fitting climax to a divine creation.

The gift of eternal life makes our condition secure. We enter into it, by a union by grace with Christ here and attain in Him to a union with God in glory.

It is this final union with God that secures our eternal happiness. For our real and true happiness depends on our sinlessness. God is omnipotent, but some things He cannot do. He cannot break His own laws or violate His own nature. He cannot make two and two five or make it right to tell a lie. And He can only permanently secure men from falling into sin but by uniting them in Christ to Himself in glory. So the blessed souls who attain that state may look down the opening avenues of eternity, and know with absolute certainty that nothing can separate them from the love and holiness of God, and that in Him their estate is eternally secured.

But it may be asked, what of those who do not attain this condition? What can we say but what Christ has said? There will come a time, how soon we know not, when the drama of creation will come to its last act; when creation shall be perfected and shine with radiant beauty, and God shall be all in all; when those who are eventually in Christ will rise up into that final union with God in everlasting bliss; when, sad as it is to say it, there will be those who miss their proffered end, and who will be lost.

But will not good eventually triumph over evil? Shall there not come a time when truth and righteousness shall triumph? Shall not God at last conquer and banish all lawlessness and sin? Surely this conflict is not to go on forever? The good must win, sin must disappear.

Very true, when the kingdom of glory begins sin will cease. God's ideal creation will be complete. But how is it that sin will cease? In this wise: Those who are gathered into the Divine Life and Light will not sin, for they will be upheld in holiness by that special union with God. Those who are left without will sin no more; for, all grace being withdrawn, they will not be able to act against it. They are in this

unhappy condition. They cannot separate themselves from the power of God, for that were to annihilate themselves, and to annihilate
is an act of Deity as great as to create. They cannot thus separate
themselves from God and destroy themselves, but they have separated themselves from the grace of God and so ruined themselves.
They continue in existence, but their spiritual life is gone. They are
in the darkness, not in the light.

But should they ever repent could not God receive them?

A superficial view might lead us to think this possible, but there
are difficulties in accepting it. The idea seems based on the theory
that whenever man repents God is bound to forgive him. Now God
has provided a way by which man can escape from the evils he has
brought on himself; if man does not accept it, is God bound to do
any more? If man may go on, not only in this world but indefinitely
for ages in the next, defying God, and God is bound, whenever man
chooses to repent, to forgive him, we have the spectacle of God de-
throned, for God has not conquered man, but man has conquered
God.

Another difficulty is, that those in this condition will feel no desire
to repent. As they cannot sin because they have no spiritual life nor
grace to sin against, so also they cannot repent, for they have no
grace to repent with. One can no more repent without grace than
an animal can breathe in an exhausted receiver.

What we must realize is that creation is a majestically progressive
work. It proceeds under the impulse of the Eternal Infinite Energy
from stage to stage. When one period, with its own productiveness
and work is past, another succeeds. There is no return; the door is
shut. We see this written everywhere in the great parable of nature.
Take the monkeys whose antics amuse us as children, but whose
strangely human faces repel us in later years. As some biologists
have said, we are descended or developed from the same primor-
dial germs. Only there were some germs that corresponded to their
environment in one way and became humans, and the others corresponded differently and became monkeys. If the latter had at an
earlier stage taken another direction they would have developed to
the higher range of life. But they failed. They missed it. It became
lost to them. It is a permanent loss. They are forever condemned to
be monkeys. So it will be for those men who will not correspond to
their Christian environment. They will miss their end, forfeit what

they might have been, and be lost.

But we say, if a man is a good moral man, a good citizen, good to his neighbors, public spirited, why should he be lost? The reason is because he was so self-willed and self-opinionated that he would not use the means to be saved. Eternal life is not immortality. It is a gift of God in Jesus Christ. It is, being a gift, something added to nature. It is thus a supernatural end offered to man. And a supernatural end cannot be attained by natural goodness or means. It can only be gained in Christ. There is no other name given under heaven whereby we may be saved.

Unwilling to accept Christ's terms, men wrap themselves in the delusion that they are as good as most, and that God must be a merciful God, and it is inconceivable He would let any suffer an eternal loss.

True, most true is it, that God is goodness and love itself. Most true is it that He is a merciful God. He is so merciful that He sent His only-begotten Son to suffer and die for us. Every drop of blood that was shed, every agony He endured, tells of His exceeding mercy and His love.

If tempted to reject His invitation, not to use the means of union with Him, kneel down, and ask yourself these questions: What could God have done more than He has to show His love towards us? How could His mercy have made the terms of salvation easier than they are? If I reject His mercy extended now, how can I before His judgment seat claim a mercy I have refused and rejected? If obstinately acting on my own theories and opinions I remain unmoved by love's entreaty and am lost, as I shall be, whose fault will it be? Say it over again and again to thyself, self-slain soul, Whose fault will it be?

> "As froth on the face of the deep,
> As foam on the crest of the sea,
> As dreams at the waking of sleep,
> As gourd of a day and a night,
> As harvest that no man shall reap,
> As vintage that never shall be,
> Is hope if it cling not aright,
> O Lord Christ, unto Thee."[19]

---

19. Christina Rossetti, *As Froth on the Face of the Deep*.

VIII

Preface to:
CHRISTIAN & CATHOLIC

T HIS book is not controversial. In these days of unbelief we are only too glad to recognize believers in Christ, whatever degree of faith they may have attained. By whatever name nonconformists and sectarians call themselves, we recognize all baptized and faithful followers of Christ as Christians. The sins of former generations which rent us apart will not make us guilty of schisms if we do not refuse enlightenment and seek for reunion. We recognize, on the other hand, the Orthodox Churches of the East and the Roman Catholic as portions of the Church of Christ and their members as our fellow churchmen. They are most potent agencies in the preservation of the Christian religion. In the devotion of their members we recognize a zeal we might well emulate. We gladly welcome all acts of Christian recognition on their part and are ready to reciprocate them. Our Church accepts their orders and places no barriers in the way of inter-communion.

Our purpose in writing is to offer some help, if by God's grace we can do so, to any who, as they say, wish to believe but cannot; or, believing in God and Christianity, are for any cause in doubt as to their duty respecting church membership. There are, we know, many such. Yet we would sincerely say that our chief desire is not to make them converts, much as we love it, to that special portion of Christ's Body the Church to which we belong.

The reason of this is that our religious experience has developed in us a strong antagonism to proselytism. There is apt to be so much of what is merely selfish and sectarian in it. Men want to get others to join their side, their party, their church, by way of triumph over some other body, or party, or church. They want their side to win, their congregation, parish, or sect to grow. They want to enlarge their tale of converts, after the manner of a Roman triumph, that all the world may see how successful they are. This spirit leads in almost every town to jealousies and rivalries between sects and churches. It undermines, however, their spiritual life.

The professional proselytizer, as we know the class, is a repulsive character. He studies the art of injecting doubts into devout minds, of playing on the weaknesses and vanities of his proposed converts. He exaggerates the discords within their church, the contrarian opinions, the lack of discipline. Sometimes he cajoles, sometimes he seeks to terrify, sometimes he tries to influence by social advantages, sometimes he seeks to take souls captive by subtle sophisms. He is apt to be self-deceived as well as a deceiver, while asserting that he is working for the "greater glory of God." In reality he is doing what our Lord condemned in the Pharisees. They compassed heaven and earth to make proselytes, but failed grievously in making them true children of God. For themselves and their converts the result was just the opposite.

It is right to try to help our brothers who are in honest doubt, just in the same spirit as we would be glad for them to help us in need. It is right if our motive is to aid any Christian soul to come into closer union with Christ. Even should any one believe that his church was the only true one, yet to work for it in the same spirit one works for the success of an earthly project is to belie its character. We must work, not for any personal gain but as Christ did. Our guiding pole-star must be the good of others' souls. If our own words are found of help to any, enabling them to know better God's Will, in whatever way He leads them, may they have grace to follow it.

Our purpose will be also accomplished if in these days of absorbing secular interests we can aid in arousing religious inquiry. With the baubles of ambition clinking on the ear and cheating the eye, with the engrossing dream of splendid luxury captivating the heart, many impatiently push aside any suggestion of religion. Others give a slight but superficial consideration to it. By the law of association of ideas, thoughts idly come and as idly go through our minds. We cannot stop this any more than the circulation of our blood. But it is not painstaking thinking. No wonder the air is laden with murmurings and complaints of the disappointed, when so many never seriously face the problems, what are we, why are we here, what will our future be, in what does our real happiness consist, and what will bring man peace at the last?

Some deliberately refuse to entertain these questions. Religion is not like a philosophy or literature or science. She stands over against our conscience, a stern censor, and demands something. Steep and craggy is the ascent to the eternal heights, and it calls for exertion. She calls us to a life which has not self-interest for its governing principle, but to one based on the higher motive of service. The consequence is that whether a man believes or not depends largely on his predispositions and will. With the self-indulgent or self-satisfied Christianity has but little chance. God may have seemingly exhausted the resources of His entreaties, but His children stop their ears and harden their hearts.

Yet there are those who do wish help and are glad to receive it. They care not by whose hands the Lamp of Truth is held up to them; it is the light they want. They are alive to the folly of neglecting investigation and longer postponing decision. Opportunity has been likened to an Angel that presents herself with bandaged eyes and winged feet. Her eyes are bandaged, for men so often fail to discern her presence; her feet are winged, for she so quickly takes her flight. The Voice of God speaking within the souls says "To-day is the accepted time, to-day is the day of Salvation."[1] The call is a loving and an imperative one, and our prayerful response should be, "O God, make me willing in this day of Thy power."[2]

---

1. 2 Corinthians 6:2.

2. Psalm 110:3

IX

The Rule of Faith

THERE are not a few believers in Christ who are sincerely anxious to know what, as His followers, they ought to believe and do. Possibly they have been for a long time connected with some Christian denomination. It has been a help to them spiritually, and many associations bind them to it. They have enjoyed its fellowship and accepted its teaching. In a charitable spirit they have looked upon others differing from them in belief or practice as fellow-Christians. But they have gotten accustomed to their own church ways, are known in its social circle, and are contented with it. Yet they feel at times that they should be able to give better reasons than such as these for remaining where they are. Mohammedan in Europe, Mormons in America can give the same. While they hold their own religious body to be preferable, they charitably admit that Christians who differ from them have convictions as strong as their own.

Which is right?

One way of cutting the Gordian knot is to say that one denomination is best suited to one class or temperament, and another to another. This is the easy solution that inertia in its laziness, not wanting to be disturbed, often takes. It might help us somewhat if the denominational differences related chiefly to forms of worship. But their divergences concern not ceremonial only, but involve doctrine. The dogmas held by one body contradict those held by another. Here one sect disbelieves in the deity of Christ, while others worship Him, which is idolatrous if He is not divine. Here the Catholic churches of the East and West believe in a system of sacerdotal and sacrificial worship, which Protestants assert belong to the old dispensation and was by Christ entirely swept away. There are some who believe in the real presence of Christ in the Holy Communion, and so give Him honor, which to others who hold the service a mere memorial one is perilously superstitious and wrong.

We have to admit that the differences are of a serious doctrinal character.

Being thus aroused, the honest conscience demands some better reason for our remaining where we are than just because we are where we are.

But grant, a reply comes, that if there are doctrinal differences, are they essential? But if they are not essential, Christians have no right on account of them to divide into separate organizations. The setting up of pulpit against pulpit and altar against altar is seriously condemned in Holy Scripture as a sin. The earnest-minded men who have founded these sects believed the differences for which they stood were essential. It is obvious that they are, for they present contrarian systems of belief and practice.

Others make reply that the multiplication of sects is not so great an evil after all, for it has tended to competition. Surely it has, and it has thereby placed a severe tax on church members to sustain, in our smaller towns, seven or eight competing societies. It is not, as in trade, where competition benefits the public, by making goods cheaper, but this competition makes religion dearer. It also hinders its growth, it damages the goods. "Until you Christians can agree, don't bring me your wares," says the unbeliever; "first unite among yourselves, then we may listen to you."

What, then, shall we do? In taking any important journey, do you not make inquiries about the various routes? If going to some distant country, do you not take into consideration not only the comforts but the dangers of the way? Do you not seek, by study and forethought, to provide against all the hazards or perils of the journey? Do you say it does not matter which route or way, "we are all going to the same place"? On crossing the Atlantic, would you think it just as well to get into an eighteen-foot sailboat as to embark on a great ocean steamer? Do you not prudently say, "I don't want to run any unnecessary risk, I want to go in the safest and best way?"

The earnest and prayerful inquirer seeking the Christian truth thus often says, "I wish I really knew which was right. I wish I knew what Christ taught about these things. I love my own church, but I love Him more. If I knew what He would have me do, I would do it, no matter what it might cost." Some of the Apostles began their training under S. John the Baptist, and were devotedly attached to him, but at the Master's call they came out from under that pupillage and followed Him. Should He come to my sheepfold and call me, should I not obey His voice, go out and follow Him wheresoever He leadeth? As a Christian I do not want merely to please myself, but to obey and please Him.

The question then is, How shall a Christian, who accepts Christ as a master, know what, as a follower of Christ, he ought to believe and do?

There are two axioms, which before attempting to answer, it may be well to state. They would be accepted as such by almost all Christians.

Our Lord, we believe, was a prophet sent from God to teach men what it is necessary for their eternal welfare that they should know and do. He revealed an elevation of being to which without such guidance and provided aid they could not by themselves attain. It was a matter of such supreme importance that One must come from heaven as its revealer and guide. Its need and transcendent value cannot be overestimated, for it concerns the glory of God, the perfection of creation, the salvation of man. Coming to give such a revelation, Christ must have left some way by which sincere inquirers were to learn, with reasonable certainty, what they ought to believe and do. The opposite proposition, viz., that He would not have done so, but have left men to grope their way as best they could, is not credible. He would not only be shown thereby to be wanting in common sense, but would forfeit all claim to be the world's teacher. How could He be the world's teacher without leaving some way by which the willing should know what He taught and what they ought to do?

How could He be a revealer of the way to heaven, unless He clearly made known and established the means of getting there?

The second axiom, which is a corollary of the first, is this: — The way which Christ established by which His followers were to learn what they ought to believe and do, must be the best way, the safe way, the common-sense way, in fact, the way a Christian should follow.

Now we find ourselves surrounded by a babel of conflicting creeds and competing religions. But upon analysis they may, for the most part, be divided into three classes, according to their different rules of faith. By the " rule of faith " is not meant how a soul shall be brought by faith to Christ, or how by faith he is justified. But it here signifies the way by which, as a Christian or desiring to be one, he is to know what the faith is. It is his chart and compass, telling him how best to proceed, and learn what he is to believe and do. As enabling him to achieve this, it is called his rule or measure of the faith. It is his measure to whose test he brings every proposed doctrine, and accepts or rejects it, as it comes up to, or falls short of the standard. Now there are three well-known rules or measures of this kind to be found among Christians. However numerous their denomination-al divisions appear, they may, according to their respective rules be reduced to three groups. In seeking what as Christians we ought to know and do, it becomes us first to examine these three rules, and see which guide it is best to adopt.

First, there is a large number, embracing all the prominent Prot-estant sects, who take as their guide to correct belief, the rule, "the Bible and the Bible only." This is their favorite motto, and by a fa-mous champion, Mr. Chillingworth, was regarded as the glory and boast of Protestantism. Those who take this rule inculcate on us the duty of patient, prayerful study of God's word. We are told that if we do so go to it, the Holy Spirit will enlighten us and guide us into the truth.

This rule is defended by such texts as these: "Search the Scrip-tures."[1] The Jews were bidden by our Lord to do this, for He said they testified of Him. The Jews would be led thereby to believe in Him. But He does not say this was the way they were to learn what they were to believe, after they had done so. The Bereans, we are told, were more noble than the Thessalonians, because they "searched the Scriptures daily." But this was not the only ground of their commendation; they were more noble, because from the Apostles "they received the word with all readiness of mind."[2] The Jew was told by S. Peter that he would, by the study of the Holy Scriptures, be brought out of Judaism into salvation, through faith in Jesus Christ. The man of God could also thereby be "furnished unto all good works."[3] None of these texts, however, state that, apart from all teachers and authority, each Christian, by reading Holy Scripture, is to learn what is Christian doctrine. But, nevertheless, most eloquently has the Bible as the only rule been defended. Why, it is said, go back to past times? Why seek light from the fathers? Why perplex oneself with past controversies? The past belongs to antiquarians and bookworms. The learning it brings is covered with the dust of departed ages. We are living in the era of discovery and light. Do you want to know the truth, let nothing come between you and it. There is the Bible. It is God's word. An open Bible was the

---

1. John 5:39

2. Acts 17:11

3. 2 Timothy 3:17

gift of the Reformation to the world. Go directly to it. "It will make you wise unto salvation."[4]

While much may be said in behalf of this rule, the question we must ask ourselves is this: is it the rule of faith that Jesus Christ, who established the Christian religion, gave to us? Is it the way He ordered, by which we are to know what is the Christian religion? We must all admit that this is the true test as to its correctness and value. For we have agreed that Christ, being a divine teacher, must have left one way by which honest inquirers should know what He would have them do and believe. Preachers may wax eloquent over "the Bible and the Bible only" theory, but however attractive, was it the method instituted by Christ? If it was, we dutifully accept it; if not, we must not take it for our guide.

We can easily settle the question. There is no recorded command of Christ to His Apostles bidding them write a book and disseminate it. As a matter of fact, the Christian Church was in existence and in active operation before any of the Gospels were written. The books also of the New Testament were not collected and certified till the close of the second century. Copying by hand was expensive, and so comparatively few persons could possess a copy of the whole Scripture. Now God could have had the art of printing invented in the first century as well as in the fifteenth. He could have had the Bible put into circulation when the Apostles went forth on their missionary journeys. But here is the plain fact: He did not do it. Nor does this theory meet the condition of enabling sincere persons with reasonable certainty to know the faith. For in every denomination there are persons abler and more learned than ourselves, and just as prayerful and sincere, yet the result of the Protestant theory is a babel of conflicting and contradictory doctrines on matters admitted, by their divisions into sects, to be essential. The rule of faith upon which Protestantism is based is not Christ's rule. We ought not, therefore, as His followers, to adopt it.

Another rule of faith is just the opposite. It is the Roman rule. Christianity, it is claimed, came into the world, not as a philosophy or proclamation of pardon, but as an institution. This institution is known by themselves as the Holy Roman Church. At its head is the pope. By God's endowment he has an assisting official gift of infal-

---

4. 2 Timothy 3:15

libility. This gift makes him, when he is speaking authoritatively in the exercise of his office as teacher, and as is said *ex cathedra*, to the Church, on matters of faith and morals, by himself and apart from any council, infallible.

This rule has to many devout minds a great attraction. Not merely because they are Roman Catholics and are brought up to surround with an artificial halo the bishop of Rome, but to others disturbed with the fruitless controversies of Protestantism. What we long for is a voice that can guide us. What we desire is an authority that we may rest upon. What we seek is relief from this weight of personal responsibility. We cannot trust ourselves to the ever-shifting uncertainties of Protestantism. Let us hear the voice of the Church speaking through the holy father.

This rule, it is claimed, saves us from the chaos of Protestantism. It delivers us from the anarchy of individualism. It replaces doubt by infallible certainty. It, like the other rule, has its powerful and eloquent defenders. The will o' the wisp of private opinion, luring men into pitfalls, is contrasted with the stately throne of the Vatican and the voice of Peter's successor.

But we must hear what can be said on the other side. It is to be noted that this assistance of infallibility is not attached to the holy see. The proof of this is that during a papal vacancy it is held that the Church can make no decree. It is thus seen to be a gift with which the pope is personally invested. But it is an universally admitted fact that a number of the popes have been abnormally corrupt, monsters in iniquity. How can the Holy Spirit, the Truth-Guide, co-operate with such souls? How do it to such a degree of union with Himself as to render them infallible? Our minds may be, apart from such a special union, enlightened by prevenient or actual grace. But to be infallible we must be more than gifted with light and guarded by such grace. This assistance would not secure infallibility, for we may resist such aid and guidance, and so err. An assisting grace does secure infallibility. To be secure from error, we must be so united to God (who is truth) as to be unable, for the purpose of being His organ, of being separated from Him. This is the way in which the Church becomes to us an infallible guide. The Church is infallible because the Holy Ghost dwells in it and securely unites it to Christ, whose organ it thus becomes. How, then, can bad popes with whom the Holy Spirit might plead, but cannot by His indwelling unite to the truth, nor

compel without the destruction of free will, be the infallible organ of
His utterance? Irresistibility of divine grace and the consequent loss
of human freedom is the very touchstone of Calvinism!

We can understand how the official acts of bad ecclesiastics are
valid, for the validity of their sacramental acts does not depend upon
their morality, but on their priestly character. God, it may be urged,
may make an ass a mechanical deliverer of certain sounds, or the
Spirit may apply to the words of Caiaphas a wider than the speaker's sense; but as the Holy Spirit cannot dwell in bad men and so
inseparably unite them to God as to make them the organs through
whom He speaks, the infallibility of those who by the grossness of
their sins have become separated from Christ is an impossibility.

It has been argued that though the Bible may be God's word, yet
it is not a safe guide, since those who consult it may and often do
err. But the same objection applies to the Roman rule. Suppose the
pope is officially consulted and gives an official response, is the recipient who adopts it secured thereby from error? Sergius, patriarch of
Constantinople, wrote to Pope Honorius to declare his opinion on a
very important theological question which concerned the nature of
Christ. The pope did so, and bade Sergius declare his decision. The
result was, that both Sergius and Honorius were afterwards condemned as heretics by the sixth ecumenical council, were anathema-
tized and declared cast out from the Holy Catholic Church.

Again, the rule of faith demands that the necessary guide should
really be a guide. Thus it is objected to the "Bible only" rule that
it is not the Bible that always controls, but the inquirer often reads
into it his own presuppositions. It means what he wants it to mean.
Does not the same objection apply to the papal rule? If the pope is
the divinely authorized guide, he will know himself to be such, and
will consequently know and act on the limitations of his powers. If,
for instance, the case of Galileo was one of scientific fact, he would
have known it was one out of his province, and so would not have
condemned him. If it was for an erroneous construction of Scripture, as is sometimes claimed, Galileo was condemned, then the
pope failed of being a safe guide as to the interpretation of God's
word. In either case he was not an infallible guide.

Again, if the pope is the pastor and teacher of all Christians, it is
his prerogative and duty to guard the Church from false doctrine.
When heresies arise, he will therefore take the lead in suppressing

them. But in the Arian heresy we find Pope Liberius apologizing to the Arian bishops for ever having defended Athanasius, signing a deficient Arian creed, and giving the weight of his influence to Arianism! S. Hilary exclaims, "Anathema, I say to thee, Liberius;" and a third time, "Anathema to the prevaricator Liberius." Thus in this contest for orthodoxy over our Lord's deity the bishop of Rome was found not to be a safe teacher and guide of the Church.

In the important Pelagian controversy, which was concerned with grace and free will, we find Pope Innocent deciding correctly. But we also find his successor, Zosimus, being, as is now contended, imposed upon by heretics, siding with them. He did so until the African bishops, in council, firm in their resistance to his letters, set him right. In the last case he did not guide the Church, but the Church guided him.

In the Monothelite contest, which involved the truth of the two natures of Christ, with two wills, human and divine, we find Pope Honorius, of whom we spoke above, giving formally his sanction to the heretical side, declaring, "We confess one will of our Lord Jesus Christ." It is now, under the necessity of upholding the late decree of the pope's infallibility, contended either that he was not speaking *ex cathedra*, to the whole Church, or probably his words may bear an orthodox meaning. Granting this, it is an undisputed fact, however, that the sixth ecumenical, and two subsequent councils approved by popes, condemned him as a heretic. We have thus pope condemning pope. On the most charitable construction (and we desire to give it), Pope Honorius lamentably failed at a most critical time to be the Church's teacher and safe guide.

Another objection made to the papal rule of faith has been this: A rule or guide to the faith should not be contradictory. The Protestants say that however different interpretations may be put on Holy Scripture, nevertheless Holy Scripture itself does not change. But on the other side the popes do change, and what one has held, another pope, or the Church in council, has denied. For instance, Pope Innocent III. (198) declared, "I can be judged by the Church for a sin concerning the faith." Innocent IV. (1242) said, "A pope can err in faith, and therefore no one ought to say, I believe what the pope believes, but, what the Church believes." Adrian VI. declared "that it was possible for popes to promulgate heresy in decrees."

Eugenius IV. said that the decision of a council is to be preferred to the sentence of a bishop of Rome. Innocent I. and Gelasius held, contrary to modern opinion, that "infants who died without communion went straight to hell." Stephen II. taught that baptism administered with wine was lawful. Nicholas I. assured the Bulgarians that baptism in the name of Christ was valid. Gregory II. decided that marriages between a freeman and a slave (they might be of the same race) might be dissolved. Celestine III. held that the marriage tie was dissolved if either party became a heretic. Urban II. declared the lawfulness of killing an excommunicated person. Eugenius IV. in a formal document misstated the form and matter of holy order, making the delivery of the instruments, the paten and chalice, essential to its conveyance, which if true would have nullified the orders of the first thousand years.

We must, in order to uphold the modern papal theory, regard these, and other like pronouncements with them, as the private opinions of the bishops of Rome. But then we are still, so far as the rule of faith is concerned, in the same difficulty. Why did they not resort in these important matters to their infallible power and decide correctly? Not to exert a power so essential to the salvation of men is in the highest degree criminal. Either, then, the popes did not know they possessed this assisting gift, in which case their ignorance proves they did not possess it; or by giving out private and sometimes erroneous opinions they have failed to exercise it, and so shown that they are not safe, still less infallible guides.

But what shall we say in presence of the fact that for a generation or more there have been rival popes engaged in unhappy contests and excommunicating one another? If one alone was the true pope, one only was infallible. But how was the Church to know which of the claimants was infallible and which not? There were saints, we are told, ranged on all sides, which seems to show that the element of papal infallibility was not a necessary part of the rule of faith. There has been, says the Protestant, no practical difficulty as to what was the Bible, but a serious one as to who was the pope.

But be all this as it may, the real test of the papal rule is the same as that of the Protestant: is it the one ordained by Christ? Is this the way He established, by which His followers should know what they were to believe and do?

We are here obliged as before to answer in the negative. If it had been the rule of Christ, it would have been universally known as such and acted on from the beginning. We know that the Orthodox Eastern Church has never recognized its existence. In the Roman Communion, the papal infallibility was not made a dogma till 1870. Before that year it was indeed denied by persons in authority to be a doctrine of the Church. In *Keenan's Catechism*, which had the imprimatur of Roman bishops, we find the question, "Must not Catholics believe the pope in himself to be infallible?" Answer, "No; that is a Protestant invention; it is no article of the Catholic faith; no decision of his can oblige, under pain of heresy, unless it be received and enforced by the teaching body, that is, by the bishops of the Church."[5] The same was stated in a famous work, *The Faith of Catholics*, compiled by Fathers Berington and Kirk. "It is no article of the Catholic faith to believe that the pope is in himself infallible, separated from the Church, even in expounding the faith; by consequence, papal definitions or decrees, in whatever form pronounced, taken exclusively of a general council or acceptance of the Church, oblige none."[6]

Now the rule of faith, to be the guide to truth, must have been recognized as such from the beginning. If it is a fatal objection to the Protestant theory of "the Bible and Bible only," that the Bible was not in the hands of the people till the fifteenth century, it is equally a fatal objection to the present Roman rule that its element of the papal infallibility was not certified to the Church till the nineteenth century. Rome, in this respect, is three hundred years more modern than Protestantism.

Let us turn to the third rule to guide Christians. Christ did not order or provide for any book to be circulated. He forbade our following any one person. "Call no man master."[7] He endowed His Church with the Holy Spirit, making the Church thereby a living organism, through which He acts, gathering souls into His saving light and life. In the Church are to be found the Holy Scriptures and the sacraments. By the Church the Scriptures are preserved and interpreted to our enlightenment, and the sacraments are administered for our reception of life. We hear the voice of Christ speaking

---

5. The Rev. Stephen Keenan's 1849 *Controversial Catechism: or, Protestantism refuted, and Catholicism Established*, Ch. IX § II.

6. Proposition XIV.

7. See Matthew 23:8–12

to us through the Church as guided by the Holy Spirit, it interprets the written word, and makes the truth known within us by our union with it.

The four points of this rule of faith are these: — Christ reveals, the Spirit guards, the Church utters, the soul comes to know it.

I. The first point means that Christ not only taught certain truths, but was Himself the truth. He is the Logos, the wisdom itself. He is the revelation. It is complete in Him. What He was, did, and said is the revelation of God to man.

We have thus an answer to the popular saying that we are living in an age of enlightenment and new discoveries and must not be tied to old truths. The answer is this: A distinction must be observed between revealed truth and all other truth. The latter depends for its progress on observation and experiment. The longer the world lasts the more time it will have to make observations and experiments, and so the wiser it will grow. But it is different with the truth revealed in Christ. It was given in Him, in its completeness, and once for all. While therefore it is no objection in any other class of truth, that a proposed theory is new or destructive of what has gone before, in respect of Christian truth, it is an obvious axiom that what is new is necessarily false.

II. The next point of the rule of faith is: The Spirit guards it. Here we must notice the office of the Holy Spirit in its relation to Christ. The Holy Spirit does not dwell in the Church to make it the organ of His revelations, for the Holy Spirit is not the revealer of truth, but Christ; who is the revealer of God to man. The office of the Holy Spirit is to guide the Church into all truth, by bringing to her remembrance and giving her an understanding of all that Christ was or uttered or did.

The Holy Spirit in the performance of this duty guides and guards the Church in two ways, by enlightening her authorized teachers, and by His overruling providence. When, in consequence of the rise of a heresy, the Church in council is obliged to defend the faith, the Holy Spirit enlightens the bishops in their decisions and the Church in its acceptance of them. By the new definition, if one is required, the Church clears away the fog of error, and enables her children to see clearly the old truth which had been held from the beginning. When, however, the Holy Spirit sees that the fathers in council, being under duress or deceived by forged decretals, are likely to go wrong, He prevents the council's decisions from having an ecumenical value. This is done in various ways. The Church does not give her consent to the conciliar action, or God overrules the divisions of Christendom to the preservation of the Church in her teaching office. Thus, while in the one case He enlightens the Church, enabling her to speak, He also, when she would go wrong, either by denying or adding to the faith, lays His hand on her mouth. Infallibility has been preserved by the division of Christendom. In these two ways the Spirit guards the faith once revealed.

III. This faith thus delivered and guarded the Church declares. It is to be found in the common consent of Christendom. What the Church has from the beginning always and everywhere declared to be the faith must indeed be so. For it is not possible that a divine teacher would so poorly have provided for the preservation of His revelation as that a great majority of His followers would fall into error. This faith so proclaimed has been also protected in the accepted creeds. It is set forth in the liturgies of the Eastern and Western Churches. It has efficaciously been proclaimed by the sacraments, which may be called the "gospel in action." In respect of the Episcopal government of the Church, the three sacred orders of the ministry, the preserved Apostolic succession through Episcopal ordination, the Christian priesthood, and the real presence and Eucharistic sacrifice, Catholic Christendom is united. Protestantism, having lost priesthood, has no consciousness of these gifts. But wherever the Apostolic priesthood has been preserved, the consciousness of all Catholics proclaims, by words and heroic lives of self-sacrifice, their possession.

We may regret the divisions of Christendom, but God has overruled them in one way to good. In consequence, the Church is protected from adding with Ecumenical authority any articles to the faith.[8] This is an advantage, for it is not the Church's duty, nor is

---

8. This particular point is a unique insight of the American Patrimony. The American Anglo-Catholic Dogmatist Francis J. Hall writes similarly in 1918:

"Schism is indeed a most grievous evil. But the fact is undeniable that God is able to overrule this evil and convert it into an instrument for good. We may believe, and be thankful, that He has made use of schisms to prevent the Church from imposing more dogmas than are really necessary for the protection of the faithful. The Church's long struggle with heresy had engendered a tendency to define with greater fullness and subtlety than the Church's total experience justifies. Whatever happens within the Church, it is the Spirit that guides the Church as

it for man's good for her to answer all the questions the curiosity of theologians may choose to ask. The Holy Spirit dwells in the Church to protect her in the truth revealed in Christ and enable man to be wise unto salvation. What she has not, by the concurrence of her several parts, declared, she merely leaves as matters of pious opinion. But as each portion of the Church, the Eastern and Western, the Russian, Greek, Roman, and Anglican, proclaims the faith of undivided Christendom, each fulfills its prophetical office and their respective members accept it on the Church's authority.

The Anglican Church has not become reduced to like "dogmatic helplessness," as Rome when for seventy years there were rival popes. She maintains the Catholic faith and her living utterance is to be found in her Book of Common Prayer. In America, Diocesan Courts and Courts of Review are established, and appeal lies in matters of doctrine to the House of Bishops. In England the Lincoln judgment shows that the metropolitan has not lost his ancient authority. And let the fundamental truths of the creed be denied and a bishop like Colenso or priests like Dr. Crapsey and Rev. McQueary are deposed.

The voice of the Catholic Church in each division of it is thus not a dead but an authoritative and a living voice. It is a living and continuous utterance. Her conciliar decisions, for example, are not like those of a secular court. What she declared of old at Nicaea and elsewhere she has continued, day by day, at thousands of altars and by hundreds of millions of her children, to declare. As one approaches Niagara, the traveler gradually recognizes the deep undertone of the falls, solemn as the judgment, unfailing as eternity. But the ears of the townspeople become paralyzed to the awful utterance and only the attentive ear hears the deep diapason of the water's voice. So it is with the Catholic Church. She is ever proclaiming, in the midst of the world's tumultuous babel of contending utterances, the faith once and for all delivered to the saints, and the wise and humble-minded listeners hear her living voice. It is a voice coming up from behind and yet as present with them, saying, "This is the way, walk ye in it."[9]

The Christian soul comes with increasing clearness of vision and certainty to know the truth. Drawn by prevenient grace to accept Christ, the newly baptized becomes united to the Church and so

---

a whole, and makes all things work out for her ultimate good." (*Dogmatic Theology*, "Authority: Ecclesiastical and Biblical," Ch. IV, Pt. II § 6)

9. Isaiah 30:21

becomes a living stone in that spiritual temple which is filled with the Holy Spirit. As a member of this temple and so spiritually illuminated, the Christian soul hears the voice of the Spirit speaking in and through it. At first, like a child it believes what it is told to believe. As it advances in light under the Church's paternal authority, the Holy Scriptures are seen to corroborate the Church's teaching and the proficient is able to give a reason for the faith that is in him. As he acts on the faith, he becomes gradually transformed by it. He then not only holds certain truths, but the truth takes possession of him. He advances from belief based on authority and reason to the certainty that comes from possession. He knows in whom he believes. For Christ dwells in him and he in Christ.

This is the Catholic rule of faith, the rule Christ established when he told us to "hear the Church," and "if any man will do His will he shall know of the doctrine."

X

The Seven Mysteries

THE gospel system is analogous to the processes of God in the natural world. In nature we see how God bestows His gifts. He loves to give them while He hides His hand. Love indeed must manifest itself, but true power loves hiddenness. "Verily," says the prophet, "Thou art a God that hideth Thyself, O God of Israel the Saviour."[1] So, hiding Himself in nature, He bestows His gifts through multiform instrumentalities. Thus life and strength come to us through ordained means. God sustains our natural life through sacraments of the natural order. So it is in the order of grace.

Our prayer-book employs two terms to describe them. It speaks of the "Sacraments" and of the "Holy Mysteries." They denote the same things under different aspects. A sacrament is an outward and visible sign of an inward and spiritual grace. It is also a mystery by which the grace of God is given unto us.

They are conveniently arranged in two classes. First, there are those sacraments whose "matter and form" were ordained by Christ and are of universal application. These are Baptism and the Holy Communion. They are necessary for salvation where they may be had, and they have relation to the eternal existence and welfare of the Church.[2] In the other class are to be found Confirmation, Penitence, Unction, Orders, Matrimony. They are not necessary for all men, and have relation to the temporal life of the Church. She needs them in her militant state and in her battle with sin.

The first in order of these is holy baptism. We shall understand Christian baptism better if we analyze the four kinds of baptism found in the New Testament.

There is first in order the baptism administered by John the Baptist. This, though often confused with it, was not Christian baptism. It is proven not to have been such by two conclusive reasons. It was not given in the name of the Blessed Trinity, as Christian baptism

---

1. Isaiah 45:15

2. "QUESTION: How many Sacraments hath Christ ordained in his Church? ANSWER: Two only, as generally necessary to salvation; that is to say, Baptism, and the Supper of the Lord." (*Church Catechism*)

must be, for the simple reason that the name of the Blessed Trinity had not been revealed to S. John Baptist. It had not connected with it any sanctifying gift of the Holy Ghost, for the "Spirit was not yet given."[3] S. John was the last and greatest prophet of the old dispensation, and his baptism was like a Jewish ordinance. It was a mere outward sign, but had no inward spiritual gift. In other words, it was not a gospel sacrament. The Apostles also baptized in like manner before Pentecost, but it was only a continuation of John's preparatory work. The manner, therefore, in which S. John baptized, whether with more or less water, would be no guide for Christian usage. And not being Christian baptism, when the baptized disciples became Christians they had, as we read in the nineteenth chapter of the Acts, to receive the Christian sacrament.

The next baptism is that of Jesus Christ by S. John. Why did He who was sinless come to a baptism of repentance? Because having taken flesh of the Blessed Virgin, He had thus identified Himself with our race and became, as the second Adam, its new representative head. As such He took upon Himself the duty of making a reparation to God for its transgressions. He thus begins, in His official capacity, His life-long act of penitence. There was another reason for Christ's action. He was to make reparation to God and work out man's deliverance by the fulfilment of His office as the Anointed One, or Messiah. He was solemnly consecrated to be the Christ at His baptism. The heavens were opened and the voice of the Eternal Father was heard: "This is My beloved Son, in whom I am well pleased,"[4] and the Holy Ghost, who from the first moment of His conception had been given without measure to Him, now was also given for His special work and office, and He was anointed with the Holy Ghost.

The next baptism we read of is the baptism by Jesus Christ Himself. During His visible or public life, Jesus, we read, did not baptize. But John the Baptist had foretold that He who came after him should baptize with the Holy Ghost and with fire. This Christ did when He had ascended. Then He baptized the Church; the outward sign being tongues of fire and a mighty wind, the inward gift being the Holy Spirit. The whole mystical body was now baptized and the

---

3. John 7:39
4. Matthew 3:17

Spirit of the Lord filled the temple.

The fourth baptism is Christian baptism. This was first administered by the Apostles to the converts on the day of Pentecost. This was with water and in the name of the Blessed Trinity.

Its subjects are both adults and infants. The condition for adults is faith and repentance. Infants are baptized because our Lord said "Suffer little children to come unto Me, and forbid them not,"[5] and showed that unconscious infancy was capable of receiving a blessing, by taking them up in His arms and blessing them. Faith and repentance are not required of infants, for not having sinned they have no sins of which to repent. And not having raised their wills against God there is no necessity for their taking them down by an act of submission or faith. Thus the passive condition of the infant is the normal one for receiving the baptismal gift. By repentance and faith the adult puts himself in the condition of a little child. We thus become like little children, and fulfill the condition necessary to enter the kingdom.

By its action baptism bestows a gift which can most easily be remembered by reference to its effects in regard to our past, present, and future.

In respect of our past, it heals the wounds of inherited or original sin, and remits all our actual sins. "I believe in one baptism for the remission of sins." This gift of God is bestowed upon us for the merits of Christ by the operation of the Holy Ghost.

A marked scriptural instance is to be found in the case of S. Paul. On his way to Damascus our Lord appeared to him. The brightness of our Lord's glorified body caused his blindness, but the Lord's words illuminated his soul. With agonized earnestness Saul cried out, "Lord, what wilt thou have me to do?"[6] He was then and there a truly converted man. It is a crucial question for sectarians whether his sins were forgiven at the time of his conversion. Their theological system requires an affirmative answer. But in Holy Scripture we read it was not so. For, three days after, Ananias, the prophet of the Lord, comes to him and says, "Brother Saul, arise and be baptized and wash away thy sins."[7] His sins not being washed away by his conversion,

---

5. Matthew 19:14

6. Acts 9:6

7. Acts 22:16

but as Scripture states by his subsequent baptism. Conversion is the turning of man to God. Remission of sin in baptism is the gift of God to man.

As related to the present time; by baptism we are born again, or "born from above."[8] This implies two things, our being begotten anew by heavenly power, and our being born out of a natural region of darkness into one of light. We are begotten anew by the Holy Spirit, which, blowing where it listeth, works the soul's conversion; and also in baptism (the Holy Spirit accomplishing that whereunto it is sent), we receive a new nature by our incorporation into Christ. "For as many of you as were baptized unto Christ did put on Christ."[9]

We discern here a distinction between our relation to God by nature and that formed by baptism. By the act of creation we are God's creatures; by baptism we are the sons of God as members of Christ. Thus baptism is not like the coronation of a king to which it is sometimes compared, for the king is one by right of his descent before he is crowned. Baptism, however, is not an acknowledgment of what we previously were, but an instrument by which we are made members of Christ and so children of God.

Next as to the future. Having been, by baptism, born into the kingdom of light, a prospect is opened before us of attaining to the further light of the beatific vision of God. We are made children of the light. We are incorporated into this new kingdom as living stones of a living temple. And so we are not merely born into and immersed in it, but it is also in us. The incipient virtues of faith, hope, and charity are imparted by baptism. These gifts received may be neglected and lie dormant, but as we respond, more and more clear becomes the heavenly vision, and we receive strength to attain it.

The effect of the loss of baptism is painfully seen in America, in the increased power of evil spirits, and the ease with which Satan deludes persons with false religions, and by teachers who come in their own name.

The baptismal faith is decisively expressed in our baptismal offices. None can be found more full of Scriptural and Catholic tradition. We utter it in the words of our Church's hymnal in praise and devotion:

---

8. John 3:3

9. Galatians 3:27

"Arise and be baptized,
  And wash thy sins away;
Thy league with God be solemnized,
  Thy faith avouched to-day.
No more thine own, but Christ's;
  With all the saints of old,
Apostles, seers, evangelists,
  And martyr throngs enrolled."[10]

The second gospel mystery is confirmation. It has three designations in Holy Scripture. It belongs to the general Apostolic ministrations of laying on of hands, which is spoken of as one of the principles of the doctrine of Christ.

It is also referred to as an anointing or unction. "Ye have an unction from the Holy One and ye know all things."[11] And "the anointing which ye have received of Him abideth in you, and ye need not that any man teach you; but as the same anointing teacheth you of all things, and is truth, and is no lie, and even as it hath taught you, abide therein."[12]

Again, it is known as the seal of the Lord. "Now He which stablisheth us with you in Christ [by baptism] and hath anointed us, is God; who hath also sealed us, and given the earnest of the Spirit in our hearts."[13]

It is administered by a bishop in the West, or by a priest with chrism, consecrated by a bishop, in the East.

In the Anglican Church it is by laying on of the bishop's hand, who in doing so in Scotland and in other places makes with his thumb the sign of the cross on the forehead of the confirmed. It is to be desired, for conformity with the symbolism of Holy Scripture, that this should be with chrism. Does it lie within the jus liturgicum of the bishop to do so?

An interesting question has been of late much investigated by Anglican theologians, concerning the difference between the gift of the Holy Spirit in baptism and confirmation.

Baptism is the sacrament of our new birth in Christ. We are

---

10. Edward H. Bickersteth, *Stand Soldier of the Cross.*

11. 1 John 2:20

12. 1 John 2:27

13. 2 Corinthians 1:21–22

brought under the converting influence of the Holy Spirit before baptism, and as a preparation for it. In baptism, by the operation of the Holy Ghost, we are made members of Christ and of His mystical body. Being thus united to the humanity of Christ in whom the Spirit dwells, we are in Him made, indirectly, partakers of the Holy Spirit. Being made living stones of the Spiritual Temple which is filled with the Holy Spirit, we are immersed in it, and the Spirit is in us. We receive in baptism both sanctifying grace and the Holy Spirit. Sanctifying grace, which is necessary for our justification, the Holy Spirit, who unites us to Christ. If we did not receive the Holy Spirit then confirmation would be a sacrament necessary to salvation. We pray in the baptismal office, "Give Thy Holy Spirit to this infant," and what we pray for, that we believe we receive.

Confirmation is a sacrament of the gifts of the Spirit. It does not merely increase the gifts received in baptism. Even if one were made full of the Holy Spirit at baptism, this would not preclude him from receiving new and distinct gifts, for the activities of the Spirit are not governed by the laws of material mechanics. So gifts, different in kind, are bestowed by confirmation. Born anew in baptism and made a child of God, in confirmation we are ordained and receive our first degree of priesthood and kingship. All the laity are made kings and priests unto God. In confirmation we receive also our mission to work for Christ in the world, and grace for its fulfilment.

The laity, in all their church work, go out "as sent" by the Lord. Receiving sanctifying grace for our justification in baptism, we receive in confirmation the sevenfold gifts of the Holy Ghost for our advancement and perfection in the spiritual life. These are the spirit of wisdom, which makes us seek after God; of understanding, which teaches us the Catholic faith; of counsel, which enables us to choose the path of duty; of ghostly strength, which enables us to perform our Christian obligations; of knowledge, which instructs us in the will of God as it pertains to ourselves; of true Godliness, which inspires us to live holy lives; of holy fear, which preserves us in reverence and the worship of God.

In confirmation we are also sealed and receive a character. In the old dispensation we read that "seals" were given by God as tokens of spiritual citizenship; but in the Christian state we receive not tokens or empty signs, we do not receive "seals" only, but by the power of the Spirit we are sealed. The distinction between the two is like unto the giving a person a ring to wear as a token of friendship, or the impressing of the ring engraved with its arms upon the wax. Confirmation imprints an ineffaceable character on the soul. This character is impressed, not on the essence of the soul, but on its intellectual and effective powers. The child of grace becomes in a degree a priest and king, and an armed soldier in the army of Christ. Thus we sing in our confirmation hymn:

"O Christ, who didst at Pentecost
   Send down from heaven the Holy Ghost;
And at Samaria baptize
   Those whom Thou didst evangelize;
And then on Thy baptized confer
   The best of gifts, the Comforter
By Apostolic hands and prayer;
   Be with us now, as Thou wert there.

Thus consecrated, Lord, to Thee,
   May each a living temple be.
Enrich that temple's holy shrine
   With sevenfold gifts of grace divine;
With wisdom, light, and knowledge bless,
   Strength, counsel, fear, and godliness."[14]

The third gospel mystery is known in Eastern and Western Christendom as the sacrament of penitence. It is the sacrament of restoration. It restores to the soul the spiritual life lost or injured by sin. Like all other mysteries it may be considered in regard to its matter and form. The three acts of penitence, which may be regarded as the matter, are contrition, confession, and satisfaction or amendment. The absolution of the priest is the form. Together these signify and effect the sinner's reconciliation with God; his spiritual resurrection and restoration in grace.

Contrition demands first a knowledge of God's love to us in Christ, and a knowledge of ourselves. This latter can only be obtained by self-examination and prayer. We must ask God to show us ourselves and Himself. We must, if we have never done so, review our life in its different parts and relationships, and see what we have done or left undone. We must examine ourselves in the light of God's command-

---

14. Christopher Wordsworth, *O God, in Whose All-Searching Eye.*

ments, the seven deadly sins, the precepts of the Gospel, the duties of our station, our privileged weaknesses and faults. We must try to see ourselves in the light of God's justice, holiness, and of His love, for, out of His love, who could bear so ghastly a sight?

Contrition combines sorrow for having offended God with a fear and hatred of sin, and a sincere determination not to offend again. It is either perfect or imperfect. It is called perfect when the dominating motive is the love of God, or imperfect when controlled by lesser religious motives, such as the fear of hell or the loss of heaven. But mere natural motives, such as the results of sin, the loss of honor, the confusion of exposure, the obstacles our faults oppose to worldly success, these do not deserve the name of contrition. For contrition must be an act of the heart and will, and be inspired by motives based on religion. There must also be with our sorrow a fear and hatred of sin; a fear, because our nature is so composite, our hearts are so self-deceiving, temptation is so subtle, our falls have been so many. Because also we grow in the love of God just in proportion as we grow in the hatred of sin; because this hatred develops the strength of will, enabling us to contend successfully with this deadly enemy.

Contrition also demands a holy determination to amend. The marks of such a sincere resolve are, fidelity in prayer, vigilance against our spiritual enemies, watchful correspondence with the interior warnings of the Spirit, a rigorous avoiding of the occasions of sin. We must learn, as S. Augustine said, to take the little ones, the first temptations, and dash them against the rock that is Christ.

Confession is the next step in the soul's restoration. It has its source in our moral nature that demands it. Its duty has been revealed in the Old and New Testament. It must be made to God, against whom we have sinned. As Christians it must be made to Him in the person of Jesus Christ, for to Him all judgment has been committed. In His great love He has left those who represent Him, and who can communicate to us His pardoning grace. They can say in His name, son, daughter, thy sins be forgiven thee, go in peace.

The form of this sacrament is the priest's word of absolution. As possessed of this power the gospel ministry is called the ministry of reconciliation. This power of absolution our Lord gave to His Church when He breathed on the Apostles and said, "Receive ye the Holy Ghost: whose soever sins ye remit, they are remitted unto them, and whose soever sins ye retain, they are retained."[15] When our Lord spoke these words most probably others besides the Apostles were present. There was reason for this. Forgiveness of sins has reference both to sin in its relation to God and in its relation to the Church's discipline and to those whom we have injured. It requires therefore both a personal forgiveness, an ecclesiastical pardon as well as divine forgiveness. To the Christian priesthood was given the power of dispensing the two latter.

It may well be noticed that our Lord gave to the Apostles their manifold powers at different times.

They were authorized at one time to preach, at another to administer discipline, at another to heal the sick, so also to ordain, to baptize, to offer the Holy Eucharist. Each power of the priesthood was given separately. So here we must conclude that a special power to absolve the penitent was given to the Apostles.

Christ, in this mystery of love, comes as the Good Shepherd seeking His wandering sheep. He comes to gather it up, trembling and with bleeding feet, and take it in His arms and bear it back to the fold. No sinner is so vile but the Sacred Heart is open to him; no sins are so black that the precious blood cannot cleanse. The reason given why frequent communions often do not advance the soul more, is that persons venture into the King's presence uncleansed and un-absolved. In the Eucharist Jesus summons us to the banquet of His love, which is a foretaste of heaven, but we must go having on the clean wedding garment. We go otherwise at our peril. He has provided most freely for our reception of one. The tribunal of penitence is the covenanted seat of mercy. It is the way of rehabilitation: "Take away his filthy garments and give him a change of raiment."[16]

"Weary of earth and laden with my sin,
    I look at heaven and long to enter in;
But there no evil thing may find a home;
    And yet I hear a voice that bids me 'Come.'

The while I fain would tread the heavenly way,
    Evil is ever with me day by day;
Yet on mine ears the gracious tidings fall,

---

15. John 20:23

16. Zechariah 3:4

'Repent, confess, thou shalt be loosed from all.'"[17]

The next mystery is that of holy unction. As penitence is concerned with the healing of the soul, unction is concerned primarily with the healing of the body. Our blessed Lord redeemed our whole nature, body and soul, and it was but fitting that He should provide sacramentally for the needs of each.

The body is the tabernacle of the soul, the house which it inhabits. It is the garden in which the soul dwells. It is entrusted to man as the fair garden of Eden was to Adam. We are placed in it to take care of it, to rule over it, and keep it in subjection. It is to be our servant, not our master. By the discipline thus imposed our souls are trained in Christian knighthood. Our bodies being the temples of the Holy Ghost, we stand guard over His honor who trusts Himself to our care. We are to stand on guard, like the cherubim at the gates of Paradise, whose eyes were like a flame, and whose hand held a blazing sword. But the body is not only to be kept under the sceptre of the will. It must be cared for in its weakness, disorder, and pain. "A merciful man," said S. Francis, speaking of the body, "must be merciful to his beast." The body and its soul must, however, temporarily, at least, cease to be companions. We all have to pass through the dark valley and bear its sorrow.

But He who knows our necessities has provided for us with a mother's care a sacrament testifying to His protection, conveying its own restorative aid, and blessing the means used for our body's recovery. So we read that, having received authority from Jesus Christ, they "anointed with oil many that were sick, and healed them."[18] They provided for the continuance of this blessing. "Is any sick among you? Let him call for the elders of the Church; and let them pray over him, anointing him with oil in the name of the Lord; and the prayer of faith shall save the sick, and the Lord shall raise him up."[19]

The occasion of its official promulgation by S. James is not given, but we may well surmise it. There were many after Pentecost who were possessed of special gifts, among them that of healing. The ill and the sick person's friends would naturally seek out those who pos-

---

17. S. J. Stone, *Weary Of Earth And Laden With My Sin.*

18. Mark 6:13

19. James 5:14–15

sessed, or who were supposed to possess, this special gift. It was probably to check a tendency not unaccompanied with spiritual dangers
both to the persons interested and to the Church's good order that
S. James gave his directions. The sick were not to seek out those accounted possessed of miraculous powers, but to send for the elders
or priests. So far as the care of the body was concerned no specially
gifted person was necessary. Let the faithful trust themselves to the
prayers of the ordained priesthood. The ordained elder was a righteous man whom God would hear just as He did His prophet Elijah.
The order taken by the Apostles was to do away with the excitement
of miracle or faith healing, and substitute a regular method promulgated by the Church.

There was also a further reason. The priest could deal with the
soul as a faith-healing or miracle-working layman could not. If the
body was to be cured, the first and most important thing for its recovery was to bring the soul into harmony with God. So the sick
was to make his confession, and prayer was to be made over him,
and then he was to be anointed. The peace and healing of the soul
would aid in the healing of the body.

S. James uses the plural form; "Call," he says, "for the elders of
the Church." Not as excluding the ministrations of a single priest,
but as teaching us the efficacy that comes from united prayer.

The anointing is not to be used when illness is but trifling, or merely when the person is in extremis, but when any illness is serious we
may resort to it, and it may be repeated.

The "matter" of this mystery is the anointing of the sick person.
The "form" is the prayer. By the anointing God is recognized as the
giver of health. A blessing is invoked on the means used for recovery,
and through this instrumentality also, if God so wills, restorative
aid is given. For the comfort of our souls, grace is also bestowed to
meet the trials and temptations of illness. Moreover, the soul, when
passing, is fortified for its final passage.

Thus by unction a blessing comes for the healing of our bodies;
and our souls are calmed, gladdened, refreshed, and fortified by a
special gift of grace.

"In death's dark vale I fear no ill
  With Thee, dear Lord, beside me;
Thy rod and staff my comfort still,

Thy cross before to guide me.
Thou spread'st a table in my sight;
    Thy unction grace bestoweth;
And oh, what transport of delight
    From Thy pure chalice floweth."[20]

The two next mysteries are holy orders and marriage. Holy order is for the generation and preservation of the priesthood. Marriage was ordained for that of the race. Holy order is indispensable to the existence of the Church, marriage to that of society. By holy order a spiritual paternity is established between priest and people; by marriage a natural one between parent and children. Order is for the ruling over the house of God; marriage gives headship to the Christian family. Order provides for the Church's spiritual needs; marriage for the support of the family's natural wants. Holy order secures to the Church good government; marriage is for the preservation in society of good morals.

We have already spoken sufficiently of holy orders. Let us now consider marriage.

It has existed under three conditions of human society: in man's state of innocence, when fallen or apart from Christ, and under the Christian dispensation. Each has its own separate law of union. We will here speak of it only in its last condition.

Christian marriage is the union of a baptized man and woman. Baptism is therefore an absolute necessity, for it lies at the foundation of this as of all other sacraments. The parties must be baptized into Christ and made members of Christ in order to be united together "in the Lord."

They must also be of legal age, not devoid of reason, with no canonical impediment existing by reason of affinity or consanguinity; must be free in their action, and not under grave fear or constraint, and neither must have a partner by a former marriage living.

The "matter" of the sacrament is the two baptized persons who purpose, and are capable, by canonical law, of making a free and mutual choice. The "form" is the words by which, in the presence of the priest, they take one another to be man and wife, and together receive as one the blessing of the priest. In this way they are united in matrimony and receive an increase of sanctifying grace, and also

20. H. W. Baker, *The King Of Love My Shepherd Is.*

the special grace needed for the fulfilment of their mutual duties. It is a grace given to enable them to live in love and peace together "until death do us part."

To this, however, it has been objected that it makes marriage rest, as it did under the Roman civil law, on contract, and if by mutual consent the estate is created, by mutual consent, as in Roman times, it might be dissolved. But the consent of the parties here is not like that to an ordinary civil contract, which is merely an agreement to do or not to do a certain thing. It is a contract which executes itself. By their mutual agreement the wills and hearts of the two parties meet and are thereby joined together. Marriage, indeed, implies the union both of body and soul, but the soul is the dominant factor, and thus the parties before leaving the church are what the priest pronounces them to be, man and wife.

The Church, however, does not recognize the character of indissolubility as attached to the union until it has been wholly consummated.

This union being a sacramental one cannot be dissolved by civil courts. But though the bond cannot thus be broken, a separation may be granted.

The unfaithfulness of a partner does not annul the bond. The text in S. Matthew 19 which apparently favors the opposite view is too corrupt or uncertain to allow us to base an argument upon it. If Christ's words are correctly given the matter still remains in doubt, as they were seemingly addressed to the Jews and had respect to marriage in their case only. Even if applicable to Christian marriage only separation, not remarriage, is allowed. In those passages where our Lord speaks to the Apostles, and clearly in relation to the Christian state, no provision is made for any dissolution of the bond. The great underlying reason is that Christian marriage is to be a witness of the indissoluble union between Christ and His Church.

The hardness and suffering thereby entailed on the innocent party is to be met by reliance on Christ's promise, "My grace is sufficient for thee."[21] For marriage is not to be considered merely in relation to our earthly state, but to our eternal reward. God calls His servants to suffer in various ways, all of us in some way. And when our sufferings are borne for Him the soul increases in sanctity and secures an

---

21. 2 Corinthians 12:9.

increment of future bliss.

There are three kinds of Christian marriage. That of the laity, of the priesthood, and that of those consecrated to the celibate life as religious.

The first is to bear its witness unto the indissolubility of the union between Christ and His bride. The second, if we construe Scripture strictly, allows of but one marriage to the bishop or priest. As the high priest under the old dispensation was allowed to marry but once, and that a virgin, S. Paul makes the same ideal the standard of the Christian clergy. By conformity to this rule they bear witness to the oneness of the Church as the bride of Christ.

The mystical marriage of those consecrated in religion to our Lord is also a true special union of the soul to Him, and, more powerfully than words can tell, bears witness to the world of the all sufficiency of the love and grace of the Bridegroom.

Of the latter Dr. Pusey has said: "Blessed, thrice blessed they whom Christ alone sufficeth, the one aim of whose being is to live to Him and for Him. He is their light, their love, their holy joy; to Him they ever approach with trustfulness; Him they consult in all things, on Him they wait; Him they love, and desiring nothing from Him but His love, desire no love but only His. 'I am my Beloved's, and my Beloved is mine.'"[22]

Of the former estate he says: "What is the pattern and measure and model of the mutual love of the husband and the wife? What but the love of Christ Himself, and of His redeemed Church for Him, its Head?"[23]

"Love, then, with a tender, forbearing love, as Christ is tender and compassionate with us; beholding us as what, by His grace, we shall one day be; cherishing one another, encouraging one another, helping one the other along the narrow road which leadeth unto Him; denying each self for the other, as Christ loved our souls more than Himself. This love shall grow with years, as the love of Christ, which is the beauty of the soul, grows and is enlarged in each. This love shall not decay, much less die. For souls which are united in Christ shall not be separated from Christ; they shall live on still, one in the

---

22. The Rev. Dr. Pusey, *Parochial Sermons*, Vol. II, "The Sacredness of Marriage," 390.
23. *Ibid.* 391.

one love of Christ."[24]

"Lord, who at Cana's wedding feast
   Didst as a guest appear,
Thou dearer far than earthly guest,
   Vouchsafe Thy presence here;
For holy Thou indeed dost prove
   The marriage vow to be,
Proclaiming it a type of love
   Between the Church and Thee.
The holiest vow that man can make,
   The golden thread in life,
The bond that none may dare to break,
   That bindeth man and wife."[25]

The Holy Eucharist is the greatest of all mysteries. It is the most grand and worthy of honor of all the sacraments; for while they convey grace, in the Eucharist we have Jesus Christ Himself, the author of grace. It is an ever-living witness of the incarnation, sacrificial death, resurrection, and ascension of the Lord. It is the consummation of religion on earth, as it affords us the most intimate and perpetual communication with Jesus Christ. It is the essence of Christianity, as being the sacrifice, in union with which the Christian makes that of Calvary applicable to himself. It is the possession of the Church on earth of Jesus Christ's real but veiled presence, as she waits adoringly for His unveiling in the state of glory.

We may for devotional and practical purposes consider the mystery under three heads:

First, as a witness. The sacraments are witnesses to the faith. The Blessed Sacrament bears witness to the incarnation, death, and resurrection of Jesus Christ, and the oneness of the Church in Him. By the necessary recitation of the words of institution, "This is my body,"[26] witness is thereby borne to the fact that Christ had a body like our own. Moreover, it is of faith that He assumed it, never to put it off. So age after age the priest repeats these words at the altar, which, if Christ had ceased to have a body, would not be true. Also

24. *Ibid.* 393

25. Adelaide Thrupp, *Lord, Who at Cana's Wedding Feast.*

26. Luke 22:19

by the consecration of the two elements the mystery tells us that the blood was separated from the body by a sacrificial death. "This cup is the new covenant in my blood poured out for you."[27] The mystery declares yet further that He who died rose in that body, for otherwise the words of the institution would be unreal. It moreover declares as well as effects the unity of the Church. We feed on Him, the living bread, and are made one loaf in Him.

The sacrament is a communion. By the words of institution and the power of the Holy Spirit the elements become the body and blood of Christ. Man's names designate, God's naming makes that He names. It is not made in the natural order, or governed by any natural laws. By the Spirit's power the elements become what the Word declares them to be, Christ's body and blood.

The Anglican Church has declared this as her faith and embodied it in her catechism. In it she declares that in the Blessed Sacrament there is an outward part or sign, and there is an inward part or thing signified, and thirdly there are the benefits which partakers receive.

First, there is a sign.

At the time of the Reformation there was a so-called Romish theory that the elements existed in appearance only. Our theologians met this error by saying, that by denying the existence of the sign, the integrity of the sacrament was fatally impaired, for a sacrament consists both of an inward thing and an outward sign.[28] On the other hand, some within the Church have mistaken the Church's meaning, and taught that the inward part was something which only signified Christ. In this way they have fallen into the opposite error of making two signs. The outward sign being one, and the inward part being only in some way another sign, — something signifying Christ and not being the real body and blood of our Lord.

There are three opinions held respecting this mystery. Two belong to the Protestant category. The Zwinglian makes the sacrament merely a memorial of an absent Lord; the Calvinistic view is that along with the reception of the elements Christ's body and blood are communicated to the faithful and elect receiver. The Catholic belief as stated in the catechism is that there is a sign and a thing,

---

27. Luke 22:20

28. "Transubstantiation (or the change of the substance of Bread and Wine) in the Supper of the Lord... *overthroweth the nature of a Sacrament...*" (*Article XXVIII*)

and that the thing signified is the body and blood of Christ.[29]

A more intelligent apprehension of the mystery of Christ's presence can be attained by considering three points.

First, the whole transaction takes place not in the natural order of things, but in the spiritual body of Christ. It is therefore governed by no natural laws of matter and space, and can be comprehended by no analogies drawn from natural life.

Secondly, by the consecration, acting through His representatives, Christ gathers up the elements into Himself, and they become His body and blood. No local movement on the part of Christ is required to effect this. The elements become what His almighty word declares them to be, and receiving them with faith we partake of Him.

Thirdly, an act of adoration is due Him from the common law of courtesy which demands that every act of condescension on the part of a superior must be acknowledged by a reciprocal act of reverence, and in case the superior is God, of adoration. We do not adore the elements considered apart by themselves, but our act of adoration has, for its terminus ad quern, His divine personality, to whom alone adoration is due.

The third aspect of the mystery is, that it is a sacrifice. Slowly the Anglican Church has recovered its grasp on this great truth. The Eucharistic sacrifice has a double relation. One to the act of our Lord's blood shedding finished on Calvary, and one to the presentation of that blood, which has passed through death to the Eternal Father.

On Calvary the offering was made in behalf and in reconciliation of the human race. On the altar it is re-presented, pleaded, and appropriated by the Church for the needs of her individual members.

It is, however, an imperfect apprehension of the truth to regard the sacrifice of the altar as a presentation by the priest of Christ's death, apart from the co-operation of the people. The deeper and fuller view is that the Church offers up herself as a living sacrifice to God. She does this in union with Christ, her head, with whom she identifies herself, by partaking of the sacrifice of the altar.

Most glorious would it be if on every altar on Sundays and holy

---

29. "QUESTION: What is the inward part, or thing signified?
ANSWER: The Body and Blood of Christ, which are verily and indeed taken and received by the faithful in the Lord's Supper." (*Church Catechism*)

days, and more frequently still, the holy sacrifice was offered. The earnestly minded have it in their power to make the Anglican Church what they desire. But it is not by mere agitation, or legislation, or change of relationship to the State, or in any like ways, will they attain their end. It is God and God only who can bring about the desired result, and the most potent of all agencies which move Him is the devout offering of the holy sacrifice.

> "Thou, who at thy first Eucharist didst pray,
> That all Thy Church might be forever one,
> Grant us at every Eucharist to say
> With longing heart and soul, 'Thy will be done.'
> Oh, may we all one Bread, one Body be,
> Through this blest Sacrament of Unity.
>
> We pray Thee, too, for wanderers from Thy fold;
> Oh, bring them back, good Shepherd of the sheep,
> Back to the faith which saints believed of old,
> Back to the Church which still that faith doth keep;
> Soon may we all one Bread, one Body be,
> Through this blest Sacrament of Unity."[30]

---

30. W. H. Turton, *Thou, Who at Thy first Eucharist didst pray.*

XI

ANGLICAN ORDERS

O UR Lord established a ministry which would be an extension of His own, and through which He would act. It would extend His own prophetical, priestly, and kingly offices and their benefits to mankind. By its means He would continue in the world going about doing good. His ministers as His authorized agents, by their official acts of consecration, blessing, and pardon, bind Him. Whom they bless, He blesses; whom they in His name forgive, He forgives; on whom they lay hands, He lays His hands; what they confirm, He confirms; what they consecrate, He consecrates; whom they join in holy matrimony, He joins together in Himself. Of all the loving gifts of the Incarnate God to His people, that of the priesthood is the most signal token of His providential care. Therefore, Christ's loyal children have ever felt it an honor to care for those set over them in the Lord, and esteem them very highly for the Lord's sake.

From its earliest formation the Anglican Church has always been in possession of this Christ-founded and Apostolic ministry. It was coeval with its earliest beginnings. It continued throughout the British-Saxon-Norman times. Its continuity was not broken at the Reformation. The reformers officially declared, and made it a part of the prayer-book, that the ancient orders were to be "continued." It has been securely guarded by canon law and an orthodox liturgy. It has extended under the divine blessing throughout the world. The loyal children of the Church do not need to be convinced concerning it. Its priests know, by its results, that they possess the gift of sacred orders. The laity ask for no further proofs than their own experience of their possession of true and effective sacraments. It is immaterial to them what those without their communion may say or think. They know in whom they believe. They know with the divine certainty what they possess. The proof vouchsafed them is of the double kind of interior verification by God's Holy Spirit, and by the outward historical and theological evidence. No more certain truth is there in the sphere of revealed religion. No better evidence, indeed, is there for the existence of God Himself than, believing in Him, exists for the validity of Anglican orders.

We do, however, meet with those who, if they do not deny, at least question them. They are divided in England into the two classes of non-Conformists, Sectarians and Roman Catholics. The reasons, when given by the first, seem based largely on ignorance, the second on technicalities and policy. We must meet both with fairness, sympathy, and charity. For only by such a spirit can Christ's honor and the true interests of His kingdom be served.

First, as to the sectarians. We must recognize that all duly baptized are united to Christ, and extend our love to all Christians by whatever name they call themselves. Their spiritual ancestors in England went out from the Mother Church, and they have inherited the results of the schism. The devout among them have found Christ and feel assured of their acceptance in Him. In their walk with the Lord they have found Him precious to their souls. So rich is the Gospel as they possess it, that it is difficult for them to realize there is a fuller spiritual life vouchsafed through participation of the sacraments of the Catholic Church. They do not see this spiritual result in the many worldly and indifferent churchmen, and so conclude that it is not to be found in the Church. God in His dear love is, however, drawing souls desirous of a closer union with Himself into the fuller embrace of those sacramental gifts which the Church alone can give.

But the sectarian is so strongly entrenched in his belief that he is ordinarily unwilling to even consider the Church's claims. If he argues at all he brings up Chillingworth's argument about the uncertainty of the transmission of orders. His argument, however, of the improbability of preserving a succession through so many ages without flaw applies to that Roman doctrine which makes the validity of a sacrament depend upon the personal intention of the priest. But it does not apply to the transmission of a divine commission according to the canon law of the Church, which requires three bishops to act in conferring it; and the validity of whose action does not depend upon their personal belief, but on their official character as agents of the Church. And as concerning the effect of such an orderly and regular transmission from Apostolic times, "there is," says Bishop Stillingfleet, "as great reason to believe the Apostolic succession to be of divine institution, as the canon of Holy Scripture or the observance of the Lord's Day."[1]

---

1. The Rt. Rev. Edward Stillingfleet, *Sermons XXII*, March 15th, 1685

But, our inquirer asks, is it probable that God would entrust such a gift to unholy and unbelieving persons as some of the alleged transmitters certainly have been? It would, however, be more improbable if, in so important a matter, God should not have left a regular and appointed method of transmission. We have indeed this treasure in earthen vessels, but the unholiness of the channel does not hinder the conveyance of the gift. The neglect or even denial of their powers would not disrobe the priests of their sacred character. "We do not become a mere creature of man though we sell ourselves to be his slave."[2] "Even if a bishop," wrote Newman, "were to use the words, 'receive ye the Holy Ghost' with little or no meaning, or a priest the consecrating words in the Eucharist, considering it only a commemoration of Christ's death, or a deacon the water and words of baptism, denying in his heart that it is regeneration, yet they may in spite of their unbelief be instruments of a power they know not of, and 'speak not of themselves' — they may be as Balaam or as Isaac."[3]

Probably the argument which in their hearts most affects sectarians is the logical outcome of the Apostolic succession in application to their own ministry. If the doctrine is true, are not their ministers without authority to officiate in Christ's name? They know and love them. They have been helped by their ministrations. They see how God has blessed their efforts. They take an honest pride in the growth and power of their denomination. They are linked to it by Christian friendships and many social ties. They cannot think, whatever is urged, that their work is not of God and dear to Him. Such a view and feeling is highly commendable. Christians ought not to deny whatever the Holy Spirit may have witnessed in their own consciousness. But a distinction is to be observed. The Church claims to have a priesthood and sacrifice and sacramental gifts of confirmation and absolution. A sectarian does not claim to have a priesthood or sacrifice. He does not call his ministers priests. He rejects all sacerdotal powers. It is therefore no want of liberality to deny to the sectarian clergy what they themselves strenuously repudiate. We do not deny that they are Christ's disciples declaring to the best of their knowledge His Gospel, and that, where sincere,

---

2. The Rev. John Henry Newman, *On the Fortunes of the Church.*

3. *Ibid.*

He blesses their work. When, however, S. John Baptist had brought his disciples to repentance and peace, they were to leave their old master, grateful for what he had done for them, to receive the fuller gifts of a more complete union with Christ. So too Apollos may be an eloquent man, mighty in the Scriptures, instructed in the way of the Lord, fervent in spirit, yet an Aquila and Priscilla must take him unto themselves and expound unto him the way of God more perfectly. In like manner, humble and devout sectarians are being led back into their old home, to find there an illumination and spiritual gifts, a wider vision and a deeper life than they before possessed.

Let us now, on the other hand, turn to our Roman brethren. A great many devout Roman Catholics, both of priests and laity, believe in their hearts in the validity of Anglican orders. They have come into friendly relations with Anglican priests and saintly laymen. They see the same effects of sacramental grace in them as they see in their own communion. "By their fruits ye shall know them,"[4] said the Lord, and their spiritual discernment tells them that Anglicans possess the sacraments as truly as themselves. A ruling of the late Pope, Leo XIII., restrains the expression of their belief, which they know to be true.

However, as has been said by Roman Catholics, this papal utterance was not of the class to which infallibility belongs; and, as it contains some errors of fact, his Holiness, by those who drew it up, was obviously misinformed. So it may be in time to come that the Roman Church, whose head is the first bishop in Christendom, may find it to its advantage, among the growing assaults of these later times, to reverse, in the interests of Christian union, its own opinion in the same manner as it reversed, concerning the conveyance of holy orders, the decision of Pope Eugenius IV. We can only say, with God all things, even this, is possible, and for Christ's sake and Rome's pray it may come to pass.

I

If any Christians, however, with honest intent, make inquiry concerning our orders, it is well to call their attention first to the fact that the Anglican Church not only claims to have them, but acts as if she had. While she holds that there are two sacraments universally nec-

---

4. See Matthew 7:15–20

essary for salvation, she does not deny there are others. She regards holy orders as the ordained means of communicating authority and grace for the work of the ministry. In one of her homilies she calls it by the term sacrament. It is placed in this category by her ablest theologians. It is the more commonly accepted belief in the Church that the character conferred by the sacrament is indelible. Once a bishop or priest, always a bishop or priest.

Again, she has also preserved carefully the distinctions between the three inherited orders. A deacon is the assistant only at the Holy Eucharist. He may baptize infants in the absence of the priest, and so bring them into the kingdom. The priest alone can consecrate and offer the holy sacrifice. It is he who ministers the word of reconciliation in the absolving of penitents. The bishop alone is possessed of the power of ordination. According to Catholic usage he alone confirms, either doing so in person or by consecrating the chrism used for that purpose. He is the source of diocesan jurisdiction. He exercises rule and authority. By thus preserving intact the distinctive powers of each of the three orders the Anglican Church officially declares her belief in them.

She holds also to the Apostolic succession preserved through episcopal ordination. In the American prayer-book, in the office of institution, she thus makes prayer for the instituted priest: "O Holy Jesus, who hast purchased to Thyself an universal Church, and hast promised to be with the ministers of Apostolic succession to the end of the world: Be graciously pleased to bless the ministry and service of him who is now appointed to offer sacrifices of prayer and praise to Thee in this house."

Again, she regards the word "presbyter" as synonymous with priest, and gives in her Articles the title of "Sacerdotes" to the ministers of the second order. In the office of institution in her prayer-book the bishop grants to the instituted minister authority for the performance of "every act of sacerdotal function among the people." The American prayer-book describes the relation between the people and the clergy as a "sacerdotal relation." The priest praises God as one who has been honored "to stand in Thy house and to serve at Thy holy altar."

Moreover, the Church regards the priest as an offerer of sacrifice. When he stands before the altar he solemnly offers the holy and consecrated gifts of Christ's body and blood to the Almighty Father. Addressing Him, he uses the liturgical words, "We, thy humble servants, do celebrate and make here before thy Divine Majesty, with these thy holy gifts, which we now offer unto Thee, the memorial Jesus commanded us to make." The sacerdotal character is thus stamped upon her priests and all their ministrations.

The Church's belief in holy order as a sacrament, conveying character and grace, is also marked in another way, for none but those episcopally ordained can minister at her altars. If a Roman priest is led to unite himself with her the Church does not again ordain him, for he is already a priest. If, on the other hand, a sectarian minister is brought into the Church, no matter how learned he may be, or whatever his attainments, the Church requires that he must be confirmed and then ordained as if he were a mere layman. He must be made first a deacon, and then in due time elevated to the priesthood. Now this attitude of the Church in respect to nonconformists can only be justified on the ground of the Church's belief in the necessity of episcopal ordination and the sacrament of order. For if the sectarian ministers are as fully and validly representatives of Christ as we are, then the Church is guilty of a great wrong, indeed of the sin of schism, in making what is not in itself essential a matter of division.

Nor finally must it be overlooked that beside her prayer-book in America she has an official hymn book. The devotions of Anglicans are not confined as they are in the Eastern Church to their formal liturgy. To understand the spirit of the Anglican Church one must study the hymns of her people. They are their devotional life. Our collects may seem cold in comparison with the East, but the spirit of devotion breaks forth in our hymns. In them we find the Church entreating the Holy Spirit to make the ordained "a holy priesthood"; she prays that they may present and spread forth to God

"That only offering perfect in Thine eyes,
   The one true, pure, immortal Sacrifice,"[5]

and that in the Holy Eucharist we may receive

"The Bread that is Christ's Flesh—for food,
   The Wine that is the Saviour's Blood."

So by her action, her liturgy, her hymns, the teaching of her theo-

---

5. William Bright, *And now, O Father, mindful of the love.*

logians, the manifestations of her spiritual life, the Church bears witness to her possession of the sacrament of holy order. However in evil times the sense of the priestly character may have decayed, her priests since the Reformation have never sunk in morals like those of the Roman communion in Mexico, Brazil, or the Philippines. There has been no such ignorance concerning the ministration of the sacraments or decadence of the priestly character as S. Carlo Borromeo found existing among the clergy when he became Bishop of Milan. When at the end of the eighteenth century so many of the French priests, with bishops, became apostates, the clergy of England in that era of unbelief remained faithful to Christ. The Church of England knows she possesses holy orders, and the lives of her sons and clergy declare it.

II

Our inquirer may ask, how have the orders been preserved and transmitted? Was there an interruption at the time of the Reformation? Through whom do the present bishops trace their descent?

An easy way of giving answer is to say that all the living Anglican bishops trace their succession to the pre-Reformation ones and so through them up to the Apostles, through Archbishop Laud. By remembering this fact the question of the Anglican succession is much simplified. For Archbishop Laud united in himself three separate and distinct lines of consecrators. These were the Irish line, the Italian line, and the English line, any one of which being good, and there is no doubt about any one, Laud was validly consecrated bishop.

Concerning the Irish line, it combined in its descent the old Celtic line, also the Roman line, to which resort was frequently made, and in pre-Reformation times and during the reign of Queen Mary the English line.[6]

It is too often overlooked that under Queen Elizabeth but two of the Irish bishops were deposed, Leverous, of Kildare, and Walsh, of Meath, for refusing to take the oath of supremacy. Most if not all of the others who had been bishops during the previous Roman Catholic period of Queen Mary conformed. Among them was Hugh Kir-

---

6. It is a fact that the Old Celtic line is preserved exclusively within the Anglican Lineage.

wan, Archbishop of Dublin, who had been consecrated by Bonner, Thirlby, and Griffin during Queen Mary's reign and according to the Roman pontifical. Some of these conforming Irish bishops were transferred in Elizabeth's time and later, to English sees. Through three of his consecrators, — John Thornborough, of Worcester, John Housen, of Oxford (one of whose consecrators had the Irish succession through Christopher Hampton, Archbishop of Armagh), and Theophilus Field, Bishop of Landafff, one of whose consecrators was George, Bishop of Derry, — Laud derived his succession.

The conveyance of orders through the Italian line is also a matter of historical interest. M. A. Spalatro, or Marco Antonio de Dominis (consecrated Bishop of Segna in 1600, and translated to Spalatro on the east shore of the Adriatic, in 1602) conformed to the English Church. He was a Roman Catholic archbishop. On uniting with the Church in England he was made Dean of Windsor. He was a co-consecrator, in 1617, of George Montaigne, Bishop of London, and Nicholas Felton, Bishop of Ely. When Laud was consecrated on the 18th of November, 1621, as Bishop of St. David's, amongst his co-consecrators were Bishop Montaigne and Bishop Felton.

Laud also derived his succession through the English line. When Queen Elizabeth came to the throne in 1559, Cardinal Pole, who was the Archbishop of Canterbury, had died. He passed away a few hours after Queen Mary's death. The see of Canterbury had thus become vacant. Nominations and elections to the see were made in legal manner. The form of confirmation followed that was used in Bishop Chicheley's case in the fifteenth century. On the 11th of December, 1559, Dr. Mathew Parker was consecrated Archbishop at Lambeth. The official original record is preserved there. A facsimile (a photo-zincograph copy) has been made and officially witnessed, and was published by Parker and Company in 1870.

Roman Catholic historians like Dr. Lingard and theologians like Canon Eastcourt have admitted the fact of the consecration. They have retreated from the former position taken by Roman writers and apologized for it. Father Brandi, S. J., in *A Last Word*, says, "One cannot be held responsible for what may be written on this or any other subject by incompetent writers, but for a long time past no English Catholic writer of any standing has used the Nag's Head story as an argument."

"With regard to Barker's consecration," says Canon Eastcourt (R.

C.), "as an historical fact it is most certain that it took place on the 17th of December, 1559, according to the description in the register."[7]

It may be added that Dr. Cyriacus, a learned Orthodox Greek ecclesiastical historian, freely admits Parker's consecration, of which he has no doubt.[8]

In the words of Dr. Döllinger, spoken at the Bonn Conference, in 1875, "The fact that Parker was consecrated by four rightly consecrated bishops, *rite et legitime*, with the imposition of hands and the necessary words, is so well attested that if one chooses to doubt this fact, one could with the same right doubt ten thousand facts;" or in the words of Courayer, "Everything concurs to set the truth in so great a light that if the fact of the Lambeth ordination is not above all doubt one must renounce acknowledging anything certain in history."

Very touching is the record of Archbishop Parker made in his own private diary: "17th of December, 1559. I was this day consecrated Archbishop of Canterbury. Alas! Alas! O Lord God, for what times hast Thou reserved me. Now am I come into the deep waters, and the floods overflow me. O Lord, I am in trouble. Answer for me." So incontestable is the evidence for Parker's consecration that the pope in a late bull abandoned all objections to it.

The consecration took place with dignified ceremonial at Lambeth. We read that the chapel was adorned with tapestry and the chancel covered with red cloth, the altar was vested with a carpet or altar cloth. The consecration, which was after the ordinal of King Edward VI., took place according to the ancient custom after the creed. The elect archbishop entered, wearing a long scarlet cassock, with four torches borne before him. He was accompanied by four

---

7. Eastcourt, *op.cit.*, p.114

8. On July 28th, 1922, the Patriarch of Constantinople, Meletios, recognized the validity of Anglican orders. On March 12th, 1923, the Patriarch of Jerusalem, Daminos, recognized Anglican orders and asserts their equality with Roman orders. In 1923, Cyril of Cyprus, Ecumenical Patriarch of Constantinople recognized Anglican orders. In 1930, the Patriarch of Alexandria recognized the validity of Anglican orders stating that, if an Anglican priest were to move to Eastern Orthodoxy, no re-ordination is necessary. On March 30th, 1936, the Romanian Orthodox Church recognized the validity of Anglican orders. On September 21st, 1939, the Holy Synod of Greece recognized Anglican orders.

bishops. The celebrant was vested in a cope of silk. In conferring the sacred order of the episcopate four bishops participated. Two of these, Barlow, the chief consecrator, and Hodgkins, had been consecrated according to the old Catholic pontifical. Bishop Barlow's consecration is certified by a great number of proofs which place it beyond any reasonable doubt. The Roman Catholic historian Dr. Lingard admits it. He was duly installed in person as Bishop of S. David's, and the mandate to install always recites the fact of the consecration. He took his seat in the House of Lords, which he could not have done but on being presented by two witnesses to his consecration. He was universally recognized as a bishop in King Henry's time and King Edward's and in legal documents by Queen Mary. His saying that the king's appointment would make a layman as good a bishop as himself would be meaningless if he were not a duly consecrated bishop. There is no reasonable doubt but that Barlow was a duly consecrated bishop, and consequently Archbishop Parker.

We must, however, notice that one departure took place from the ordinary method. It is of record that all four bishops, when they laid on hands, pronounced the formula, "Receive the Holy Ghost," etc. The occasion was a peculiar one and they felt the importance of most carefully guarding the transmission of the gift and grace of holy order. They thus departed from the customary way of the chief consecrator alone using the words. By each of them uttering the formula, each acted as a consecrator, so that if any one of them was a validly consecrated bishop the gift of orders would be conveyed. The Roman Catholic Martene declared that the bishops assisting in the laying on of hands are "not merely witnesses, but co-operators."[9] The Eastern Church holds that as many bishops as are present and act do consecrate. It can therefore be no matter of doubt that Matthew Parker was solemnly set apart and consecrated as bishop in the Church of God.

We can but note the contrast of this consecration with that of Dr. Carroll, who was consecrated in 1790 as the first Roman bishop for the United States, and upon the validity of whose consecration that of the Roman hierarchy in America for half a century depended. He was consecrated in the private chapel of Lullworth Castle, and contrary to the ancient canons, by one bishop only, and he a bishop

---

9. *De Antiq. Eccles. Rit.*, Lib. I, Pt. III, C. VIII

only *in partibus*, having no lawful jurisdiction in England and assisted, so the records say, by two priests!

Thus the preeminent caution taken in the consecration of Archbishop Parker bears witness to the Anglican Church's care in the transmission of holy orders. The fact of his consecration is now, by the admission of opponents, beyond dispute.

III

Let us next consider the ordinal.

In the opinion of a late pope the validity of the Edwardian formula was denied. Like one of the English privy council decisions it was obviously so dictated by policy as to be for Catholics without weight. It could be no more so than preceding opinions of former popes who have fallen into errors respecting the orders of other bodies, or in what the essence of holy order consists. Thus we find one declaring certain orders invalid which Rome now in uniat churches accepts, and Eugenius IV. declaring the essential "matter" to be the delivery of the instruments which is an opinion now abandoned. Pope Leo XIII. in turn contradicted the rulings of his predecessors Julius III. and also of Paul IV. The former authorized Cardinal Pole to grant dispensations touching "the office of consecration which had been granted even by bishops who were heretics and schismatics, or otherwise minus rite and without observance of the accustomed form of the Church." The phrase "accustomed form" means the customary full ritual, "minus rite," something less. The cardinal accordingly informed Parliament that he would receive "all who had obtained orders under the pretended authority of the supremacy of the Anglican Church in the orders to which they had been so admitted." Paul IV. ratified the action of his predecessor.

A question, however, had arisen whether the dispensation granted applied to certain Lutheran and Calvinistic ministers who by the king's grant had been allowed to have churches of their own. Pope Julius in his brief *Regimine universalis* decided who were to be regarded as ordained and who not. Those "alone can be said not to have been ordained, rite *et recte* who were not ordained and consecrated in the form of the Church." The phrase "form of the Church" means that part of the accustomed form which is sufficient to effect or confer a sacrament. This had been wanting in the cases above mentioned. There was no competent consecrator. But the pope ruled "that others on whom orders had been conferred by bishops ordained and consecrated in the form of the Church had received the character of the orders conferred and lacked nothing but the execution thereof," *i. e.*, papal recognition and consent. It is thus seen to be a somewhat difficult task to reconcile Pope Leo's opinion with that of his predecessors.

It is also to be noticed that Leo fell, through the way the case was represented to him, into a mistake of fact. There was an authority given by Pope Paul IV. to Cardinal Pole to condone or dispense persons who had *nulliter et de facto* obtained during Henry's and Edward's time various grants concerning orders as well as ecclesiastical benefices. As cited by Leo, the word "concerning" was omitted and the word *nulliter* was translated "null" and made to refer to the orders. It thus made the sentence convey the idea that these orders were declared null. But it has been shown that *nulliter* in mediaeval Latin, as given by Ducange in his *Glossary* means "unjustly," "extra-legally," "illegitimately." It was so used within a short time in the English ecclesiastical courts. The meaning, therefore, is that certain irregularities might be dispensed, but not that the orders were declared to be invalid. These errors of fact vacate the papal opinion of Leo of any value. As the members of the great and learned Society of Jesus have come to disregard the condemnation of their order by Pope Clement, so in time to come they may learn to disregard this political one of Leo.

However all this may be, the question of Anglican orders is not affected by any papal decision. It must stand on its own merits.

In respect of the ordinal, the Anglican Church provided that the ancient orders of the priesthood should be preserved and rightly transmitted. As the ordinal was in hopeless confusion, perplexing differences existing between the Roman and the Sarum rites, and no one was able to say with certainty at what time in the service the priest was ordained, it was of the first necessity that the ordinal should be revised. In the Roman rite there are two laying on of hands by the bishop. One when the words "Receive the Holy Ghost" are said. But this is said after the ordination; for the ordained has been acting as a co-consecrator of the Holy Eucharist with the bishop, which unless ordained he could not do. The other laying on of hands is at the beginning of the service, when the hands of the bishop are laid on, but nothing is said. For the removal of these difficulties a revision was deemed advisable.

As no one universally received rite existed to which the Anglican Church was bound to conform, it cannot be inferred from the rectification of her ordinal that she had any intention of departing from Catholic faith or usage. She declared officially and many times the contrary. In the changes she made she had resort to Holy Scripture, ancient practice, and Catholic tradition. The alterations were not made because she accepted the Lutheran or Protestant view of the ministry, for she rejected the proposal of the foreign Lutheran Reformers[10] to frame an ordinal after their belief. She set forth one founded on essentially different and on Catholic principles.

It was not framed on a denial of priesthood and sacrifice. If it had been, the title of *sacerdos* or priest, which implies sacrifice, would have been stricken out of the prayer-book as the sect of Reformed Episcopalians in America has done. The Church's intention was to preserve the inherited ancient orders. This is proved by two facts: First, by the ordinal itself, where the distinction between the three orders is preserved, and ordination is required by one of the Episcopal order. The proper "matter" is provided by the laying on of the bishop's hands. An efficient "form" is set forth, namely, prayer for the ordinand, with designation of the order to be conferred and authorization for its work, together with the gift of the Holy Ghost bestowed for its exercise.

---

10. In fairness we must temper the Saintly Bishop's words by asserting that *some* forms of Lutheranism held to a Catholic understanding of Holy Orders, and *some* Lutherans still retain them. Archbishop Laurentius Petri —a Lutheran Reformer of the Church of Sweden— wrote:

Therefore, since this ordinance [Episcopacy] was very useful and without doubt proceeded from God the Holy Ghost (who gives all good gifts), so it was generally approved and accepted over the whole of Christendom, and has since so remained, and must remain in the future, so long as the world lasts, although the abuse, which has been very great in this as in all other useful and necessary things, must be set aside. (*Kyrko-ordningat*, 144)

Bishop John Wordsworth said that in this regard, the Swedes are of the same mind as the judicious Hooker: "[Episcopacy] had either divine appointment beforehand or divine approbation afterwards, and is in that respect to be acknowledged the ordinance of God."(*Laws*, Bk. VII, Ch. V §3) Furthermore, the Rev. Gustaf Elias Unonius — another Swedish Lutheran and the first graduate of Nashotah House — wrote regarding his ordination in the Episcopal Church: "The rest of us believed, however, that in joining the Episcopal church we were not guilty of lapsing from either the [Lutheran] church or the confession." (*The Memoirs of Gustaf Unonius*, Vol. II, 18) It is unfair to say that the Anglican Tradition is altogether unlike some Lutheran Bodies.

Secondly, the Church explicitly declared her intention to preserve the ancient orders in their integrity. She declared her intention that her priests should be what they were in pre-Reformation times. She did this in a preface to her ordinal. And here we must expose a common error of interpretation into which clerical writers are apt to fall. The private opinions of the authors of any law cannot logically or legally be appealed to in aid of its construction. The opinions, for example, expressed in the debates in Parliament cannot be cited in court to explain the meaning of a statute. The reason is, the statute is the utterance of the whole body as an entity, and not merely of those who planned or advocated it.

Now the ordinal was adopted by the whole body of bishops, all save one being in favor of it. This body putting forth the ordinal expressed its intention officially, as we have said, in its preface. We cannot legally or logically go behind it to get at the ordinal's meaning. It is clearly stated in words which cannot be misunderstood or explained away. It states that "from the Apostles' time there have been these orders of ministers in Christ's Church: bishops, priests, and deacons, . . . and therefore to the intent that these orders may be continued, no man shall be accounted or taken to be a lawful bishop, priest, or deacon except he be admitted thereto according to the form hereafter following, or hath had formerly Episcopal consecration or ordination."

This explicitly declared intention legally governs the interpretation of the ordinal. It also does so morally, for a principal in common law is bound by the "holdings out" or representations of an authorized agent. So it is with the Church. She uses the well-known terms, bishops, priests, and deacons. On the "holding out" that she possesses them in their ancient sense men are induced to enter holy orders and give their lives to her service. She is therefore estopped from explaining them away, or putting any other than the recognized Catholic sense upon them.

So much for the intention of the ordinal. As for the intention of those who used it in Archbishop Parker's case, it must be observed that the bishops were the officials of a Church whose ordinal was provided for them. They could not alter its meaning by any interior views of their own. It is not, therefore, to be construed by their own private opinions whatever they may have been. Acting as they did seriously and with the intent of doing what the Church ordered, their intention, as well as that of the Church's ordinal, must be taken to be that of making and continuing a Catholic priesthood.

The care of the Church is also seen in the preservation of the "matter and form" essential to the sacrament. "Matter" expresses the outward sign, and "form" the words that accompany it. Although Pope Eugenius IV. declared the proper matter to be the delivery in the service of the paten and chalice, yet that decision had to be admitted erroneous when it was discovered that this ceremony was unknown for many hundred years. The commonly accepted belief now is that the "matter" is the laying on of hands by the bishop. This the Anglican rite provides for in the giving of all the degrees of order.

There can therefore be no question concerning the validity of the "matter."

When we come to consider the "form" we are met by the fact that there never has been one universal formula, but it is generally agreed that there should be prayer for the ordinand, with a recognition of the order to be given and the gift of the Holy Spirit for its exercise.

We must here draw attention to the fact that here are two views regarding the connection between the matter and the form. One is that they must be coincident, the other that the service being considered as a whole, they are legally and morally united though in different parts of it.

The validity of Anglican orders is not affected whichever opinion is adopted.

Let us examine the first as applied to the ordinal in use at the time of Archbishop Parker's consecration. There, in the ordination of a priest, the bishop, laying his hands on the head of the ordinand, says, "Receive the Holy Ghost: whose sins thou dost forgive, they are forgiven: and whose sins thou dost retain, they are retained: and be thou a faithful dispenser of the Word of God, and of His Holy Sacraments: In the Name of the Father, and of the Son, and of the Holy Ghost."

We have here a bestowal of the Holy Spirit for the exercise of a power exclusively sacerdotal, which thus designates the priest's office, and empowers him to minister the "Word" and "the Sacraments." The ministering of the sacraments includes all of them, and all they include. The authorization and empowering therefore includes the offering of the gospel sacrifice of the body and blood of Christ.

It is well known that the essence of the priesthood lies in its function of ministering in the Church and for it, as it offers itself up in union with the sacrifice of the altar to God, and as it ministers for God to its members. It offers the holy sacrifice of the altar to God, it dispenses from God the pardoning word of reconciliation. These are the two special works cited in Trent as characteristic of the priesthood. In order to express the *Sacerdotium*, or priesthood, it was only necessary to incorporate one of these into the ordaining form. The Anglican Church took the one used by our Lord when He breathed upon the Apostles. To insist that it is necessary more explicitly to express the sacerdotal function of the priesthood would be to invalidate all the orders of Christendom.

The Anglican "form" of conveying priesthood is thus seen to be sufficient and valid.

In the bestowal of the episcopate the form given in the ordinal was, "Take the Holy Ghost, and remember thou stir up the grace of God, which is in thee by imposition of hands: for God hath not given us the spirit of fear, but of power and love and of soberness." This is equally as valid a form as that for the priesthood.

It is to be remembered that this is the text cited in the Council of Trent to prove holy orders a sacrament.

Now the same reason that led the Anglican Church to take for the "form" in the ordination of a priest the words of Christ when He bestowed a sacerdotal power led to the taking of the most significant words in Holy Scripture connected with the character belonging to the episcopate. The episcopate is the order of authority and power, it ordains and consecrates and rules. It therefore requires a gift of "power" for ordination and consecration, which is here implied, and the spirit of love and soberness to rule wisely and well. Thus, by this text according to Trent, the episcopate is designated, and the bishop consecrated is empowered with the gift of the Holy Ghost coincidently with the laying on of hands.

If, on the other hand, the other opinion is adopted and the service is regarded as a whole, the gift of priesthood and of the episcopate is equally evident. This opinion has two reasons in its favor. First, it is common sense. Seeing that the purpose and object of the service is to ordain or consecrate a person a priest or bishop, the whole service should legally be construed together. Again, it is the way our

Lord Himself ordained the Apostles. He bade them at one time offer the holy sacrifice; at another gave them authority to forgive sin;
at another commanded them to baptize; lastly, gave them mission
and jurisdiction. But their consecration was not complete until He
ascended and made them "able ministers of the Word"[11] by the gift
of the Holy Ghost.

It seems to be suggested, as the Anglican Archbishops say, by the
Pope that our present form of ordination ought perhaps to be considered sufficient, if it were not for the fact that between the years
1549 and 1662 the words, "For the office and work of a priest" were
lacking. But this is a quite groundless objection, as the archbishops
pointed out in their reply to the Papal Bull, because during that time
words designating priesthood, which the Pope considers necessary,
were contained in the prayer, "Almighty and everlasting God, giver
of all good things, who by Thy Holy Spirit has appointed divers
orders of ministers in Thy Church, mercifully behold these Thy servants now called to the office of Priesthood." This prayer, it must
be remembered, was at that time part of the ordination proper, and
not, as now, the Collect of the Mass, of which fact the Pope seemed
to be unaware.

But even now, however, this Collect is not separated in time so far
as the potential words of Christ to the Apostles to offer the Holy
Sacrifice and the effective gift of the Holy Spirit at Pentecost which
enabled them to do so. If thus the "matter and form" must for validity be absolutely coincident, then the Twelve, including Peter, were
never consecrated Apostles.

Let us then consider the service as a whole. We are compelled
by the declaration in the preface to interpret the terms priest and
bishop in their ancient sense. We find in the ordinal, as set forth,
the "intention and form" declaratory of the priesthood and episcopate wrought into every part. The titles of the offices are, "The
form of Ordering Priests," "The form of Consecrating a Bishop."
The person presenting the deacons has to say, "Reverend Father in
God, I present unto you these persons present, to be admitted to the
order of Priesthood." In the presentation of the elect bishop, "We
present unto you this godly man to be Ordained and Consecrated
Bishop." In the case of the deacons the bishop says, "Good People,

---

11. 2 Corinthians 3:6

these are they whom we purpose to receive unto the holy Office of Priesthood." In the Litany the bishop prays God " To bless these Thy servants now to be admitted to the Order of Priests." He prays in the Litany for the elect bishop that God would send His grace on him that he may duly execute the office to which he is called. In the collect for the Communion, which expresses the intention of the holy sacrifice about to be offered, the celebrant prays God, "Who hast appointed divers Orders of Ministers in the Church; Mercifully behold these now called to the Office of Priesthood and so replenish and adorn them, that they may faithfully serve Thee in this Office." The collect for the consecration of bishops recognizes their distinctive office as based upon that of the Apostles, and prays for grace on all bishops.

In the exhortation made to those to be ordained priests they are put in charge how "high a Dignity, and to how weighty an Office" they are called. In the solemn and deep words of Holy Scripture, they are as priests "to be Messengers, Watchmen, and Stewards of the Lord." "Messengers," that is, angels. Messengers sent with a heavenly message and divine authority. They are, as S. Paul calls them, certified and authorized "ambassadors of Christ,"[12] speaking in His name and by His authority. They are "watchmen," that is, guardians, to whom is committed the guardianship of the kingdom of Christ and the faith. They are "stewards," who by their office are official mediators between the members of the mystical body and its head; the offerers up of all the body owes its head in connection with the appointed gospel sacrifice, and the dispensers of all that the head, by His sacraments, bestows on the members.

In the response made by the elect to the bishop, he declares, in the name of God, that he believes himself called to "the Order and Ministry of Priesthood." The Holy Ghost having been solemnly invoked by the recitation of the *Veni Creator Spiritus*, prayer is said over the persons to be ordained or consecrated. Then follows the laying on of hands by the bishop, who says the grace-bestowing form, "Receive the Holy Ghost," and, as we have seen, at the same time in the Edwardian Ordinal by words significant of the office.

Thus the ordination of the Anglican priest is utterly unlike in kind and character to the authorization of a Protestant minister, where

---

12. 2 Corinthians 5:20

priesthood and sacrifice are not recognized.

Not without its significance also is the fact that in the Edwardian Ordinal, and our present one, the ordination and consecration service are incorporated into the mass. The ordination does not form a separate service by itself. It does not come before or after the Holy Communion. It is, as liturgical writers say, "farced" into it and so becomes part of it. It comes in before the Offertory. The Church is about to offer herself, body, soul, and spirit, to God in connection with her head. She does this by an identification with Him in the sacrament of the altar. Hither come those to make an offering of themselves to be priests or bishops, as identified with Christ's offices and for their extension.

To say there is not a *sacerdotium* or priesthood designated in our ordinal is like saying in broad daylight the sun is not shining. The Anglican ordinal from beginning to end is full of priesthood, and penetrated and illuminated by it.

O sad perversity of the human spirit that blinds itself to the truth! O foolish and deceived by party zeal, who, though unconsciously, hinder the divine purpose. O weak and doubting hearts that fail to see the mountain full of protecting angel hosts. A day of gloom it was when years ago Newman addressed his memorable apostrophe to England's Church and then bade her farewell. But the grace of her sacraments has transformed her life and given another meaning to his words. "O Mother of Saints! School of the Wise! Nurse of the heroic! Of whom went forth, in whom have dwelt memorable names of old to spread the truth abroad or cherish and inculcate it at home! O thou from whom surrounding nations lit their lamps!" How hast thou arisen as from the dust! How hast the reproach upon thee of a "miscarrying womb and dry breasts"[13] been done away. Marvel of marvels! Miracle of repair! The branch again puts forth her leaves and buds, and bears fruit an hundred-fold. A new enthusiasm for man as well as love of God fills her with fresh missionary zeal. Her educated sons have gone down to live in the slums of great cities among the poor, to elevate them by their friendly intercourse. Her daughters have given themselves by hundreds to the religious life with its noble service. Again the voice of the ancient bishops and fathers is heard in her pulpits. Again is the one sure and certain faith

---

13. Hosea 9:14

Nicaea taught of old proclaimed. Again the daily sacrifice is being restored to her altars. She is being recognized in her true character. She is the shrine of truth, guardian of the faith, teacher of the nations, blessed home for the lonely, refuge for the distressed, ark for the perishing, body of Christ in which He dwells, through which He acts. The truth of the old prophecy, as Neale wrote, is being fulfilled.

"Again do long processions sweep through the cathedral pile;
Again do banner, cross, and cope gleam thro' the incensed aisle;
& the faithful dead do claim their part in the Church's thankful prayer,
And the daily Sacrifice to God is duly offered there;
And many an earnest prayer ascends from many a hidden spot;
And England's Church is Catholic, though England's self be not."

XII

ANGLICANISM & REUNION

THERE are among others these glories which belong to the Anglican Church. The first is her continuity. She is not a sect of yesterday. She is not a man-made organization. She did not begin, as is falsely asserted, with King Henry the Eighth. He had about the same relation to her as Pontius Pilate had to Christianity. She reaches back in her history to Apostolic times. The authority and spiritual powers the Lord gave His Apostles have been transmitted to her. The golden network of the Apostolic succession binds its bishops and clergy to Christ. At the Reformation no new Church was founded. The Catholic Church in England rejected the mediaeval growth of the papacy as the great Eastern patriarchs and the Orthodox Churches of the East had done before. The ancient faith, as declared in the creeds and the undisputed Ecumenical councils, was retained. The appeal the Church made in the conduct of her reforms was to Holy Scripture and antiquity. While the general principle was correct in the undertaking, no doubt some mistakes were made, and the Church, while gaining much, suffered some loss. "We buy," as Burke said, "our blessings at a price."[1] But no new church was created, no change made in the orders of the ministry. The priesthood was preserved; the validity of the sacraments was secured; the torch of living truth was handed on.

One proof of this is to be found in the fact that of the fifty-six hundred clergy who celebrated mass in Queen Mary's reign, only about some three hundred beneficed clergy are known to have refused to accept the book of common prayer and conform in the reign of Queen Elizabeth. It is stated, on the authority of Chief Justice Coke, in a charge delivered by him at Norwich, that the pope offered to allow the use of the book of common prayer if the queen would only submit to his supremacy. "There is no point," said the non-Conformist Professor Beard in his Hibbert lectures, "at which it can be said, 'Here the old Church ends; here the new begins.'"[2]

---

1. Burke's *Works*, Vol. III, p. 383.

2. Charles Beard, *Hibbert Lectures*, 300.

The historian Freeman, the Lord Chancellor Selborne, the great statesman Gladstone, emphatically said so likewise. Judge Sir Robert Phillimore declared, "It is not only a religious, but a legal error to suppose that a new church was introduced into the realm at the time of the Reformation. It is not less the language of our law than of our divinity that the old church was restored, not that a new one was substituted."[3] Thus the church founded and organized by Christ and His Apostles has come down to us through the ages, bearing the majestic treasures of the Apostolic order, the life-giving sacraments, and the Catholic faith.

It is to be admitted that there are differences of doctrinal expression, ceremonial, and practices to be found. These are often made a target by Roman critics. But the existence of different schools of theology is a sign of interest in religion. The Western Church has its Thomists and Scotists, its Gallicans and Ultramontanes. So long as the creeds and dogmas proclaimed and certified by the whole Church are held, differences of opinion on subordinate points are allowable. We have not any such bitterness and party spirit as has been found existing between contending schools in Rome. There are extreme dogmatists and men of exaggerated utterances on both wings. But the differences between the great body of churchmen are not so great as they seem to superficial observers, or as the interested advocates would make them out to be.

It is a help in understanding these differences to remember the theological distinction between dogmatic and systematic theology. By the first we mean the great underlying and essential facts of the Christian faith, and the creeds and the accredited dogmas put forth by conciliar authority which express and guard them; by systematic theology, the philosophical expressions, theories, and explanations which unite them scientifically together. Now leaving out the extremists, there is concerning the dogmatic faith and creeds comparatively little difference. The Anglican Church puts the creeds and liturgy and ordinal and catechism and prayer-book into the hands of her clergy, and bids them interpret Holy Scripture according to the ancient fathers. Where this is honestly done, men will find themselves standing not so very far apart.

It, moreover, is to be observed that the high and low schools are

---

3. Sir Robert Phillimore, *Paper at the Norwich Congress*, 52.

not in principle antagonistic, but are supplementary to each other. The low churchman emphasizes the subjective side of religion. He dwells on the sinfulness of man's nature, and his redemption by the atoning efficacy of Christ's cross, and the necessity of conversion and a living faith. The high churchman dwells on the objective aspect of religion. Christianity came into the world as an institution. An Apostolic ministry is essential to connect us with Christ's authority. The sacraments are the ordained channels and instruments of conveying grace. The two aspects do not exclude one another. The truth lies in their combination.

Every school, high, low, or broad, has its own danger. The subjective or low church system, unbalanced by the objective side of religion, leads to a denial of the visible Church, its priesthood, and the sacraments as instruments and effective signs of grace; the broad, or rationalizing, to a denial of all that is supernatural in God's Word, and of authority, and the Church's inherited dogmatic faith. The extreme Catholic or pro-Roman one, by his devotion to Western scholasticism, centralization in government, mistaken interpretation of Scripture, impatient with the condition of the English Church, turns in faint-heartedness to the papacy.

But these errors lead to their own cure. The divine life of our Church is no more forcibly shown than in her inherent power of self-purification. Christ is in her, and she shares in His indestructible and resurrection life. The faith is preserved in her, not by ecclesiastical trials, necessary as they must be. Extremes lead to their own elimination; and so we have found the extreme low churchmen, who deny priesthood and sacramental grace, seceding from the Church and founding a new sect, called the Reformed Episcopalians. They tried in America to get the Church to alter the prayer-book, which they admitted was not in accord with their theology. It taught, they said, the Apostolic succession, priesthood, baptismal regeneration, and the real presence. The Church refused to change the prayer-book, and they withdrew. It was the honest course to pursue and the logical outcome of their theology. Likewise Catholics, who have become pro-Romans, believing in the divine power of the papacy, and our duty to submit to its dominion, naturally gravitate to Rome. They go out from us because they have ceased to be Catholics and become papists. The rationalizing broad churchmen who deny the fundamental facts of the creed, such as the virgin birth and the resurrection of Christ's body, are eventually pricked by conscience, which tells them they have no right to go on saying one thing at the altar and denying it in the pulpit. It is like leading a double life. They are in a false position. It is dishonorable to eat the bread of the Church whose creed they do not teach. It is far better for all those who do not believe in the creed and sacramental system of the Church to be outside of it. They then are delivered from the sin of saying what they do not believe, or not discerning the Lord's body in the Eucharist, and so eating and drinking to their own condemnation.

In Western Christendom a tremendous struggle is going on. It takes two forms, — one in the Roman, another in the Anglican communion. They are alike in this, that Rome is having her struggle with the State in France, and the Anglican with the State in England. Both churches are assailed, in France by unbelief in Christianity, in England by unbelief in Catholicity. For all that is Catholic our sympathies must be with the French Catholics, and we can but sorrow that so many priests there are leaving the Church. There is, however, a difference between the struggle of the English Church to restore the Catholic faith and worship, and that between the papacy and the Italian Government. The two contests differ radically. The English Church is trying to free herself in things spiritual from State control, while the papacy is trying to recover her lost temporal sovereignty. The one is seeking to be loosed from bondage to the world's power; the other is trying to make herself a worldly power. The English Church is struggling to resume her spiritual rights; the papacy is plotting to regain her earthly sovereignty.

The positions also of the two bodies in England are very different positions. The Church of England, as possessed of a continuous life from the establishment of Christianity in England, alone has lawful jurisdiction; while the new modern Italian mission is an intruding schismatical organization. Moreover, as the sin of schism lies with that party that compels withdrawal, by demanding uncatholic or uncanonical terms of communion, the Church of Rome is in schism everywhere. She is in schism in the city of Rome, though not equally and for the same reasons that she is in London. Again, the English Church (unlike other portions of the Anglican communion) is suffering from her present connection with the State, and so is feeble in the exercise of her own courts of discipline; but since she declares the faith in her formularies, Catholics are not committed to heresy by communicating with her. On the other hand, while the Anglican Church is succeeding in recovering the faith as once delivered, and by all everywhere received, the Romans by late additions and the turning of what were once acknowledged to be but opinions into dogmas of the faith are failing in holding fast to it.

Again, the Anglican Church has not added to the faith, while the Roman has. The doctrine of the papal infallibility and the immaculate conception of the Blessed Virgin cannot bear the test of Catholicity. Neither can that of the treasury of merits accumulated by the saints' works of supererogation, and placed at the disposal of the pope, on which the modern system of indulgences is based. The withdrawal of the chalice from the laity is in contradiction of the universal custom of the Catholic Church for over a thousand years, and that of the Eastern Church to-day. And while no one would question the marvelous grace bestowed on the ever-blessed *Theotokos*, the Bringer-Forth of God, yet the assigning to her the position and office of the neck of the mystical body through whom all graces must pass from the head to the members, is no part of the original deposit of the faith. It is not the language of the fathers to say "God has constituted Mary as the ordinary *dispensatrix* of His grace," nor that it is safer to go to the Blessed Virgin than to our Lord, or that "Mary so loved the world that she gave her only begotten Son." "Mary is the most faithful *mediatrix* of our salvation." "Thou, O Mary, art the propitiatory of the whole world." "From whom thou turnest away thy face there shall be no hope of salvation." "It is impossible any sinner can be saved, save through thy help and favor, O Virgin." "For whom the justice of God save not, Mary saves by her intercession, by infinite mercy." "The nation and kingdom which shall not serve thee, shall perish."

The Anglican Church is thus seen to be free from the charge of schism, and her formularies from heresy. On the other hand, Rome is both schismatical and, as testified by her decrees and accredited teachers, in error. It follows that while Anglican Catholics are not committed to heresy by communicating in the Anglican Church, because there may be some heretics in it, yet to enter the Roman communion is to make oneself responsible as a partaker of authorized schism and formally promulgated heresy. It is painful to write this, for all that is Catholic in the Latin communion we love, but in the presence of efforts to unsettle the faith of English Church members, loyalty to the Catholic faith requires it.

If Anglicans are ever desponding, they have only to look to the past and see how God has protected their communion. A branch cut off from the tree must perish, but a living branch is known by its persistent vitality and fruit. Assaulted, as seldom any portion of the Church of Christ has been, during the past three hundred years, it has by its inherent power resisted all attacks and emerged a victor. Neither the assaults of Rome under Mary, nor of the Puritans under Cromwell, nor the disaster of the non-jurors' withdrawal in the seventeenth, nor the Erastianism of the eighteenth century, nor all the worldly combinations of the nineteenth, have crushed out her Catholicity.

And not least of God's goodness to her is seen in two great providences. The first was the early death of King Edward VI. He was followed by Queen Mary of unhappy memory. But the evils wrought by Mary were temporary ones. Had, however, King Edward lived, the Church would have lost its Catholic heritage. With all the tyrannous spirit of a Tudor monarch and all the narrowness and self-conceit of a reforming Calvinist, the King would have made the Church like unto the deformity of the Continental reformers. We read in Strype's "Memorials of Cranmer" that the king had determined to make further changes, and if the bishops refused, to make them on his own authority. The continuity of the Church would have become so broken, and her Catholic doctrine so marred, that she would have largely lost her heritage and become a withered branch of Christ's Church. God preserved the Church by Edward's merciful removal.

Another, and we deem it the next great providential blessing vouchsafed the Anglican Church, was the denial of the validity of our orders by Leo XIII. It, like the former providence, has wrought in a wonderful way for the preservation of the Anglican Church. It has helped to unite her members, has painfully revealed to us the worldly policy that governs the papacy, has destroyed the possibility of any belief in the papal infallibility, has dissipated the dreams of corporate reunion with Rome, has helped to fill the Church with new courage, and, fixing her gaze on her true mission, to discern the mighty work of evangelization she may do for God. Had the pope decided otherwise, it is impossible to estimate the strong tide of love and trust that would have impulsively turned towards him. But providentially he did not so declare. Anglicans know they possess valid orders and sacraments. They can no more doubt this than the existence of God or any essential fact of Christianity. So that when the pope decided against what Anglicans knew, with a divine certainty, to be true, they knew with the same certainty that he was not infallible. It was seen to be a decision as contrary to the truth as when he condemned Galileo and the planetary system. So, for many, the glamour of the papacy passed away, and the papal curia, looked at calmly and dispassionately, was seen to be but a piece of skilfully constructed human machinery. The papal idol, to which some, not discerning its real worldly origin and character, had begun to turn, went down like that of Dagon before the Ark of the Lord. Corporate union with Rome, as she is, is seen to be beyond the range of human possibility, and not the terminus of the Tractarian movement, or the leading of Divine Providence.

But while this is so, there are brightening prospects in the East. Thither, it would seem, God's providence is directing us. The venerable orthodox Russian and Greek Church is turning to us with friendly expressions of interest. She says, "We do not ask you, as Rome does, to 'submit' we only ask, 'Do you hold the same Catholic faith we have inherited from the Fathers? 'If you do this, we are brothers." When we consider that the East has been but little affected by the schoolmen, and had not to pass through the convulsions of a Reformation, and has for nine hundred years borne consistent witness for the faith once delivered, and against Roman errors, Anglicans should be willing to free themselves from their prejudices and somewhat self-conceit, and listen to her kindly words.

The Church, indwelt by Christ, guided by the Holy Spirit, is a living organism, and we may trust the Voice of God speaking through her before she was rent into Eastern and Western divisions. The Voice of God speaking to the churches is not confined, as some Anglicans seem to think, to any particular centuries. But in the seven Ecumenical councils we have the Voice of the Spirit and in the seven holy mysteries, the means of grace.

The question presenting the most difficulty has to do with the *Filioque*. There is no difference in belief between the Anglican communion and the venerable East on the doctrine of the Filioque, but without Ecumenical consent it has no right to be in the Creed.

May God inspire the wise men of the Church to solve the difficulty. Each church in the case of restored intercommunion would retain its own independent government and liturgy. Anglicans and Easterns must be content with agreement in the ancient faith, — not in the uniformity of its outward expression. While the faith is unchangeable, the Church, as the bride of Christ, has been led to follow her Lord's life, and sometimes has been more absorbed in devotion to His incarnation, sometimes to His passion. The faith abides from age to age; but ceremonies and practices of devotion are the fresh outcome of the Church's love. The East and the West have their own ceremonial traditions, and the differences existing should not hinder the restoration of Christian recognition and fellowship.

If a reunion of Christendom is to be attained, it will come through the union of the Anglican and Eastern Churches. It is in this direction the safe guiding providence of God directs His people. It requires largeness of vision and generous toleration of unessential differences, and much of the charity that hopeth all things, believeth all things, and of the faith that believes that with God all things are possible. For so glorious a consummation Anglicans must be willing to recognize the devotion, the missionary zeal, and the orthodoxy of the Russian and Greek Churches. The cause of the reunion of Christendom is the dearest to the heart of Christ. What saints have longed and prayed for, let the Catholics of to-day labor to accomplish. We can do much by learning more of the Easterns and their worship, and studying their catechism. The all-availing power of the Holy Sacrifice is ours and the promise of answer to prayer in His Name. May the sacrifice of the altar be more frequently offered for the reunion of Christendom, and the prayer of blessed Bishop Andrews[4] be more in use among us! —

Bless, O Gracious Father, thy Holy Catholic Church; fill it with truth and grace; where it is corrupt, purge it; where it is in error, direct it; where it is superstitious, rectify it; where it is amiss, reform it; where it is right, strengthen and confirm it; where it is divided and rent asunder, heal the breaches of it; O Thou Holy One of Israel; through Jesus Christ our Lord.

Jesu hear, Jesu bless, Jesu answer our petition, for thy Mercy's sake.

Laus Deo.

---

4. The following is actually a prayer of Archbishop William Laud.

XIII

THE CHURCH IN BRITAIN

W E do not know at what time, or by whom, Christianity was introduced into Britain, any more than we know who carried it to Rome. Doubtless as the disciples were dispersed by persecution and went hither and thither, they told of Christ and proclaimed the Gospel.

There is a beautiful legend of St. Joseph of Arimathaea, who was banished from Palestine by the Jews, and who, with twelve companions, came to Britain bringing with him the Holy Grail. He preached in the Isle of Avalon, where in confirmation of his teaching, he stuck his staff of thorn into the ground, where-upon it blossomed like Aaron's rod, and grew into a tree. Here the famous church and monastery of Glastonbury were founded. There is another story that Lucius, the British King, sent to Eleuthereus, Bishop of Rome, a letter expressing a desire to be a Christian. This statement has been traced to a fabrication in Rome in the fifth century. For lack of authority, the story has led modern historians to reject it. The Abbe Duchesne says: "This legend had a Roman, not a British, origin, and may probably have been invented in the fifth century." There is also a Welsh legend about Bran the Blessed, found in the Welsh Triads, collected in the thirteenth century. It relates how Bran, the father of Caractacus, having been detained by the Emperor Claudius for seven years at Rome, as a hostage for his son, was there converted by St. Paul, and on his release carried the faith back to Britain, and planted the Church there.[1] Oddly enough, the idea that St. Peter came to Britain has cropped up many times, and in widely different places, an error probably owing to a misapprehension of the fact of the sending of the monk St. Augustine to England by Pope Gregory. This view has even been put forth by a Roman Catholic clergyman of our own day. We have to be ever on our guard against accepting like untrustworthy legends for, as Professor Collins says,[2] "when there was a demand in the Middle Ages for any conceivable information on any conceivable subject, there was always some one

---

1. Cutts, *Hist. Eng. Ch.*, p. 6.

2. Collins, *Eng. Christianity*, 43.

ready to supply it." However controversialists may have adopted any of these stories, truth bids us not to use them.

The Account of St. Paul

The account of St. Paul visiting Britain has more probability attached to it. Caractacus, the noble British Chief, had been pardoned, and sent by Rome back to his native country to rule over his tribe as a Roman official. His father Bran, and his son and daughter Lyn and Claudia, were retained in Rome as hostages. They were there at the same time St. Paul was there in residence. He lived in his own hired house, and made converts among Caesar's household.

In his Epistle to the Romans, St. Paul makes mention of Linus, Pudens, and Claudia. A Claudia is commemorated by the poet Martial as married to Pudens, the son of a Roman senator. It would seem therefore that the Linus and Claudia, mentioned as his converts by St. Paul, were the children of the British chief. Now it is a fair inference, indeed a certain one, that Lyn and Claudia would urge St. Paul to visit Britain and preach the Gospel to their own people. Certainly, St. Paul would have regarded this as a providential opening, and a call from God. The commission he had received from Christ and the Apostles ran to all the Gentile world. As he was on his way to Spain, why should he not extend his journey to Britain? Lightfoot, in his commentary on the Epistle to the Galatians, says St. Paul probably went to Gaul. It would be easy for him then to cross over to Britain. This theory has for its corroboration the statement of St. Clement that "St. Paul is said to have come to the boundary of the West," or, as it is otherwise translated, "furthest limits of the West." Now Spain was not a boundary of the Roman Empire, but Britain was.[3] The expression "furthest limits of the West," is a phrase which in Roman literature of the time was understood to include Britain.

We may agree with Dr. Bright and Professor Collins in holding St. Paul's visit not to be an ascertained historical fact, but yet hold it to be one of considerable probability. It seems like unto that of St. Peter's residence at Rome. Our Lord did not bid blessed Peter to go to Rome, as he did St. Paul. There is no explicit statement in Scripture that he was ever there. There is no contemporary witness to the fact. There is no clear statement of St. Peter, nothing in contemporary

---

3. Lane's *Illus. Ch. His.,* p. 6.

history to confirm it. There is the tradition that he was martyred there, and upon this it is claimed that his body was buried there. So we may accept his having been there as a probable event. It is not, however, an ascertained historical fact, upon which a dogma can rightly be based.

In like manner, may we not hold as probable that St. Paul visited Britain? May we not believe with Irenaeus, who was born in 97, that the Church was extended "by the Apostles to the utmost bounds of the West, and to the Celts" ? Gildas, the British historian, after describing the defeat of Boadicea in 61, wrote: "In the meantime, Christ the true Son, for the first time cast His rays on this island." Eusebius, in his history, says: "Apostles crossed the ocean to those islands which are called British." Charles Butler, a Roman Catholic wrote: "It is probable that Christianity was disseminated over parts of Britain during the Apostolic age." Hore, a notable scholar, in summing up the authorities, says: "There can be no reasonable ground for doubting that the British Church was not only a very ancient one, but also of Apostolic foundation."[4]

THE PLANTING OF CHRISTIANITY

It is regarded as probable that either in the Apostolic or sub-Apostolic age, Christianity had entered into Britain. It was certainly there, in organized form, by the latter part of the second century. It came, not from Rome, but from Gaul. "In the reign of Marcus Aurelius, about 170, a mission consisting of Bishop Pothinus and a presbyter, Irenaeus, a pupil of St. Polycarp, who had been a pupil of St. John, left Asia Minor. Sailing along the Mediterranean, they came to Marseilles and thence up the Rhone to the middle of Gaul. There at Vienne, near Lyons, they founded a church. From thence Christianity went, perhaps pushed by persecution, further north, until finally missionaries crossed the Channel and planted the Church in Britain."[5] Not only is Christianity thus early found in Britain, but it is in its organized form of Episcopal government. The proof of this is that we have the names of three Bishops of Britain who attended the great Council of Aries, called in the year 314 to pass on the Donatist heresy. The records of this Council give the

---

4. Hore, *Eighteen Centuries.*

5. Cutts' *Hist. Ch. Eng.,* p. 30.

names of these three British Bishops who attended, Eborius of York, Restitutus of London, and Adelphius, Bishop of Colonia Londinensium (probably from Caerleon, Wales). These were accompanied by a presbyter, Sacerdos, and a deacon, Arminius.[6] This fact shows that by the beginning of the fourth century, the Church was established in Britain as far north as York, and probably as far west as Caerleon; that it had a diocesan Episcopate, and the three orders of the ministry; that it was in communion with other churches of the Empire; and that it was of sufficient importance to be summoned to a great and important Council. Later on also, in 359, we find British Bishops taking part in the Council of Ariminum. The poverty of these Bishops is expressly mentioned by Sulpicius Severus, who bears witness to the existence and temporal condition of their church.

There are also many subordinate evidences of an early existence of the Church in Britain. The remains of an early church building have been discovered at Silchester. Fragments of pottery with the holy sign have been upturned, a coin bearing the Alpha and Omega, and grave-stones with the inscription "a Christian sleeps below" have been found.[7] The Church came, as we have seen, from Gaul, not from Rome or directly from an Eastern source.

In 410, a great political event happened. The capture of Rome by Alaric shook the foundations of civilization. "To St. Jerome, in his cell at Bethlehem, the news came like the shock of an earthquake." He says, "My voice falters, sobs stifle the words I dictate; for she is a captive, that city which outrivaled the world." To St. Augustine, it was the judgment of God upon "the profligate manners, the effeminacy, and the pride of her citizens." The Roman government was forced, for its own self protection, to withdraw its garrison from Britain, where they had been for nigh four hundred years. The Romans had done much there for civilization, and somewhat for Christianity. Converts had been made, and churches had grown up about their settlements. The literary remains are scanty of this time, but two interesting incidents relating to this period are commonly stated by historians. One of them is of the ennobling heroism of Britain's first martyr, St. Alban. While Alban was still a heathen, we read that one day there came to his house a priest, to

---

6. Hore, *Ch. of Eng.*; Cutts' *Eng. Ch. History,* p. 14.

7. Bright's *Early Ch. Hist.,* p. 11.

whom Alban gave shelter from his persecutors. Alban saw that the stranger was very devout and holy, and marked his spending many hours in prayer. He opened the Gospel to Alban, and led him to believe in our Lord Jesus Christ. But at last the hiding place of the priest was discovered, and the soldiers came and surrounded it. St. Alban, perceiving the danger, dressed himself in the priest's clothes, so that the soldiers, breaking in, and seeing him in the habit of a priest, seized him and dragged him before the Judge. With fearless courage, Alban declared that he was a Christian. Though he was tortured to make him deny the Faith, he remained faithful, and was led out to execution. The soldier whose duty it was to execute him was so struck by Alban's splendid courage, that, throwing away his sword, he declared himself also a Christian. It was an instance of the extension of the Faith from one brave heart to another by the power of the Spirit. The great Abbey of St. Albans, lately restored, is a memorial of the heroic devotion of these early Christians. The other instance is that of the Alleluia battle.

In the early days of the fifth century, a momentous theological controversy arose. Pelagius, whose Celtic name was Morgan, went astray by over-rating the power of the human will and denying the necessity of internal grace. The heresy, as all rationalistic speculations are, was attractive to some of the laity. Britain naturally made an appeal to her Mother Church of Gaul for aid in the controversy. The Gallican Church, we read, summoned a synod, which sent to the aid of the Church in Britain two of her greatest Bishops, Germanus and Lupus.[8] The authority for this statement is found in the life of St. Germanus, by Constantius of Lyons, who wrote some sixty years after the decease of St. Germanus, with full access to local information. With respect to this controversy Constantius gives as his authority the action of the synod. His account is copied by the Venerable Bede, who states that the prelates, Germanus of Auxerre and Lupus of Troyes, were sent over by a synod to uphold in Britain the belief in Divine Grace.[9] Prosper, another writer, says that Germanus was sent by the Bishop of Rome. But properly the official record of the synod is to be taken as a more reliable evidence than the unsupported and probably hearsay report recorded by Prosper.

8. Bright's *Early Eng. Ch. Hist.*, pp. 15, 16.

9. Cults' *Eng. Turning Points*, p. 16.

Possibly the Pope might have sent his blessing to Germanus, but the fact remains that the British Church in its need appealed to Gaul, and not to Rome. This was about the year 429. We are told that at a conference between the Pelagians and the Gallican Bishops, the Gallic party triumphed. After this, the invasion of Picts and Scots followed.

We now come to the Alleluia battle. Germanus and Lupus, the Gallic Bishops, encouraged the Britons to resist the invaders. They preached the Gospel and brought a large number to Christ and to baptism. Here we quote largely from Professor Bright: "On Easter Eve, the baptisms were administered, the great Feast was celebrated in a church formed out of the boughs of trees, the British host advanced to the battle, the greater part of it fresh from the laver. Their General drew them up as if in ambush, under the rocks of a narrow glen which he had ascertained to lie full in the path of the enemy. As the first ranks of the heathen, expecting an easy triumph, drew near, Germanus made the British people shout after him the one sacred joyous word, which they had so lately uttered in their paschal solemnities. Three times he and Lupus intoned it, Alleluia, Alleluia, Alleluia. Their followers with one voice made the sound echo through the valley. It rang from cliff to cliff. It struck the invaders with panic. They fled as if the very skies were crashing over them. The Britons, successful without striking a blow, exulted in a victory won by faith, without bloodshed." This is the story of the great Alleluia victory.

On the withdrawal of the Romans, the Britons, who had been originally disarmed by their conquerors, and thus rendered unaccustomed to warfare, were left practically defenseless. The country was left open to a great invasion of Jutes, Angles, and Saxons, coming from different parts of the continent. The three are commonly spoken of as Anglo-Saxons. The first work of the new invaders was to stamp out with fire and sword every trace of Roman civilization. "They seemed," says Professor Rollinston, "to have a great aptness for destroying and great slowness in elaborating material civilization."[10] These heathen Anglo-Saxons, we read, drove away or enslaved the Romanized and Christianized Celts, broke down every vestige of Christian civilization, destroyed the churches, burnt the villas, laid waste many of the towns, and reintroduced a long peri-

---

10. *Anglo-Saxon Britain*, Allen, p. 25.

od of pagan barbarism. We quote from Grant Allen:[11] "These Anglo-Saxons were a horde of barbarous heathen pirates. They mas-
sacred or enslaved half the civilized Celtic inhabitants with savage
ruthlessness. They let the roads and cities fall into utter disrepair.
They stamped out Christianity with fire and sword from end to end
of their new domain." As Gildas the historian, with Celtic fervor,
phrases it: "The red tongue of flame licked up the whole land from
end to end, till it slaked its horrid thirst in the western ocean." There
is, however, a difference among scholars to-day as to the extent of
the Saxon destructions. The remains lately found go to show it was
not so complete an extermination as has been represented by some
historians. The Church, though enfeebled, continued to exist.

The Scotic Church

When we look to the Scotic Church, we find it existing in an early
period of the fourth century. Here came St. Ninian, about 397, and
"preached the word to the southern Picts." The work was developed
under St. Kentigern, and St. Columba in the latter half of the sixth
century. The latter, having done much in Ireland, desired to "so-
journ abroad for Christ's sake," and at Whitsuntide, 563, settled at
Iona, and there founded that famous missionary monastery. "He
was," says Adamnan, "angelic in aspect, clear in speech, holy in
conduct, great in counsel; never did a single hour pass in which he
was not engaged in prayer or pious work." "He was," writes Bright,
"a grand saint, and a man of extraordinary courage, perseverance,
energy, and determination, born to guide minds and also to win
hearts." Most have heard the story of his passing when the old
monastic horse thrust his head into Columba's bosom, and the old
monk said, "Let him alone, he loves me." His dying suggestion to
his monks was to mutual charity: "But you who must rule after me;
remember no deed can last, but only Love."

The Native British Church

At the dawning of the fifth century, the whole of the west coast of
England, Cornwall, Wales, Cumberland, from Land's End to the
Clyde, was being covered by the native British Church. "At this peri-
od" says Dr. Bright, "the headquarters of the British Church was
Wales." In the middle of the sixth century, a religious revival took

---

11. *Ibid.*, p. 46.

place. The Welsh Episcopacy then became regularly diocesan. It had its yearly synods, but it had no Metropolitan. It is of interest to observe how David, commonly known as St. David, when traveling in the Holy Land, in the sixth century, was there consecrated by the Patriarch of Jerusalem. He became the Archbishop of the See of St. David's, which subsequently was named after him. In the year 1115 the Welsh Bishops became united with the English Church, under the Archbishop of Canterbury. Eventually the Bishop of Landaff, a successor in this line, united with Laud in his consecrations and thus passed on the ancient British succession from the Patriarch of Jerusalem.

The Celtic Church

The planting of Christianity in Ireland is obscure. It was carried there probably by Christians from Britain. Palladius, in 431, is spoken of as the first Bishop of the Irish, but he is reported as practically failing in his work. The great name that looms up before us is that of St. Patrick. So many legends have surrounded his life that it is difficult to know what is true. The only reliable sources are a book of Confessions written by him, and some prayers, or hymns. He was of British parentage, his father or grandfather being a clergyman. When a lad, with others, he was stolen and carried away to Ireland. He became a shepherd, and while looking after his sheep, he was drawn to meditation, and "he remembered his own sins and was converted." A strong desire filled his soul to serve Christ. Escaping from his captivity, he found his way back to his home and native land. But having a call, as he believed, from God, he went back to Ireland, and being ordained, became its missionary. He does not tell us who ordained him. His success is probably exaggerated. Along with St. Patrick, the name of St. Columbanus is prominent. There is no more typical Irish missionary. Bright calls him a "pious, fearless, self-devoted man, with not a little of Celtic passion in his nature." Having addressed Pope Boniface as "head of all the Churches of Europe, and Pastor of pastors," he nevertheless lectured him as having appeared to compromise the faith.

One mark of the old Irish Church was its love of teaching and study. Bede remarks upon the open-hearted, generous hospitality extended to Anglican students attracted to Ireland by the fame of its monastic schools. What the old Irish Church lacked conspicuously was organization. The Episcopal character was bestowed very freely on priests, and the monasteries were ruled over by Abbot-Bishops. A tribal influence affected the Church, and Bishops were often members of some particular family within the tribe. It was at the Synod of Kells that Ireland gained its first hierarchical organization, with four provinces having four Archbishops, a primacy being reserved to Armagh.

It may be noted that the line of Bishops from St. Patrick extended down to the Reformation, when some of the Irish Bishops, whose consecration has never been questioned, conformed to the Anglican Church in the time of Queen Elizabeth, and imparted to Archbishop Laud the Episcopal order. The gradual re-Christianizing of the major part of Britain, which came to be called the Heptarchy, we will treat of in a following chapter.

XIV

Condition of the Medieval Church

I T is more agreeable to turn now to the consideration of the Church and clergy during the Middle Ages. The Church developed under the Normans, who were Christians, and Churches began to be multiplied. There was also a considerable revival of the monastic spirit, and many noble monasteries were founded. Lands and money were freely given for their endowment. In Saxon times the land had been divided into parishes; now we find the establishment of Vicarages, which were served by monks from the neighboring monasteries. A striking social feature of the time was the way in which the Church gathered her ministry from all classes of the people. The lords of the manor might present their younger sons, and the vicars might be the nominees of the Religious houses. The middle classes, however, supplied a great number of the clergy. There were also cases where a serf obtained leave from his lord to send his son to school. There were always some who took a less liberal view; and we find, even in the vision of Piers Plowman, the more liberal sentiments satirized. He says that bondsmen and beggars' children belong to labor, and should serve lords' sons, and that lords' sons should serve God as belongeth to their degree. When this principle was urged at the Reformation at the founding of King's School at Canterbury, Archbishop Cranmer resisted it, saying, "To exclude the poor man's son from the benefits of learning, is as much as to say that Almighty God should not be at liberty to bestow His gifts according to His most goodly will and pleasure."

The career that mother Church thus threw open to all extended not only to the offices of the Church but also to those of the State. From the monastery or cathedral school, the earnest or ambitious student went to some more famous center of learning, to Bologna for law, to Paris for theology, to Salerno for medicine, in England to Oxford or Cambridge, which were organized universities early in the thirteenth century. The clergy were not, unless by their own will, uninstructed.[1] The course of reading was, in the grammar schools: four years in the Latin language, literature, rhetoric, and logic; three

---

1. Cutis' *Parish Priests*, p. 139.

years in science, i.e., arithmetic, music, geometry, and astronomy; afterwards seven years' study in theology; and three years in the Bible. They went up to the university at about fourteen years of age. In the thirteenth century there were about 3,000 students at Oxford.[2]

An interesting account of his own life is given by Bishop Latimer in a sermon preached before the king, which gives us an account of the farmer who sent his clever son to school. 2 "My father," he said, "was a yeoman, and had no lands of his own, only a farm of three or four pounds a year by the uttermost, and hereupon he tilled as much as kept half a dozen men. He had a walk for a hundred sheep, and my mother milked thirty kine. He was able, and did find the king a harness and his horse. I remember that I buckled on his harness when he went to Blackheath Field. He sent me to a school, or else I had not been able to preach before the King's Majesty now. He kept hospitality for his poor neighbors, and some alms he gave to the poor, and all this he did of the same farm."[3]

It was easy for the student to get into minor orders, but he could not be priested without passing the Bishop's examination, and obtaining a title, i.e., a. definitely assigned place where he could practice the ministry. There were, of course, a number of men whose vocation became wrecked, as is the case now. We find the worldly and unconverted clergy throwing off the clerical habit and adopting the secular dress of the time. From disciplinary canons which were made, we learn of their wearing girded belts, rings on their fingers, and long beards, and concealing their tonsure. We see, in our own day, clergy asserting that they are "men before they are priests," throwing off the clerical attire and wearing a secular dress. "Clergy then persisted," says Cutts, "in wearing their hair cut like other people's, and short skirted coats, and their ordinary dress was of red or blue, or other colors, instead of grey or black, and they ofttimes carried a short sword."

The costume worn in Church continued to be practically the same as in early times, a long under garment or tunic, white, with long sleeves, known as the alb. At the time of Augustine, the chasuble, or *plenida*, had come into use, and continued to be worn during the Middle Ages. The *arearium*, or stole, was placed round the neck, and

---

2. *Ibid.*, p. 140.

3. Cutts' *Parish Priests*, p. 140.

was enriched with an embroidered border, the deacon wearing it over one shoulder. The amice was a square piece of linen which was put over the head before the chasuble was put on, and served to protect it from being soiled. The dalmatic was another over-garment, and shaped like a short tunic split at the sides, which became the distinctive vestment of the deacon at mass. A little later than the tenth century, the sub-deacon wore a tunical, which was a similar, but somewhat scantier, vestment. The cope was simply a cloak. It was originally a protection from the weather. It appears as a clerical vestment about the end of the ninth century, being worn in processions and in choir. The surplice, a shortened alb, which is the most modern of all vestments, came to be used in the saying of the divine office. In the Cathedrals, the Canons wore over the surplice a short furred coat or cope.[4]

The priests were bidden to address the people on the Lord's Day in sermons. Bishop Grosseteste, 1235–1254, gave directions to his clergy to preach on Sundays, and gave them the heads of their teaching. Bishop Exeter drew up a similar book for his clergy, requiring every parish to have a copy. Bishop Breitingham of Exeter assumed, in his directions, that a sermon was preached in all parish churches on Sunday. Other Bishops put forth similar injunctions. The subjects given them to preach upon by the Provincial Synod of Lambeth in 1281 were the Fourteen Articles of Faith, the Ten Commandments, the Two Evangelical Precepts of Charity, the Seven Works of Mercy, the Seven Deadly Sins, and the Seven Sacraments of Grace. Five of these Sacraments, it was declared, ought to be received by every Christian: Baptism, Confirmation, Penance, Holy Eucharist, and Extreme Unction. The two other Sacraments of Order and Matrimony were for individual application. The prayer to be said by the sick before receiving unction, is declarative of the evangelical spirit found in the Church. "My God, my God, my mercy and my refuge, Thee I desire, to Thee I flee, to Thee I hasten to come. Despise me not, placed in this tremendous crisis, be merciful to me in these my great necessities. I cannot redeem myself by my own works, but do Thou, my God, redeem me, and have mercy on me. I trust not in my merits, but I confide rather in Thy mercies, and I trust more in Thy mercies than I distrust my evil deeds, my faults, my great faults. Now

---

4. Cutts' *Parish Priests*, 191–195.

I come to Thee because Thou failest none, I desire to depart and to be with Thee. Into Thy hands, O Lord, I commend my spirit; Thou hast redeemed me, Lord God of truth. Amen. And grant to me, my God, that I may sleep and rest in peace, who in perfect Trinity livest and reignest God, world without end. Amen."[5]

The priests had many homiletic books to help them in their delivery of sermons. Among them were the *Speculum Christiani*, by John Watton, *Pars Oculi Sacerdotis*, put out in the year 1350, and *Liber Festivalis*, by John Myrk. There were also works of a spiritual character such as *The Prick of Conscience*, by Richard the Hermit, 1349, and the *Speculum*, by Archbishop Rich. The people were provided with various books of private devotions. There were primers, and layfolk's mass books, which explained the meaning of the service and the ritual. *The Mirror of Our Ladye* was a popular book with the devout laity.[6]

THE WORSHIP OF THE CHURCH

There were daily services in the Churches. Amongst the higher classes were to be found domestic chaplains, who daily performed mass in the private chapels. There were altar lights. A law of Edmund directs that a priest shall not celebrate without a light, not for use, but as a symbol. At low mass, one candle on the Gospel side of the altar was regarded as sufficient. More often two wax candles were placed on the altar, symbolizing Christ in His two natures, as Light of the world. An oil lamp was also bidden to be hung in front of the high altar in honour of the reserved Sacrament. A large ornamented wax light, called the Paschal Candle, was lit at Easter, and burnt through the Easter season. It symbolized the resurrection of our Lord. The lighting of the candles, it was written, was not to dispel darkness, but to show that the saints are lighted by the light of heaven.

Beside the ritual lights, it was customary to place torches at funerals about the bier, symbolizing the fact that the souls of the departed were in the land of light. It was customary, also, to place a chandelier in the church at the Purification of the Blessed Virgin Mary, and for the congregation to bring tapers with them. It was this custom that gave to the Feast of the Purification the title of Candlemas. The

---

5. See Cutts' *Parish Priests*, 126–240.

6. *Ibid.*, 249.

names of those departed belonging to the parish were read out in church, and the prayers of people asked for the repose of their souls. A custom which united the parishes together was to make an annual procession, if it was not too far, to the Cathedral, or mother church, carrying banners, and chanting or singing hymns. At Christmas, in addition to the Christmas services, there was often a grotto arranged in the church, with representation of the shepherds and the holy family.

On Ash Wednesday, there was an office for the signing of the people with ashes. The veiling of the rood took place at Passion tide. A procession, bearing palms, marched round the churchyard on Palm Sunday, and the Blessed Sacrament was taken from the high altar and placed on a special altar on Maundy Thursday, where it remained till Easter. Whitsunday was a time especially kept for baptisms, and the baptized were arrayed in white dresses, a symbol of baptismal purification. The fields were blessed on Rogation days. The festival of the dedication of the parish church was yearly kept. The Church in her services became thus the chief object of interest and the bond of the social life among the parishioners.

The devout priest of those times looked upon himself as the pastor of his people and the administrator of the sacraments. He had not on his shoulders the burden of a modern parish. The priest has now to keep up the various organizations associated with the modern parish, which make it like a great mill with its machinery, in comparison with the old handlooms that stood by the fireside. The priest of our time is so pressed with the burden of work that he gives less time to his own spiritual life than did the priest of old. The mediaeval priest said the seven canonical hours in church. On Sundays and holy days, having finished Terce, he offered the Holy Sacrifice. Thrice in the year he heard the regular confessions of his people. Under some circumstances, mass was offered daily. There were those who, striving after greater holiness, would resort more frequently to the tribunal of penitence. There were few priests who did not have some sort of school for the children and communicants' class for the adults.

We are, however, obliged to note that there were some abuses and evil customs which sprang up in those days. People made the churchyard a place of general meeting, and used it for sports of a worldly nature, so that it was found necessary to prohibit them by

canon. There were abuses by the Popes of putting foreigners, especially Italians, into English benefices for the purpose of taking the
revenues.

Again, the evil of pluralities sprang up, and Bishop and clergy
would hold the revenues of several benefices together. They would
farm them out, taking the larger portion of the income for themselves.[7] This corrupt and worldly spirit indubitably tended to lower
the spiritual standard of the clergy. What affected them perhaps still
more was the endeavor to force celibacy upon them. It was found
not possible to enforce the decrees which had been made on this
subject. King Henry I. raised a large revenue by permitting the
clergy to retain their wives, on payment of money for a license to
do so. Many of the secular clergy argued that matrimony was a
divine ordinance, whilst prohibition of it was only an ecclesiastical
rule. It is well known that in the fifteenth century there were many
ecclesiastics who had wives. Warham, the last Archbishop of Canterbury before the Reformation, is said to have had a wife, who was
not secluded from the knowledge and society of his friends. Dean
Colet, in his famous sermon preached at St. Paul's, 1511, before
Convocation, sternly rebuked the faults of the clergy of his day. He
dwelt upon their secularity, worldliness, and concupiscence. "They
give themselves to feasts and banquetings; they spend themselves in
vain babblings, they give themselves to sports and plays, they apply
themselves to hunting and hawking. They drown themselves in the
delights of the world." The bold, fearless words must be taken with
some allowance. Many of these faults might be seen amongst the
clergy of today.[8] We may believe that the standard of clerical life in
England was higher than on the continent, and that on the whole,
the clergy led moral lives.[9] There was nothing like the prevalence
of evil lives and ignorance of the clergy in the dioceses of the land
that marked the advent there of Carlo Borromeo at Milan.[10] "Religion, then, in the Middle Ages," says Wakeman, "played a larger
part in man's life than it does now. The large number of clergy enabled much more attention to be given to the wants of each individ-

---

7. Cutts' *Parish Priests*.

8. *His. Ch. Eng.*, Wakeman, p. 165.

9. *Ibid.*, Wakeman, p. 165.

10. *The Reformation*, Cazenove, p. 34.

ual soul than is possible nowadays." For those who could not read, rhyming paraphrases in English, to be committed to memory, were largely used. The Creed, the Lord's Prayer, the story of the Passion, the Ten Commandments, the Seven Deadly Sins, the principal festivals and fasts, were thus learned by heart by the ignorant. For the more learned who could read, and the rich who could buy, there was no lack of books. The primers were in the hands of every well-educated man or woman in the fourteenth and fifteenth centuries, and answered in no small extent to our Book of Common Prayer.

Thus in the Middle Ages, the Church, teaching her children either orally or by book, put them in possession of the seed-plot from which might grow the fairest forms of devotional life. By the creeds, she taught them the faith. In Holy Scripture, she pointed them to the basis of all meditation. In prayer, she trained them in the devotional life. By the Commandments and the list of the seven deadly sins, she led them to self-examination and penitence. By her public offices she taught them due harmony of praise, of intercession, and of prayer. Finally, in the weekly or daily Eucharist, she brought them to renewed self-consecration in the fullness of corporate worship.[11]

---

11. *His. Ch. Eng*, p. 184, Wakeman.

XV

THE REFORMATION IN ENGLAND

WHATEVER the view one may take of the Reformation, it is hardly possible to exaggerate its importance. It was like an avalanche, which was long preparing for its descent. It could but come; and a small event was enough to give it instant action. On the continent, the immediate cause was the sale of indulgences by Tetzel; in England, the king's divorce.

Christendom had already been divided into East and West, and the two portions had lived and grown separated from each other. In the West, the papacy had been moved to Avignon; subsequently, the papacy was restored to Rome. It descended from being an international representative, and became nationalized. At Avignon, it was a French power, and the mouthpiece of French policy; at Rome it became Italianized, and so continues to the present day.

The claims of the papacy had not been unquestioned in the Middle Ages. Marsiglio put forth a powerful book called *Defensio Pacis*, about the end of the thirteenth century, which denied that St. Peter had had any authority over the other Apostles, or had ever been proved to have been Bishop of Rome, or to have given the Popes a prerogative of government as Peter's successors. Wycliffe had attacked the iniquity of the Popes, and denied their right to rule. William of Ocham had contended that the Pope, even in discharge of his spiritual functions, was subject to the general voice of Christendom. At the Councils of Pisa and Constance, it was held that the Church in General Council was superior to a Pope, and could compel the Pope to obedience. The latter Council authorized a new election, after securing the deposition of two Popes and the resignation of one. In England, it was always maintained that the papal decrees were not binding, even on questions of faith and morals, unless accepted by the national authorities.

Again : the papacy had lost moral influence through the luxury and sensuality of the papal court. Its tyrannous greed, in demanding the first year's revenues of vacant bishoprics and other oppressive taxes, alienated both clergy and laity. This taxation was grievously felt by the laity in England, and prepared them for a revolt. As we have previously stated, the Pope had filled up a number of sees with Italians, who never visited England, but drew their revenues. In Europe, the sale of indulgences aroused the moral indignation of the German people. It was not true that the indulgence gave to its holder the right to commit sin, but relieved him from the punishment of it, which is all the sinner usually cares about. The burning zeal of Luther shook the continent with opposition to such an immoral practice. In 1453, the fall of Constantinople, while it brought disaster to the Eastern Church, brought, through its fugitives, a reinforcement of classical literature into Europe. With the discovery of printing, and the renewal of classical learning, many had become fascinated with the old pagan life. The discoveries of the New World filled men with a spirit of enterprise, and made their hearts beat with a golden vision of conquest and wealth. Popes themselves felt its influence. These were some of the precedent causes of the great forward movement which we call the Reformation.

The further rent in Christendom caused by the Reformation could not take place, however, without much harm, whatever blessing might come with it. As Wakeman says, "In the Church, division, however we may palliate it, is, after all, sin, and carries with it its consequence of sin." The fact of the divisions of Christendom has been amongst the great hindrances to the effective representation of the Gospel. While a reformation was necessary, a division might have been avoided. The Church, herself, had earnestly demanded a reform. The call had been reinforced by committees of cardinals, who demanded a reform; both in the head and in the members of the Church. As the papacy would not lead in the way of reform, it had to come in other ways. Looked at in its political aspects, the Reformation was a part of a great general movement towards liberty, freedom, and the better government of mankind.

In England, the movement began under Henry VIII. and his parliament, as a political one. There were antecedent causes, as we have seen, but the king's matrimonial scheme was the match that touched the magazine and caused the explosion. In England, on its religious side, it was a removal of erroneous accretions of doctrine, and so a reformation, not a revolution.

On the Continent, it had first of all a religious aspect. It was a revolt against the immorality of the papacy and the sale of indulgences. It was also a gospel desire for justification by a living faith, in place of a formal observance of sacramental ordinances. In England, the Church, expressing her mind through her convocations, passed, in 1534, a resolution that "the Bishop of Rome hath not by Scripture any greater authority over the Church of England than any other foreign Bishop." It thus denied anew, what it had denied ever since the time of the Conquest, that the Pope had a supremacy, spiritual or temporal, over the Church of England, in virtue of anything declared in Holy Scripture. This was made effective by Act of Parliament, forbidding all appeals from English courts to the papacy.

HENRY'S DIVORCE

Here we may observe why the king was personally interested in the passing of measures restrictive of the papacy. It was necessary for the king's purposes to secure an acknowledged legal separation from Queen Catherine. He had been told by Cranmer, who was an ecclesiastical canonist, that he had a good case. "It would have to be legally presumed," Cranmer said, "whatever Catherine herself, as an interested party, might say, that her marriage with his brother Arthur was consummated." Consequently, the marriage with Henry, being against the Divine Law, according to the opinion of most theologians, could not have been allowed by the Pope. A former Pope, Innocent III., had said that "in decrees prohibited by Divine Law a dispensation cannot be given." The Pope had, however, undertaken to dispense this marriage, for Catherine had a bull in which the Pope had granted permission for her marriage with Henry, though perhaps her marriage with Arthur had been consummated. The Pope had thus undertaken to do what most theologians held was beyond his power. The papal dispensation for Henry's marriage to Catherine, therefore, being invalid, the marriage was not merely voidable, but "void," *ab initio*. Cranmer stated that this judgment would be the decision of the court. But what was to be guarded against was Catherine's appeal to the Pope, who would be bound to hear the case; for he, being under the control of Charles V., the German Emperor, uncle of Catherine, would reverse the English decision. Thus Henry, through his parliament, reaffirmed the old laws of the kingdom, which forbade all appeals to the Pope. Therefore, while a great and cruel injustice was done to Queen Catherine, the Church and nation thereby recovered their national rights and pre-Norman independence.

Some Romans have tried to prove the Pope in this matter the upholder of the sanctity and indissolubility of marriage. Here we quote from Brinckman: "But, while Clement gave his legates a special commission in the form of a decretal, in which he declared the marriage of Henry and Catherine null and void, and authorized them to give judgment for the king and notified the king by a Papal Brief what he had done in the matter, the Pope at the same time gave the legates secret instruction to burn the decretal letter embodying the commission, and charged them on no account to act upon it."[1] However badly the king, and all the parties concerned, came out of this miserable business, the Pope himself is far from being blameless.

There are some popular errors in regard to the Reformation to be noted. It is a habit of Roman controversialists to say the "Church of England was founded by Henry VIII." That is an historical misstatement that dies hard, but is, nevertheless, untrue. "Nothing," says the great historian, Professor Freeman of Oxford, "was further from the mind of either King Henry VIII. or Elizabeth. Neither of them ever thought for a minute of establishing a new Church."[2] Queen Elizabeth, in a letter to a Roman Catholic Princess of Europe, asserted that "there was no new faith propagated in England; no new religion set up but that which was commanded by our Saviour, practiced by the primitive Church, and approved by the Fathers."[3] Archbishop Bramhall thus expressed our position: "We do not arrogate to ourselves a new Church, or new religion, or new orders. Our religion is the same as it was, our Church is the same, our Holy Orders the same." The administrative power of Rome was in the king's way, and he swept it aside; but at heart and in religion he was a Roman Catholic. He had persons burnt for not believing in transubstantiation. He died, leaving a will providing for masses to be said for his soul.

Another popular error is that the Reformation under King Henry was a casting off of the Catholic Faith, and the adoption of what is popularly known as "Protestantism." Protestantism is both schismatical and heretical. It rejects Church authority and the Gospel's sacramental system. Mr. Gladstone said: "I can find no trace of the

---

1. *Anglican Brief,* p. 308; *Catherine of Aragon,* Froude, 67, 69, 84, and 85.

2. *Disestablishment and Disendowment,* Freeman, 21–26.

3. *Life of Queen Elizabeth,* Camden, Book i, p. 32.

opinion, which is now common in the minds of unthinking persons, that the Roman Catholic Church was abolished in England at the period of the Reformation and that a Protestant Church was put in its place. The Church of England is the same Church that existed from the beginning. There was no new Church created and endowed by King Henry."[4] Sir Robert Phillimore, a noted legal authority, said: "It is not only a religious, but a legal error, to say that a new Church was introduced into the realm at the time of the Reformation. It is no less the language of our law than our divinity that the old Church was restored, and not a new one instituted."

Again, it is sometimes ignorantly asserted that the Church separated from Rome. Now we did not separate from Rome, but Rome separated from us. The Church before the Reformation was always known as the *Ecclesia Anglicana*, or the Church of England. She continued to exist at the Reformation as the same identical Church as she was before. No division took place during the period of the reigns of Henry VIII., Edward VI., and Mary. The people all, whatever their views, worshipped together as one Christian body. But in 1570, the Pope, excommunicating Queen Elizabeth, called on his followers to leave the old Church. Some did so, and it was not until 1854, nearly three hundred years later, that the Romans in England were organized into dioceses. This schismatical body is commonly known as the Italian Mission. "We are a new mission" says Father Humphreys, S.J., "straight from Rome."[5]

Thus we see how the Anglican Church, while rejecting the papacy, holds the ancient faith, essentially the same as it was held in Apostolic times; and by the Celtic, the Saxon, and the Eastern Churches and undivided Christendom. The Church, in all that she did in England, asserted that her members were Catholics — she was maintaining the Catholic Faith. Thus, in the statute passed, the twenty-fifth of Henry VIII., it was denied that the sanction of the Pope was essential to the validity of the consecration of Bishops and to the valid celebration of the sacraments. But this denial was based on the verified, historical fact that "divers Archbishops and Bishops have heretofore in ancient times been so consecrated, and they asserted that they were as obedient, devout Catholics, and humble children of God, as

---

4. *The State in its Relation to the Church*, p. 127.

5. Humphreys' *Divine Teacher*, p. 54

any people within any Christian realm."

THE REFORMERS & THEIR PRINCIPLES

There is a great diversity of opinion amongst partisans concerning the character and the motives of the reformers. They differed amongst themselves. But they have passed to the judgment seat of God, and the duty is not imposed on us of passing judgment on them. It is both wise and charitable to avoid exaggerated expressions. All that Anglican Churchmen are practically concerned with is the work they accomplished and the avowed principles of their action.

In the reforms she made, history shows that the Church appealed for her guidance to the Holy Scriptures, as interpreted by the Fathers, and the ancient Councils, and sought to maintain the faith as it had been held in the Church from the beginning. She appealed thus to Holy Scripture as corroborated by tradition. The Convocation of 1571 declared that "the clergy should never teach anything to be believed by the people but what is agreeable to the doctrine of the Old and New Testament, and collected out of that very doctrine by the *Catholic Fathers and ancient Bishops.*" No new Church was founded. "The continuity of the Church," says Aubrey Moore, in his very able work, "was as true and real as the continuity of the nation."

CATHOLIC DOCTRINE

On its religious side, the movement did not begin with favoring Protestantism. In 1529, when the movement is said to have originated in the Reformation Parliament, as it was called, Convocation forbade the circulation of the works of Wycliffe, Knox, Luther, Zwingli, and the English Tyndall. The only authoritative doctrinal formularies put forth in King Henry's reign were the Ten Articles and a book called A Necessary Doctrine and Erudition for Any Christian Man. This book was put forth in 1543, by the authority of Convocation. It set forth the Creed, the Seven Sacraments, the Decalogue, the Lord's Prayer, the Hail Mary, and the four articles of Justification, Good Works, and Prayers for the Departed. It held the doctrine of the Real Presence in the Sacrament of the Altar, and the validity of receiving it in one kind, and the duty of fasting communion.

In the reign of Edward VI. we have the first Prayer Book put forth. It was drawn up by a commission consisting of an Archbishop, six Bishops, and six Doctors of Divinity. It had the authority of the

Church and parliament. It "was accepted by Convocation," as Bishop Stubbs remarks. It was not a new book, but one composed out of materials previously existing. These were the old Service Books, including the rites necessary for the other Sacraments, as well as the Holy Eucharist; the Pontificale, containing the Ordinal, and others. In this Prayer Book of Edward VI., the Holy Communion was called the Mass. The words of administration were the first sentence of the present form. This was meant to mean a recognition of the Real Presence. The ancient ritual was practically unchanged. The priest wore the Eucharistic vestments, which symbolized the ancient Eucharistic doctrine. By the ordinal the three orders of Bishops, Priests, and Deacons were continued. The power to ordain or consecrate was shown to lie with the Bishops, who alone could give valid orders. The Anglican Church, in the interests of the Faith, recast her ordinal. It was with the intention, as is seen by the office itself, to hand on that divine succession of an Apostolic ministry and priesthood, which she believed her Bishops and orders then possessed.

About this time was put forth what is commonly known as "Cranmer's Catechism." It was a translation, and is chiefly noticeable as showing what Cranmer's views were at this time. It is the latest expression of them. The Real Presence, the Power of the Keys, and the Apostolic Succession are all plainly affirmed. We may omit dwelling on the later four years of Edward's reign, at which period there was an influx of foreign Protestants, whose object was to conform the doctrines of the Church of England to the sects of Zurich and Geneva. They effected, however, very little. But it was under their influence that a second Prayer Book was compiled. It is a comfort to find, however, that "this Prayer Book never had the slightest claim to ecclesiastical authority." It cannot even plead acceptance by the Church, for it was only in force about eight months, and probably it was never used at all in many parts of England. It was one of the most signal blessings of God on the English Church that Edward VI., "the young tiger cub," was early taken away. The loving presence of God, watching over the Anglican Communion, thus preserved it in Catholicity.

The Interlude

Mary succeeded Edward, and the Church and nation were reconciled to the papacy. Then, after five years, Elizabeth succeeded, and in her time the Prayer Book was put forth by the Church's authority, and secured for ever to the Church the liturgy in the common tongue. This is one of the greatest blessings derived from the Reformation.

In Elizabeth's reign, the orders and the faith and the continuity of the Church were preserved. Cardinal Pole, who was Archbishop of Canterbury, was dead when Elizabeth came to the throne, and Matthew Parker was legally and validly consecrated as Archbishop. Roman Catholics, now ashamed of their attacks upon the fact of his consecration, have granted that, according to the register preserved at Lambeth, Parker was consecrated on December 17, 1559. We have full and minute accounts given in the Lambeth Register.

There was a foolish story started forty-five years after the event, by Romans, denying the fact of Parker's consecration, and which was known as the Nag's Head fable. It has of late years been apologized for and repudiated by Roman authorities.

In the *Civita Cattolica*, the organ of the Pope, we find it said, "Let us admit the falsity of the Nag's Head fable, and deplore its use as an argument to cast doubt on Anglican orders." Objections to the consecration of Parker on the part of Romanists have now ceased, and have been apologized for. There was no doubt of the fact of his consecration.

The Earl of Nottingham, a Roman Catholic and a relative of Parker's, declared that he was present at the service. " There are at least nine distinct contemporary officials and authentic documents to prove it."[6]

Parker was consecrated by four Bishops — Barlow, Hodgkins, Scory, and Coverdale. Barlow and Hodgkins had been consecrated by the old Roman Ordinal. One of Barlow's consecrators was Clerk, Bishop of Bath, who in his turn derived succession from Italian Bishops. The King's mandate for Barlow's consecration is still in existence, and also it is of record that he was installed and enthroned in his See. He was involved in many legal contests, and his being a Bishop was never questioned. Moreover, he took his seat and voted

---

6. *Anglican Orders and Roman Claims*, p. 29.

in the House of Lords, which he could not have done unless it had been certified that he had been consecrated. His consecration has been fully vindicated by Courrayer, Mason, Bramhall, Haddon, and Lingard. De Augustinis, of great renown as a modern Roman theologian, in the late Conference about Anglican Orders, said: "Barlow was unquestionably a true Bishop."

As for Scory, who was consecrated under the Edwardian Ordinal in 1551, he had conformed and acted in Mary's reign as Suffragan Bishop of London.[7] This would show that the Edwardian Ordinal was accepted by Roman authority as valid.

Through his consecration, Parker's succession is thus traceable up to Archbishop Theodore, who was consecrated (668) by Pope Vitalianus.[8] Matthew Parker, in tracing thus his succession back to Archbishop Theodore, also does so to that old Saxon succession whose Bishops united under Theodore.

Along with Matthew Parker, we must consider the case of Archbishop Laud, who was one of his successors. He not only received his consecration through the old Anglo-Roman line of Parker, but through the Irish line of Bishops. For at the time of Queen Elizabeth, some of the Irish Bishops conformed — all but two, it is said. The record is as follows: St. Patrick was Archbishop of Armagh in 432. Christopher Hampton, in 1613, was the ninety-second Archbishop from him. He consecrated the English Bishop Thomas Morton in 1616, Bishop of Chester, who consecrated John Howson, Bishop of Oxford, in 1619, who, in 1621, consecrated Laud.[9]

Laud also received the Episcopate through the modern or Italian

---

7. Bonner's *Register,* fol. 347, July 14, 1554.

8. There were many other Archbishops of Canterbury consecrated by Popes or Cardinals: Theodore, at Rome, by Pope Vitalianus, A.D. 668. Northelm, at Rome, by Gregory II., 736. Lambert, at Rome, by Paul I., 763. Wulfred, at Rome, by Leo III., 803. Celnotus, at Rome, by Gregory VI., 830. Athelard, at Rome, by Adrian II., 863. Plegmund, at Rome, by Formosus, 891. Richard, at Avignon, by Alexander III., n 74. Stephen Langton, at Viterbo, by Innocent III., 1207. Boniface, at Lyons, by Innocent IV., 1244. John Peckham, at Rome, by Nicholas III., 1278. Henry Chichele, at Sens, by Alexander V., 1409. Robert Winchelsea, consecrated by Gerard, Cardinal of Sabina, 1294. Simon Mepeham, consecrated by Peter Cardinal Praeneste, 1348. John de Stratford, consecrated by Vitalis Cardinal Albano, as Bishop of Winchester, 1323. Thomas Bradwardin, consecrated by Bertrand, Cardinal of St. Mark, Archbishop of Embrun, 1349.

9. Moore, *The Reformation,* p. 280; Macbeth, *Ireland and Her Church,* 166, 168.

line. Mark Anthony, Archbishop of Spalatto, Italy, joined the Church of England, and was appointed Dean of Windsor. He, with others, consecrated George Monteigne in 1617 as Bishop of Lincoln, who consecrated the Bishop of London in 1621, who consecrated Laud.

We have also seen how the Patriarch of Jerusalem in the sixth century consecrated St. David. This Welsh line became in 1115 united to the English Church under the Archbishop of Canterbury. William Murray, the Archbishop of Llandaff, was, with Archbishop Laud, a consecrator in 1634 of Bishop Wren of Hereford, and from Wren and Laud all our present English and American Bishops have their spiritual descent. Our Anglican Episcopacy is thus derived from Roman, Irish, Welsh, and Eastern sources, the validity of whose orders has never been disputed.

In the consecration of Matthew Parker, it is of record that all four Bishops laid on their hands, and invoking the Holy Ghost, all said the words of consecration, the order being designated in the service. Thus the four acted as co-consecrators. This shows the great care that was taken to validate their action.

The matter and form of Parker's consecration as attested by the ancient liturgies was valid. Our Lord had given no one form as He had in respect of the sacrament of Baptism. There was no one form that had been universally used in the Church. The Roman ordinal was obscure, and it could not be told with certainty when the ordinand was ordained priest. It was therefore within the rights of the National Church, having expressed her intention to continue the orders as they anciently were, to improve her ordinal. She preserved in it all that was necessary for the conveyance of orders. There was the laying-on of the Bishops' hands, with the designation in the service of the order to be conveyed, and with prayer and invocation of the Holy Ghost. The intention of the consecrators was to do that which the Church proposed to be done. This is all that Cardinal Bellarmine says is necessary. The Church in her preface to her ordinal explicitly stated that her intention by it was that the ancient orders should be continued. The consecrators could not, by their own private opinion, if they had any, alter the intention of the Church of which they were the agents. Moreover, as de Augustinis held, "It is not necessary for the minister to intend to produce the effect or end of the sacrament, but only to do what the Church orders to be done." Thus the consecrators had a right intention, and the matter and form were correct.

As to Matthew Parker's jurisdiction, like all other Bishops, habitual or potential jurisdiction is conveyed by the consecration. Actual jurisdiction is the limitation of that which is inherent by consecration, and it limits the exercise of spiritual powers to certain places and over certain persons. It is regulated by canon law. This right to exercise Episcopal authority in a certain locality, or over certain persons, flows back on the death of its Bishop into the See, subject to the confirmation of the Bishops of the Province, or, in the case of an Archbishop, it goes to his comprovincials. On Elizabeth's succession there were nine Bishops who were in canonical possession of their Sees, and all these, except two, accepted Matthew Parker as their Archbishop. None of the uncanonically intruded Marian Bishops made any formal protest. So Parker's jurisdiction was confirmed.

We Anglicans know that we are possessed of orders, and real sacraments, and therefore we have a true priesthood. The truth of our orders rests not only on an historical argument, but on their spiritual effects. Their enlightening power and saintly-making efficacy demonstrate to us, their recipients, their validity.

When the Pope lately denied the validity of our orders, he declared what we know with divine certainty to be untrue, and proved he was not infallible.

WORSHIP & CEREMONIAL

The English Church thus preserves the Priesthood, the three Holy Orders, the ancient Faith as set forth in the Creeds and in the undisputed Councils. She preserved the ancient worship and ceremonial, which the Ornaments rubric of 1661 authorizes. As we of the American Church are not very familiar with this rubric, we here quote it in full: "And here it is to be noted that such Ornaments of the Church and of the Ministers thereof at all times of their ministration, shall be retained and be in use, as were in this Church of England by the authority of Parliament, in the second year of the reign of King Edward VI."

It is to be remarked that this rubric was not merely the republication of a former rubric; but by the introduction of new words it has the legal character of a new law, the legal effect of which, as Justice Coleridge said, was to "wipe out all the intervening legislation, and to establish for the Church's Ornaments those which were legalized at the time specified."[10] These were the Eucharistic vestments of amice, alb, girdle, stole, chasuble, surplice and cope for priests; and mitres and other regalia for Bishops; and the use of lights on the altar, and incense, etc. Thus the Ornaments Rubric provided for the use of the old ceremonial. We know that Queen Elizabeth had on the altar in her private chapel a silver crucifix, candlesticks, images of St. Mary and St. John. There were also a surpliced choir, priests in copes, and Eucharistic vestments were worn by her chaplain; also the great Bishop Andrewes, in his own chapel, used the same. The Anointing of the Sick, according to the injunction of St. James in the New Testament, was provided for in the First Prayer Book of Edward VI. The Rubric reads thus: "If the sick person desire to be anointed, then shall the priest anoint him upon the forehead or breast, making the sign of the cross; and we pray that God may restore him to bodily health, and release him from all troubles and diseases both of body and mind." In the book, newly edited, by V. Staley, *Hierurgia Anglicana*, we can see how these usages were continued in subsequent times.

DOCTRINE & THE REAL PRESENCE

The Church was no less careful in preserving the ancient doctrine of the Real Presence of Christ in the Holy Eucharist. There had been some question in the Church as to the right interpretation of her formularies. The Zwinglian theory that the communion was but a memorial service had obtained but little acceptance, yet the Calvinistic theory had received some encouragement. Calvin, having lost the priesthood, was compelled to assert that consecration was unnecessary, and he held constantly that the elements were not changed into the Body and Blood of Christ. They were only set apart, he affirmed, as holy things. On the delivery of them to the faithful believers, Christ's Body and Blood were, however, simultaneously given to them. The Presence depended thus upon the faith of the receiver, not on the consecration by the priest. This teaching is known as the theory of Reception. It is technically called virtualism.

Calvin's theory had been contradicted, however, by the 28th Article of Religion, which said that the "Body was given and taken and eaten in the Supper, after a heavenly and spiritual manner." If

---

10. *Hierurgia Anglicana*, Part I.

Christ be not in the priest's hands as he holds the consecrated bread before the communicant, and says, "This is My Body," how can he be said to give the Christ? And if Christ be not in the communicant's hand as he receives that from the priest, how can he be said to take Christ? It was because Christ was present in the Sacrament by virtue of the consecration that the communicants were bidden to leave their seats, to come forward and kneel down, and in that posture of devotion receive the Sacrament. But questions arising, the Church herself pronounced judgment upon the opposing theories and condemned Zwinglianism and Calvinism. This she did officially by making additions to her Catechism in the year 1604; the last portion of the Catechism, on the Sacraments, being written by Bishop Overall, whose belief in the Real Objective Presence of Christ in the Sacrament is well known.

In the Catechism it is stated that baptism is an "outward and visible sign of an inward and spiritual grace given unto us." Baptism is an act which consists thus of two parts. The Sacrament of the Lord's Supper has three things said of it: First, it is an outward and visible sign, and secondly an Inward Thing, which is the Body and Blood of Christ, which are verily and indeed received by the faithful, and thirdly, a grace which follows faithful reception. The difference between Baptism and the Lord's Supper is, that in Baptism there is no necessary consecration of the element, or change made in respect of it; whereas in the Blessed Sacrament a change takes place, so that the Body and Blood of Christ, which is the inward part or Thing, is given by the priest and taken by the faithful. Thus the Church herself pronounced that her doctrine was that which is called the "Real Objective Presence of Christ."

And here we would reverently make a statement which may help souls to realize this great mystery of Christ's Presence. The unfortunate blunders and mistakes theologians have been led into have come in a large measure from arguing about the Presence in the Sacrament as if it were something taking place in the ordinary natural material order of things. It is an action on Christ's part which takes place in the spiritual organism of the Church, and is governed by laws of its own. Christ stands in the midst of His Church ever present to all the members of it. He does not have to move locally in order to manifest Himself in any portion of His Mystical Body. "Our Lord," says Cardinal Newman, declaring the present Roman doctrine, "neither descends from Heaven upon our altars, nor moves when carried in procession. The visible species change their position, but He does not move. We can only say He is present, not according to the natural manner of bodies, but sacramentally. His Presence is substantial, spirit-wise, and sacramentally, an absolute mystery."

Christ, at the time of the Institution, took the elements into His hands, and gathered them into sacramental union with Himself. And now, ever present and standing in the Church, through His ministers, who act as His agents, He does the same thing. This tremendous act of loving condescension demands from us an acknowledgment by worship: and our act of adoration has for its object, not the elements, but the divine Person.

As one proof that there was no denial of the Catholic Faith by the English Church at the Reformation, we note that out of nine thousand clergy who said Mass under Queen Mary, only some two hundred or two hundred and fifty beneficed clergy refused to conform at the accession of Queen Elizabeth and the promulgation of the new Prayer Book. As at least a large number of these Marian priests conformed, we cannot suppose that there was anything in the new Prayer Book that they regarded as denying the Catholic Faith, or as making a new religion. It seems to be an historical fact that the Pope himself offered to accept the changes, and was willing to allow the use of the Book of Common Prayer, if Queen Elizabeth would only acknowledge his supremacy.[11] We see in all this how the Anglican Church, while rejecting the papacy, and rejecting it now more strongly than ever, since it has added new doctrines to its creed, holds the ancient Faith.

The English Reformation began in 1529 and was not completed until 1662. It had two phases, one in respect of Rome, and one in respect of Puritanism.

The Church Repudiates Puritanism

The Church, having thus met Romanism, had next to meet with Puritanism and Protestantism. There had arisen within the Church of England, largely derived from the Continent, Calvinistic opinions. These developed in the time of Cromwell into the Great Rebellion; and overthrew for a time the monarchy and the Church. The Puri-

---

11. *Elizabethan Clergy*, Gee. *Queen Elizabeth*, Camden.

tan theological positions had been met by the Church's great theologians, Hooker, Andrewes, and Laud. When in power, the Puritans, displaying their true spirit, forbade the use of the Prayer Book, broke the stained-glass windows in the churches, stabled their horses in the old Cathedrals, removed the altars from their ancient eastward position and substituted tables in their place, around which they gathered in unseemly and irreverent fashion. They denied the authority of the Church, the power of the priesthood, and the sacraments.

God's providence again preserved the English Church and overthrew the intruders. In 1661 the restoration of the monarchy took place, and with it the revival of the Church. Perhaps never so able a body of Bishops came together as those who assembled after the Restoration and put forth the Prayer Book in its last revised form. But first, in order to be fair, they sought, if possible, to unite the nonconforming bodies and to restore them to the Church. Thus, in 1661, the Savoy Conference was assembled, consisting of twelve Bishops and twelve Protestant ministers. Baxter, who led the Protestant side, produced a rival Prayer Book of his own making, and demanded its acceptance as an alternate. These ministers also demanded the disuse of the word " priest' ' in the Prayer Book, and the permission to use extempore prayers at the discretion of the ministers. They asked that the observance of Lent and Saints' Days be abolished. They objected to the sign of the cross in Baptism and the ring in marriage. They required that the practice of kneeling at the reception of the Holy Eucharist be discontinued. They objected to the teaching of the baptismal service, which taught that each person so baptized was "regenerated." They demanded that the Ornaments Rubric should be abolished, so that the Eucharistic vestments, and lights on the altar, incense, and other ceremonials should no longer be permitted.[12] They demanded also that those who received Presbyterian ordination should be admitted as Church clergymen, without any further form of laying-on of hands by the Bishop. These Protestant ministers also asserted that the Church was not merely acting inexpediently but sinfully, in making the sign of the Cross, in allowing the wearing of surplices, in the kneeling at Communion, and the declaring those baptized to be "regenerate." It is obvious that if their demands had been accepted the Church of England would have

---

12. *Catholic Brief,* Burnie.

been wrecked, and it could no longer have been a branch of the Catholic Church. The Bishops refused, in obedience to the divine trust they had received, to grant these revolutionary demands. The Prayer Book was thus reestablished practically as we now have it. We cannot be too thankful to God's providence that in this critical time He so saved it, and that the Church was thus found loyal to Catholic doctrine and worship, in resisting the attacks of Protestantism.

Final Repudiation of Romanism

Not long after, through her Bishops, she resisted the political influence of the Roman Catholic King, James II., who sought to make her subservient to his purpose; and when, in 1688, the king commanded the Bishops to cause his declaration, which was to be a step towards the revival of Romanism, to be read from every pulpit, we know how the demand was met. Archbishop Sancroft summoned a conference of Bishops and clergy at Lambeth. The discussion lasted for a week. Legal advice was sought. Seven Bishops presented a petition to the king, stating that his declaration was founded on a dispensing power which had already been declared illegal. The clergy and laity of the Church stood unitedly behind the Bishops in defense of national liberty. The Bishops, as being guilty of a libel, were committed to the Tower. We quote the vivid description of their committal as given by Wakeman: "Their passage to the prison was a triumphal procession. Never since the days of the Crusades had the stolid natures of Englishmen been so deeply moved. As their barge passed swiftly down the Thames, hundreds of sober citizens assembled on the river banks, and kneeling in the black mud, craved their blessing and thanked God for their courage. On the 29th their trial began. The judges were divided in opinion whether their petition could be in law a libel or not. The jury, unable to agree, were locked up for the whole of the night. At 10 o'clock in the morning they came into court and gave their verdict, 'Not guilty.' In a moment broke out a scene of wild excitement, un-paralleled in the history of English courts of law. The crowd within and without Westminster Hall broke into a frenzy of enthusiastic joy. Men fell upon each other's necks, and wept and shouted and laughed and wept again; and amid the cheers of men and the boom of cannon the humble heroes of the Church passed in safety to their homes."

Thus the Reformation was made secure in England, and the Cath-

olicity of the English Church vindicated both against Rome and
Puritanism.

XVI

PUSEY & THE CHURCH REVIVAL

THE Church was planted in Britain in very early times. It met
with reverses and almost destruction at the hands of the Saxons
and Danes; was strengthened by the coming of the Monk Augustine
in 596; became consolidated under the great Archbishop Theodore;
was brought in loser connection with the Roman See at the time of
the Norman Conquest; came fully under the dominion of the Papacy as its power culminated under Hildebrand and Innocent III.;
was aroused by the voice of Wycliffe to the struggle for its ancient
rights;[1] passed through its struggle with the Papacy in the sixteenth
century, maintaining the continuity of its organization, its holy orders, and its inherited Catholic Faith; emerged from the contest with
Puritanism in the seventeenth century; and then, fortifying its Prayer
Book with more emphatic statements of Catholic doctrine in 1662,
completed the work of the Reformation.

During all this period we can but note the loving Providence of
God, watching over and developing the Church, purifying it by its
trials and sufferings and preparing it, freighted as it is with the balanced wisdom of the ages and with all the endowments and ministries of grace, for its development throughout the world, opening
now under advancing civilization to Christianity as never before
since the days of Constantine.

It will not be uninstructive to review together that remarkable
development of spiritual life which took place in the Church of
England during the nineteenth century; a movement which has so
transformed and vivified her anew with spiritual life as to seem like
a revival of those early days when the Church was trembling under

---

1. Some may be surprised — even scandalized — by Grafton's favorable citation
of the Rev. Dr. John Wycliffe. Despite a handful of unfortunate beliefs, Wycliffe
has historically occupied a significant place in the hearts of Anglicans of all
churchmanships, titling him "The Evangelical Doctor." Notable Anglo-Catholic
Dogmatist C.B. Moss (who also cites Wycliffe) writes: "Wycliffe was a theorist
who had no opportunity of working out his ideas." (*The Christian Faith*, Ch. 54
§ VI) His errors may be charitably dismissed as a product of his generation and
circumstance. For the good Anglican, Wycliffe occupies a similar space as the
Father Origen — *wary* veneration.

the Divine afflatus of her lately received Pentecostal gifts.

I

In order that we may more fairly estimate this work of God's Holy Spirit in our Communion, we would first call attention to the condition of the English Church in the century that preceded it. We find the Church in the beginning of the eighteenth century, to quote from the historian, Wakeman, full of vigorous endeavor, secure in her position, bright with hopefulness. Her great theologians, Hooker, Andrewes, Laud, Overall and Montague, had discriminated and vindicated her position as against Papalism and Puritanism. "The writings of George Herbert, and Donne and Crashaw and Jeremy Taylor had proved that the fairest flowers of devout literature could spring from the garden of her faith. The lives of holy Nicolas Ferrar, and Bishops Juxon, Gunning and Ken show that a special type of restrained devotion, second to none in reality and sacrifice, was attainable by her children. The trials which she had suffered at the hands of Cromwell and of James II. witnessed to her steadfastness and tested her reality."[2] It was at this time the great Christian Society, the *Society for the Propagation of the Gospel*, was founded, and her foreign missionary work begun.

But with the accession, in 1714, of George I., and the coming into power of the Whig party, a change came over the Church. Most active measures were taken to cripple the Church's activity.

For eleven centuries the Church had met together for deliberation and legislative action in Convocation. From 1718 to 1850 convocation was practically suspended. The living voice of the Church was thus suppressed. The erection of fifty new churches, voted by Parliament in Queen Anne's reign, was changed by the action of the King and only twelve were erected. Since the Restoration, most of the practical activity of the Church had been the work of high Churchmen, and the suppression of high Churchmanship practically meant the suppression of religious energy. The plan of appointing four Bishops for the American Colonies was shelved. As the century advanced, the lower condition of the spiritual life is discernible. The saintly line of the Carolinian Bishops had given place to the classical

---

2. Henry Offley Wakeman, *An introduction to the history of the Church of England : from the earliest times to the present day*, 418.

scholars of the Georgian period. The King said all his Bishops were gentlemen and probably they were, but the visitor to the great hall of Christ Church, Oxford, adorned with so many portraits of her distinguished sons, can easily pick out, by their full, rubicund countenances, the appointees of the Hanoverian dynasty from the older divines whose faces wear the purified livery of prayer.

While the clergy as a body lived moral lives, yet the saintly ideal of the Priest's life was lacking. "The patronage lavished upon a worldly-minded clergy stimulated the growth of Latitudinarianism in doctrine and unspirituality in life."[3] They came to regard the Church as merely a human institution. They had little apprehension of the sacredness of their powers or their ministerial priesthood. Their ideas of Eucharistic doctrine differed not materially from that of Zwingli, seldom rose higher than that of Calvin. Thus in this dark age of England's Church, we find, along with Clayton and Hoadley's riotous unbelief, as Dr. Neale has said, "a Blackburne running his career at York, and a Cornwallis dancing away his evenings at Lambeth, till George III. had peremptorily to interfere."[4]

The spirit of the age aided the spiritual paralysis. It was rationalistic. Canon Liddon says: "The eighteenth century was marked by a shallow common sense."[5] Also, the hysterical phenomena at times attending Wesley's preaching, which the good man said he did not know whether to ascribe to God or to the devil, made sedate Churchmen dread what, under general terms, they called enthusiasm. Enthusiasm became synonymous with piety without morality. The Archbishop of Canterbury counseled the famous missionary, Heber, on leaving for his work in India to preach the Gospel and to put down enthusiasm. Moved by this fear of an emotional religion, preachers confined themselves more and more to an inculcation of

---

3. Grafton is quoting his own essay in the Church Review: *The Rise of Ritualism in the Church.*

4. Also quoted in *The Rise of Ritualism in the Church,* but it is not there attributed to Dr. Neale.

5. The "shallow common-sense" referred to here by Fr. Liddon belonged to none other than the young Rev. Dr. Pusey. It was his early letters which "savoured somewhat of the shallow 'common-sense' of the eighteenth century, the traditional language of which he had not yet revised, and was unconsciously repeating. Thirty years later he would have judged it severely." (The Rev. H.P. Liddon, *The Life of Edward Bouverie Pusey,* Vol. 1, Ch. VI.

morality, and consequently got themselves labeled as "formalists," "dry-as-dusts," and "legalists." The received ideal sermon of the period, as described by Robert Hall, was "a discourse upon some moral topic, clear, correct, and argumentative; in the delivery of which the preacher must be free from all suspicion of being moved himself, or of intending to produce any emotions in his hearers."[6] Blackstone, the well known jurist, has given us his experience of the pulpit, when he came to reside in London: "As to its morality, it did not always rise, in his opinion, to that of Plato or Cicero; and as for the religion, it was difficult to say whether the preacher believed in the Koran, Confucius, or the Bible."[7]

The religious decadence expressed itself in the neglect of the Churches. The old Church buildings of England were thoroughly Catholic, and each part of their structure proclaimed some doctrine of the Nicene Faith. The threefold divisional arrangement into sanctuary, chancel, and nave bespoke the doctrine of the Blessed Trinity. The cross-form of the Church proclaimed the truth of man's redemption through Christ. The nave was symbolical of the ship of the Church passing through the waves of the world; the font, near the door, of our entrance into the ark of Christ's Church by Baptism. The chancel, filled with the white-robed choristers, spoke of the Church in Paradise. The Altar evidenced the fact that while Christ was reigning in glory, He was yet ever present with His people. All this had faded from the spiritual sight of the eighteenth century. Symbolism lost its significance. Worship became a lost art.

The late Beresford Hope thus describes the condition as existing far into the last century: "The aisles were utilized by certain family pews or boxes, raised aloft and approached by private doors and staircases. The pulpit stood against a pillar, with a reading desk and clerk's box beneath. There was a decrepit western gallery for the band, and the nave was crammed with cranky pews of every shape. The whitewashed walls, the damp, stone floors, the high, stiff pews, with faded red curtains, allotted to all the principal houses and farms in the parish, the hard benches, without backs, pushed into a corner, or encumbering the aisles, where the poor might sit, spoke eloquently of the two prevailing vices of the time's apathy and exclusiveness.

---

6. *The Works of the Rev. Robert Hall*, Vol.1, 350

7. Quoted in several of Grafton's works, all without citation.

The grand old fonts were frequently removed to the rectory garden to serve as flower pots, while their place was supplied by a small stone basin standing on a pedestal in some remote corner of the church. In the place where once the Holy Altar stood, vested in fair array, was to be found a mean table with a moth-eaten red cloth upon it."[8] The practice of daily service in town churches was given up. Congregations not infrequently sat through the Psalter as well as through the lessons. In the ordinary parish church, chanting was unknown. Public catechizing in the afternoon had ceased. Celebrations of the Holy Eucharist were very infrequent. In most parishes it was celebrated on the three great Festivals only. We read that in St. Paul's Cathedral, on Easter Day, 1800, there were only six communicants, and at the only celebration.

Such was the condition of the Church in the eighteenth century; "Its corporate activity destroyed by suppression of Convocation, its practical energy sacrificed to State policy, its mission spirit evaporated by Latitudinarian leadership, its conscience dulled by the repression of enthusiasm," its very life blood chilled by its decay of faith and its loss of worship. Was it possible for these dry bones to live? While religious bodies which have lost the Apostolic ministry, the Priesthood, the gifts of Sacramental grace, necessarily, under the strain of never-ceasing conflicts, decay and divide; on the other hand, where the Priesthood and Sacraments are preserved, there, through the abiding Presence of Christ, is an ever-present resurrection power. The Church might slumber, but she could not die. No weapon formed against her could prosper, the gates of hell could not prevail against her. As in times past, when the Church seemed to be overwhelmed by the tempest, Christ had manifested Himself, so it was now. At the close of the century, moved in part by the tragic Nemesis of the French Revolution and the wars which followed, the spiritual perceptions of Christians were quickened to the discernment, amidst the thunderings and voices and showers of blood, of man's need of divine succor and to call upon the Master who seemed asleep in the Ship.

First, there arose within the Church of England, a body of earnest preachers who came to be known as the Evangelicals. Their spiritual

---

8. Sir Alexander James Beresford Hope (1820–1887) was a conservative politician and author.

progenitors were Romaine, Henry Venn, Law, Harvey, John Newton, Richard Cecil, Charles Simeon. Under their leadership the *Religious Tract Society* and the *Church Missionary Society for the Evangelization of Africa and the East* were founded. They awakened England to the evils of the slave trade, which was abolished in 1807. In 1833, largely by the exertions of those known as the Clapham sect, the further act for the emancipation of the slaves was passed. Under their teaching personal piety revived. The characteristic of their preaching was a vivid presentation of Christ crucified. In contrast with the preceding morality and formalism, the Evangelicals dwelt largely on man's lost condition, his deliverance through the satisfaction made on Calvary, and the need, in order to its individual appropriation, of a living faith. They were somewhat strict in their discipline. They assembled frequently in each other's houses for Bible expositions and prayers. "To be religious meant, in the language of the day, to foreswear [sic] dancing and the theater, to keep Sunday strictly, to sit under a popular preacher, to be sober in dress and staid in manner, and to be interested in foreign missions."[9]

The Low Church movement, however, was not an especially learned one. It was not necessary that it should be. Theologically, it had to dwell largely on the subjective side of religion. It was of the nature of a St. John Baptist awakening. It preached conversion and pointed to Christ. It rapidly increased throughout the country up to the year 1833. Then political events began to force the Church into the consideration of other portions of her Creed. A supplementary religious movement began, called by various names the Oxford, the Tractarian, the Catholic Movement. I have called it a supplementary movement, for it was supplementary rather than antagonistic to that which had preceded it. By the laws which govern human thought, we are obliged to look at truths both in their subjective and objective aspects; and different minds, according to their temperament, will be drawn to dwell more exclusively upon one than the other. The Evangelical theology was, in its application, essentially subjective; but truth, for its completeness, requires to be supplemented by its objective side. The Evangelicals had earnestly proclaimed the necessity of a living faith in Christ and His sacrifice. They strove to bring men by their preaching under the conviction of sin, to make then

9. Henry Offley Wakeman, 454

an act of submission and trust in Christ's promises, and to find in the peace that ensued an assurance of acceptance. It was an earnest presentation of Christ crucified and the subjective religion in which emotion and feeling played a large part.

The supplementary movement brought out the objective side of religion. Contradicting, denying nothing the Evangelicals asserted, and believing equally with them in the necessity of a true conversion and a living faith, it was shown that Christ's Religion came into the world not merely as a proclamation of pardon, but in the way of an Organization. This organization was something more than a mere aggregation of individual believers. It was not a voluntarily formed one like a human society. It did not take its inception from Roman burial guilds. It had Christ for its Founder, the Apostles for its authorized Ministers, the Sacraments for its means of grace. Yes, it was something different from a divine society. It was more even than an organization. It was an Organism. An Organism is something that has life in Itself and can communicate life. It was a spiritual living Organism, through which Christ, ever present in it, acted. An Organism in which the Holy Ghost dwelt. An Organism by whose Ministry and Sacraments the life and light of Christ was conveyed to individuals. An Organism which was to be eternal and was to be the Bride of Christ.

The two schools of thought thus supplemented each other. But at first this was far from being understood, and only in these latter times is becoming commonly recognized, as high Churchmen and low Churchmen are coming together in more loving accord, agreeing to differ in matters of opinion, members of one common household of faith, divided as the waves, but one as the ocean is one.

II

It would be profitable, if here we could linger on the fascinatingly interesting period of the inception of this movement, and its rapid progress between the years 1833 and 1845 by means of published tracts and treatises; on the healthful checks it met — "Our checks," said Pusey, "have been our greatest blessings" — on the sad loss of adherents, the trials and bitter assaults its leaders sustained, its widening influence as the century went on, the gradual acceptance by the larger portion of the Church to-day of the principles for which it stood.

The names of those who are best known as influential leaders in this movement are those of Keble, Pusey, and Newman. Concerning the one whose name is published in connection with this treatise, it is to be said that one distinguishing characteristic of his was that he shrank in every possible way from putting himself forth, or allowing himself to be regarded, as a leader. The Church is full of the history of those who, having gathered followers about themselves, have led them eventually out of the Church into a schismatic and sect condition. A true and loyal son of the Church, ever submissive to her authority, Pusey, in the spirit of deep self-abnegation and humility, shunned what would be called leadership. Indeed, one peculiarity of this movement, which has so revived the Church's life, and brought the long-neglected objective side of truth into prominence, is that it has been under the guidance of no one man. This has saved it from disaster in times when a few prominent persons fell away, and has also protected it from the narrowness of echoing any one man's opinions. God raised up for the blessing of the English Church a body of men learned and devout, conspicuous among whom, for the vastness of his learning, and saintliness, was Pusey. He was a man of gigantic learning, vast acquirements, intense nature, profoundly spiritual; and more remarkable for the sweetness of his nature and his profound humility.

"I had known him well," said Newman, in his Apologia, "since 1837, and had felt for him an enthusiastic admiration. I used to call him 'the Great' [ὦ μέγας]. His great learning, his immense diligence, his scholar-like mind, his simple devotion to the cause of religion overcame me."[10]

He was born in the year 1800. At the age of ten years, he could easily have passed examination for entrance into Oxford. When taking his degree, the senior examiner predicted his greatness, and always considered him the man of the greatest ability he had ever examined or known. He had the capacity of studying sixteen hours a day, and the tenacity of his memory was remarkable. He pursued his theological studies in Germany, studying Oriental languages, and attending the lectures of Schleiermacher, Neander, and Hengstenberg. At the early age of twenty-nine, he became Regius Professor of Hebrew, and Canon of Christ Church. One feature of his

---

10. John Henry Newman, *Apologia pro vita sua*, Part IV.

scholarship was the exhaustiveness of his research on every subject with which he dealt. His mind was unsatisfied until he had examined all that could be known relating to any matter, and all arguments for or against any question he was considering. There was a fixed determination, before arriving at conclusions, to make his investigation thorough and complete. He has been fairly criticized for over-burdening his statements with needlessly accumulative argumentation.

He not only wrote himself, but he set others to work, and the Church is indebted to him for the translations of the Library of the Fathers and the Library of Anglo-Catholic Theology. The work he loved most was the interpretation of Holy Scripture; and his Commentary on the Minor Prophets, for its learning and spiritual insight, will always stand in the first rank of Commentaries. He enriched the Church with many devotional books, but it would be impossible to enumerate, without tediousness, the number of volumes he gave to the Church on matters of controversy and doctrinal questions. Along with Pearson and Hooker, he will rank as one of the greatest Doctors of the English Church.

Vast as was his learning, he had none of the graces of the pulpit orator. There was no attempt in his composition at literary finish or arrangement. It was little relieved by aught that would strike the fancy. But the neglected, unpolished framework was vivified by his burning devotion to God and souls. "Each sentence," says Liddon, "was instinct with his whole purpose of love as he struggled to bring others into communion with the Person of Him who purified his own soul. It was this attribute of profound reality which characterized his discourse from first to last, and, as it fell on the superficial and somewhat cynical thought of ordinary academical society, at once fascinated and awed the minds of men."[11]

Crowds came to hear him, but his sermons owed nothing to those arts and accomplishments which have been carried to their greatest perfection in the Church of Massillon and Bourdaloue. He had no pliancy of voice, no command over accent or time, or tone. He did not relieve or assist the attention of his audience by changing from fast to slow, or pausing between his paragraphs, by looking off his page; his eye throughout was fixed on the manuscript before him and his utterance was one strong, unbroken, intense, monotonous

---

11. The Rev. H.P. Liddon, *The Life of Edward Bouverie Pusey*, Vol.3, p.61

swing, which went on with something like the vibrations of a deep bell.

As he moved slowly through the vast crowds which came to hear him, his very appearance affected one. We can almost see him as Dean Church has described him. "His perfectly pallid, furrowed, mortified face, looking almost like jagged marble, immovably serene withal, and with eyes fixed in deep humility on the ground,"[12] bore the impress of that other world in which he so constantly dwelt. When he stood up in the pulpit, even before he uttered a word, you felt yourself in the presence of a saint.

His theological standpoint was that of a Catholic. He believed in the One, Holy, Catholic, Apostolic Church. He believed it was the appointed guardian of Holy Writ, of the Faith, and the organ through which Christ proclaimed it to men. All that had been taught and held from the beginning and by all, he implicitly believed. If he was a liberal in politics, he was conservative in religion. Great as was his intellect and profound his learning, before the Church, which he called his "dear Mother," he was as a little child. He submitted himself entirely to her. The writer well remembers having been with him on one occasion after the Doctor had been reading a violent attack on his *Eirenicon*, the Doctor, placing his hands behind him, as he was wont, slowly remarked, "The only question is, what has the Church of God said?"

Unlike his dear friend Newman, who was of a speculative mind, and passed through many forms of belief, being an Evangelical, a Whatelyite,[13] a High Churchman, eventually a Roman, Pusey was always stayed on authority. The voice of God came to him through the Church, and this gave grandeur and solidity to his convictions.

But great as he was intellectually, he was greater still in his spirituality. The principles of the Sermon on the Mount he practically made his own.

His life was entirely consecrated to the glory of God and the service of Jesus Christ. He lived most simply. He gave largely and at the expense of his own comfort. He built a Church at his own expense at Leeds; the only inscription referring to the donor was that it came "from a penitent." He gave most generously to the building of

---

12. Ibid, p. 60, Letter by J. B. Mozley.

13. The Rev. Richard Whately (1787–1863) was a leading Broad Churchman.

Churches in the east of London. His bodily discipline was excessive. He would have taken the discipline every night with the fifty-first Psalm, only his confessor would not let him. He has been known not to break his fast after his Maundy Thursday communion till Easter.

He rose daily at six, commending himself to God. He used a hard seat by day and a hard bed at night. He would never wear gloves nor protect his hands. He traveled poorly as possible in third-class carriages, excepting when health, or pressure of time, or duty to his mother obliged him to do otherwise. He ate his food slowly and penitentially, making a secret confession of unworthiness to use God's creature before each meal. He abstained from wine and beer unless obliged to use them by order of the physician. He mortified his curiosity; he asked himself before reading anything if it was God's will he should read it. He never set aside solid work to read newspapers or letters. "His rules about the use of speech," said his biographer, "will explain to those who remember it the peculiarity of his conversation; its profound seriousness, its unexpected pauses and silences, its grave and charitable protests. He determined not to speak of himself or his work whenever he could help doing go; to blame another only after asking himself the question, Would my lord have me say it? And to accompany the blame with an act of self-humiliation; he softened, if possible, any unfavorable judgment of others that he heard. He resolved always to give way in argument whenever it was not a duty to maintain his opinion; to interrupt no one else when speaking; to stop if interrupted; never to complain of anything which happened either to himself or to the Church, since his own sins were the cause of the one and might contribute to the other; not to mention bodily pain except as an explanation of silence which might be misunderstood; to address every one, especially his inferiors in rank, as his superiors in the sight of God."[14]

He did nothing by halves. He brought all his devotions and ministerial work under the domain of penitential rule. If you ask, Why did he do this? Had he ever been an unbelieving worldly-minded man? Was he like an Augustine, repenting of the sins of his youth? the answer is "No." He had grown up almost like a Samuel. He had a most profound, awful, supernatural sense of the holiness of God, and the pitiable, weakened, and unspiritual condition of the English

---

14. The Rev. H.P. Liddon, *The Life of Edward Bouverie Pusey*, Vol.3, p.105

Church. God had such great designs for her. How feebly she was realizing it! As the Saints of old had mourned for their people, and the prophets had girded themselves with sackcloth, so did Pusey gird himself with the robe of penitence. "He would join in intercessions as 'unfit to be heard for any one;' in the *Gloria Patri*, and *Pater Noster* as 'unworthy to take on my lips the Name I have so dishonored;' in profession of duty in the Psalms as 'what I would do, but the contrary of what I have done;' in the responses after the Commandments as to 'pray for the conversion of the worst sinners myself chief;' in thanksgiving 'to thank God I am not in hell;' and in my Absolutions that the devil did not enter into me altogether as he did into Judas."[15]

He prayed God to enable him to pray before each break in the service, at the beginning of Psalms, Canticles, before the Creed, the Lessons, three times in the Litany, immediately after any distraction, and then to try to throw his whole soul into the prayers. He would repeat the penitential Psalms when walking alone; he prayed for some grace at every Communion, and to be watchful to treasure it, and first of all for humble penitential love. He prayed God daily if good for him, to give him sharp bodily pain, and His grace in it.

The same spirit was carried into his ministerial work. He did everything in the spirit of a penitent. He would aim with commencing every ministerial act with confession that he was so unfit to be a minister of God. Another rule was, "Always in taking his place in the Cathedral, or on going to the Altar, to make an act of humiliation, as one who ought to be shut out from it" — the first should be last. Another rule was, "To hear all the very worst confessions, very penitentially, as worse myself." "In undertaking any plan to pray that it be not marred through my sins; to aim to offer all acts to God and to pray for His grace in them before commencing them as conversations, while people are coming into the room, or before I enter a room, each separate letter which I write, each course of study, and in the course of each if continued long."

It would be a great mistake to suppose that what he imposed upon himself he thought wise for others. The Elijahs, John Baptists, the Chrysostoms, a Basil, an Ambrose, a St. Francis Assissi, a Bernard, a St. Vincent de Paul, the Kens, the Wilsons, the Andrewes, and Puseys have laws of their own.

---

15. Ibid, p.106.

"All the world cannot and should not," says Liddon, "wear a hermit's garb and live austerely; but the example of the Baptist is not therefore less valuable, as a reformer of society no less than as a saint of God, for men of all nations and of all times."[16]

What a life he led! What trials he underwent! What heart-breaking sorrows he endured! Early he lost his wife. His saintly daughter was taken from him at the time he looked to her to found a Religious house and work of mercy. His son was deformed. Slander never ceased to assail him. He was called a Jesuit, a Romanizer, disloyal to his Church, the teacher of soul-destroying heresies. The hatred of theological opponents obtained an unjust and illegal censure on one of his sermons, and he was suspended from preaching in the University pulpit for three years. He quietly submitted. The doctrines he taught were misrepresented. All the inbred hatred and unreasoning prejudice against Rome, latent in the English mind, was stirred up against him, in the strange panics which would ensue. Bishops fulminated charges against doctrines which were Catholic and enshrined in the Book of Common Prayer. Men got discouraged. Newman's mournful apostrophe as he left found an echo in many hearts: "O my mother, whence is this unto thee, that thou hast good things poured upon thee and canst not keep them, and bearest children, yet darest not own them." The heart of Pusey was again and again saddened by the defection of friends. No wonder that in dark hours, under injustices and condemnations some despondent ones fell away. Not least among all the pain and bitter heartache of Pusey's penitential life, was the loss of one whom he loved as David loved Jonathan. But through all these multiplied trials, like some great rock, abiding unmoved amidst the hurtling storms and maddening waves, Pusey never wavered in his loyalty and trust in the Anglican Church. He knew God was with her and in her. God had not deserted her in her days of neglect and coldness; and He would not give her up, he said, now that she was on her knees. His unchangeableness, his constancy, unconquerable faith, his intense loyalty to the English Church as a branch of the one Catholic Body, steadied the hearts of men in troublous times and saved the Anglican Communion.

---

16. Ibid, p.111.

III

Thus, the doctrine of the Incarnation and the Church as the extension of It became the foundation of the revival. As a consequence the revelation which God has made to man was placed upon a more secure and logical foundation. It had been customary for all the sectarian bodies to base their teaching exclusively upon a book. Their foundation principle was that the revelation which God had made of Himself to man was the Bible. This Book, they claimed, was written by its various authors under the direct inspiration of God. Many held that the writers were mere mechanical instruments for recording the words given them by the Almighty. This system was embarrassed with the difficulty of giving any satisfactory reason, without calling upon the authority of the Church, for the acceptance of the several books of which the Bible is composed. It was a greater logical difficulty to demonstrate the inspiration of it. And when it came to its interpretation, the divergent opinions of a hundred sects proved the futility of independent individual interpretation. Modern discoveries and critical examinations of authorship and text are fast sapping the foundation of the theory of the "Bible and the Bible only." Now, in contrast with this discredited system, which bases its belief on a Book, the Church teaches us that God has revealed Himself to us in a Person. In contrast with the Protestantism which makes religion rest on a book, the Church makes it rest upon the Person of Christ. It is true that the revelation, which God has made of Himself to man, and of man's duties and responsibilities has been made through various channels and in many ways, and adapted from the beginning to the degree of man's intelligence, and has been gradual and progressive. It has been made through man's intelligence, understanding, imagination, conscience, spiritual nature. It has been made through thinkers, philosophers, poets, prophets, seers, in all nations and all times.[17] It has been made with

---

17. St. Justin Martyr's *Logos spermatikos* theory — the belief that "whatever things were rightly said among all men, are the property of us Christians" (*Second Apology*, 13) — was a common theme among the writings of the Tractarians and their successors. The Rev. John Keble writes in his *The Christian Year* for the Third Sunday in Lent:

"The olive-wreath, the ivied wand,
　'The sword in myrtles drest,'
　Each legend of the shadowy strand

clearer illumination, greater certitude, far-reaching spiritual vision, through the Hebrew race. It is, however, all one revelation of God; made through nature to man and in man himself, until at last the revelation became consummated and perfected in Jesus Christ. In the fullness of time, the Eternal Word or Reason of God wrapped round Himself our human nature, and the Divine Light and life shone forth through Him on the sons of men. It is thus on Christ, not on a book our religion is based. First and foremost the Tractarians made Christ their basis and Christ was their all-in-all.

The next distinguishing principle of the Revival was its Rule of Faith.

We mean, by that, the rule or way by which all the followers of Christ are to know what is essential for them to believe and do. Now it is obvious that, if Christ is the revelation of God to man, He must have left some one way by which, with reasonable certainty, those who desire to be His disciples should know what they were to do and believe. Distracted as many are in their pursuit of religious truth by the babel of conflicting sects, they must admit, if they could but discern Christ's method of solving the problems which concern their immortal destiny, such a method must be the best, and the wisest and the safest one to follow.

What then was the method Christ established for our knowing His truth? For the last three centuries sectarianism has proclaimed that the true way of learning Christ's religion was by the study of the Bible. The formula which they were never tired of repeating was, "The Bible and the Bible only the religion of Protestants." Every truth seeker was to prayerfully peruse its pages, and by the covenanted aid of the Holy Spirit, he would arrive at the truth. The babel of conflicting voices on matters essential has proved, however, the futility of this rule and made men heart sick. Moreover, it is evident, it is not the way established by Christ. If He had wished that by such means His truth was to be made known, it would have been as easy for Him by His Almighty power to have paper and printing invented

---

     Now wakes a vision blest;
      As little children lisp, and tell of Heaven,
       So thoughts beyond their thought to those high Bards were given."

This passage of Keble's was later quoted approvingly in Cardinal Newman's *Apologia Pro Vita Sua* Part III.

in the first century as in the fifteenth. The fact that He did not do
so shows that it was not by the individual study of the Bible each
person was to come by himself to the knowledge of Christian truth.

What Christ did was to establish a Church whose duty it was to
preserve and, in His Name, teach the truths God made known to
man through Him. The Church teaches, the Bible confirms. By the
abiding gift of His Holy Spirit, that Church was to preserve the
truth from age to age, defining its dogmas as heresies arose, and by
her united utterance throughout the ages proving her faithfulness
to her trust. She speaks with paternal authority to the illuminated
reason and conscience of her children. Thus, against an individual interpretation of the Scripture and the supremacy of private
judgment, the Tractarian upheld the truth that Christ had made
the Church the Keeper, Guardian, and Proclaimer of His Gospel.[18]

In reply to the speculative and rationalistic spirit which pointed
to the progress made everywhere in arts, literature, learning and
science, and declared that religion must also advance in order to
keep in touch with the spirit of the age, it was replied that a vast
chasm separated the revealed from all other kinds of truth. It was
obvious that the apprehension of all other kinds of truth, depending
as they do upon observation and experiment, must, as the ages go
on, increase and develop to the better well-being of man. But the
revelation which God made to us in Christ was made once and once
for all. It was not man's discovery, nor did it depend on his observation or experiment, but it was the gift of God. It was given in and
through Christ, once for all and for all time and for all mankind. To
His Apostles Christ gave His Holy Spirit to lead them into all truth,
bringing to their remembrance all they had heard from Him. The
Apostles declared that "they had not shunned" to declare to those

---

18. "The visible Church of Christ is a congregation of faithful men, in the which
the pure Word of God is preached..." (*Article XIX*) The Tractarian Bishop Forbes
of Brechin comments in his *An Explanation of the Thirty-nine Articles*: "Thus the
visible Church... is the Son of God Himself, everlastingly manifesting Himself
among men in human form, eternally renewing His youth, the permanent Incarnation of the same... If Christ the eternal Truth hath built the Church... The Divine truth, embodied in Jesus Christ, must thereby be bodied forth in an outward
and living phenomenon, and become a deciding authority... It is, then, the duty
of the Church to preach the pure Word of God... by preserving and interpreting
Holy Writ."

who succeeded them in office "the whole counsel of God."[19] The faith thus delivered by them has under the Spirit's guidance been summed up in the Creeds, set forth in action by the Sacraments, embalmed by the churches in her liturgies, and declared by the common utterance of united Christendom. While therefore, it is no objection in every other department of knowledge that a thing is new, because as the ages go on man must make progress, yet in religion, seeing it is revealed by Christ primarily and once for all, any proposed truth, which has not the marks of antiquity, universality, and consent upon it, could not have come from the Master, and is necessarily false. While error may thus be detected, the truth, revealed by the Holy Spirit speaking authoritatively through the Church to the illuminated reason and spiritual understanding of its members, is confirmed by its results. They come not only to believe in a Creed but in God, and not only to believe in Him but to know Him Father, Son, and Holy Ghost for He dwells in them and they in Him. Thus the Tractarians' principle was that the Church, indwelt by the Holy Spirit, is the living organ of the revelation of the Light and Life made by God in Christ to man.

Another feature of the Tractarian teaching had regard to the ministry. It startled an Erastian age bent on degrading the Church to a mere State establishment by proclaiming its true spiritual character. It was not from man or by man that the authority and power of the clergy came. They were ambassadors of Christ, clothed with His authority. They were something more than preachers of righteousness, but stewards entrusted with divine mysteries or sacraments. The commission that clothed them with authority to speak and act in Christ's Name could be historically traced to the Apostles and so to Him. The power that made them "able ministers of the Word,"[20]

---

19. Acts 20:27 — This verse took on significance for the Oxford Movement. The Tractarians were insistent that the Faith must be approached in its entirety; a particular doctrine could not be set aside merely because it was tertiary or *adiaphora*:

"[I]t is no matter as regards our practice, whether the doctrine is primary or secondary, whether the duty is much or little insisted on. A Christian mind will aim at obeying the whole counsel and will of GOD; on the other hand, to those who are tempted arbitrarily to classify and select their duties, it is written, 'Whosoever shall break one of these least commandments, and shall teach men so, he shall be called the least in the kingdom of heaven.'" (*Tract 11*)

20. 2 Corinthians 3:6

was the same Holy Spirit that had descended at Pentecost and had never left the Church.

Naturally opposition was aroused from the Erastian quarter and from the Puritan one. Within the Church there was also much theological controversy as to the origin of the Christian ministry and its powers, and the mode of their transmission. But today, as the result of unfettered discussion together with a growing desire for the sake of the common cause for a better understanding, a great rapprochement if not concord has been effected. No one can read Dr. Moberly's[21] *Ministerial Priesthood* without recognizing its moderation and balanced wisdom, or wonder that Professor Sanday,[22] a representative of a different school should profess himself satisfied with it. It argues well for that unity so much to be desired when men so eminent find themselves at one.

It has been helpful in this matter to note more discriminately than formerly how Christ commissioned the ministry that was to represent Him. The process was a long one. It had reference to His own life and ministry. His ministerial life was divided in three parts. There was His public life when He was in an especial manner exercising His prophetical office. Then followed the period when as Priest and Victim He offered Himself up on Calvary. Finally, during the great forty days He as Victor over death and hell manifests His Kingly power.

Now in each of these periods He began to associate the Apostles with His special office and commission them. When He was exercising His prophetical office as the teacher of the world, He clothed them in a degree with it and said, Go and teach.

When He was entering on His great high priestly function, after the significant inauguration into their office by the feet washing, He authorized them to offer the Eucharistic sacrifice as a Memorial of His death, saying: "Do this in remembrance of Me."[23] Having won

---

21. The Rev. Robert Cambell Moberly (1845–1903) was the son of the Rt. Rev. George Moberly — Bishop of Salisbury — and the first principal of St. Stephen's House, Oxford.

22. The Rev. William Sanday was the Dean Ireland's Professor of Exegesis of Holy Scripture from 1883 to 1895 and the Lady Margaret Professor of Divinity from 1895 to 1919. He had previously been Master of Bishop Hatfield's Hall, University of Durham.

23. Luke 22:19, 1 Corinthians 11:24

His victory as a King, He gives them jurisdiction in all nations and bids them gather disciples into the Kingdom, baptizing them in the Name of the Father, Son, and Holy Ghost. As it belongs to sovereignty to pardon as well as to grant citizenship, it was at this time, breathing on them, He said: "Whosesoever sins ye remit they are remitted, and whosesoever sins ye retain they are retained."[24]

Thus were the Apostles gathered into fellowship with Christ's three offices of Prophet, Priest, and King. But as yet they were only parts of a structure not yet vivified, of a Temple not yet Spirit-endowed, of a body not yet quickened with life. On Pentecost the Holy Spirit that filled and sanctified the whole Body, making it a Ministerial one and all its members Kings and Priests unto God, consecrated and empowered the Apostles for their special functions in that Body. They were then made "able ministers of the Word," i.e., enabled to do those things which Christ had commissioned them. In this way the Apostolic Order or College was founded. Thus the Church came into being complete with Christ as its Head and the Holy Ghost as its Indweller, and the Apostolic Order as its Ministry. But it had no written constitution. It was, however, a living Organism and must grow. Some might assign its growth to mere natural causes, others might refer it to the laws of evolution and correspondence to environment. Others would say that as the Holy Spirit dwelt within the Church and Divine Providence orders all things, it was by the Divine action the three Orders were formed. First, as need arose the Order of Deacons was created, then that of the Presbyters, finally as the Church extended and troubles arose and the Apostles were passing, the higher Order of Bishops. So it was that pressed by external circumstances and guided by the Spirit within, the Apostles gathered, by laying on of hands and prayer, others into different degrees of fellowship with themselves, and so sharers with themselves in the Triple offices of Christ. And as thus guided, we find at Jerusalem the local Church possessed of its resident and permanent Apostle with its presbyters and deacons, so as the Church extended into all lands it gradually conformed itself to the type given by God in the Mother Church.

What Pusey brought out was the divine character and authorization of the Christian ministry in its threefold orders. While the

---

24. John 20:23

validity of any other than an episcopal ordained ministry is open to serious objection (and our Church recognizes no other), yet it might be charitably admitted that a prophetical office, if this is all that sectarians seriously claim, might be exercised by license and not by ordination. However this may be, yet apart from technical questions all Churchmen can loyally and lovingly meet together in the belief that an apostolic ordination is needful for our being gathered into union with their fellowship and so with the commissioned powers given to the Apostles by Christ.

Another principle of the Tractarians was the value of the Sacraments. The initial sacrament is Baptism. This first engaged their attention. The teaching of Holy Scripture and the Prayer Book was thought to be quite plain that Baptism conveyed a gift. It took men out of their old relation to God and made them members of the Body of Christ, faith and repentance were the necessary conditions for a beneficial reception on the part of an adult. Infants were fit recipients, for as they had committed no sin there were no sins to be repented of, and as they had not raised their wills against God, there was no need by an act of submission and faith to take them down. The infant was in a passive state and thus capable of receiving a gift as Christ had showed by taking them up in His Arms and blessing them. The adult by faith and repentance becomes a fit recipient by thereby putting himself in the position of the little child. We must become like little children in order to enter the Kingdom of Heaven.[25]

In contrast with the Baptism of John, the Church teaches that Christian Baptism conveys a spiritual gift. The Baptism of the forerunner was not Christian Baptism. It was not in the name of the Blessed Trinity, for that same had not then been revealed. It conveyed no spiritual gift for the Spirit had not then been given. It was only an outward sign of repentance on the part of those who re-

---

25. "Then our Lord gives us a reason why children should be brought, 'Of such is the kingdom of God.' And He says again, that unless adult believers become conformed to the image and likeness of little children, they cannot enter into the kingdom of God... Our Lord then evidently considers infants to be in a better spiritual position for receiving the grace of His kingdom than such believing adults as the Apostles were at that time." (M.F. Sadler, *The Second Adam and the New Birth*)

ceived it. It was called "the Baptism of repentance."[26] The Christian sacrament on the other hand is said to convey a gift from Him who gave the sacrament and it is called from the gift it conveys, a Baptism "for the remission of sins."[27]

This is strikingly brought out in the case of St. Paul. He was powerfully converted on his way to Damascus. But were his sins remitted when he was converted? The Scripture says they were not. For after he had come to Damascus the prophet Ananias came to him and said, "Brother Saul, arise and be baptized and wash away thy sins."[28] It thus appears that his sins were not forgiven at his conversion but by his subsequent Baptism.

However clear this and numerous other passages in Holy Scripture are, and in Sadler's *Church Doctrine, Bible Truth*, they are well set forth, great commotion was raised by this teaching.

It was said that the lives of many of the baptized did not show that any change had taken place for the better, and that this doctrine of baptismal regeneration was a soul destroying one and productive of false peace. And so we believe it is if persons rest their hope of final acceptance on the mere fact that they have been baptized or confirmed or taken the Sacrament.

In respect of Baptism it must be ever kept in mind that unless we are truly converted and become "new creatures" by the power of the Holy Ghost no outward observances will be of any avail. The Tractarians therefore most earnestly preached faith, repentance, and conversion.

The truth seems to be this: that an adult coming to Baptism must, like St. Paul, be converted first and so coming the acceptance and peace he had will be sealed to him, he will also receive the remission of sins, and be made "a member of Christ, a child of God, and an inheritor of the Kingdom of heaven."[29] The case of infancy is this: the infant does not need faith or repentance to enable it to receive a gift. It can be grafted into the body of Christ's Church, and receive a seed principle of that new nature that Christ imparts. For in the spiritual order as in the natural one life precedes consciousness. The

---

26. Luke 3:3

27. Acts 2:38

28. Acts 22:16

29. *Church Catechism.*

gift implanted if neglected comes to naught. The gift becomes active and there is a conscious birth of the spirit when the necessary subsequent conversion, which may be gradual or otherwise, takes place.

Sectarians had looked upon the Sacraments chiefly as symbols or signs of what Christ had done for them, or signs and pledges of His mercy and love. They were not, in their view, as the Church has ever taught, channels of grace. They were only badges of a Christian man's profession, a doctrine our Articles deny.[30] Baptism conveyed nothing to the recipient, a theory our Baptismal service repudiates. Baptism was only a proclamation of what the child was by birth, or a mere proclamation of God's favor. His favorite illustration was the coronation of a king, who is a King before he is crowned, a view which fails to recognize the difference between our state by nature and that by grace. Holy Communion was only a touching remembrance of the death of Christ. The Christian Sacraments were thus placed on the low level of Jewish ordinances. They were signs, not sacraments.

No wonder, so regarded, they fell into neglect, and persons argued that if this was all they were, they could be as good Christians without as with them. But Pusey and those with him showed how this was to degrade and empty Christianity of its high purpose, which was, not only to forgive man, but to restore, recreate, transform his nature, and, inoculating it with Christ's own Humanity, elevate it into a new union with God. This was, as we have said, the grand purpose and object of the Incarnation. Christ came not to be a mere teacher, illuminator, example-giver, sin and death destroyer, but the Head of a New Creation, into whom we being incorporated and "made partakers of the Divine Nature,"[31] were finally to be further united in glory with God.

The Sacraments, therefore, were not mere empty signs, but "effectual" ones, as our Articles declare. That is, they effect in those who devoutly and rightly receive them what they signify. By Baptism, our sins are remitted and we receive the seed-principle of a new nature,

---

30. "Sacraments ordained of Christ *be not only badges or tokens* of Christian men's profession, but rather *they be certain sure witnesses, and effectual signs of grace*, and God's good will towards us, *by the which he doth work invisibly in us*, and doth not only quicken, but also strengthen and confirm our Faith in him." (*Article XXV*)

31. 2 Peter 1:4

become "members of Christ, children of God, and inheritors of the Kingdom of Heaven." By Absolution, pardon for our post-baptismal sins is assured to us, and the soul fortified by renewing grace. By the gift in Confirmation, we are sealed by the Holy Spirit of promise, and receive the anointing of the Lord which makes all in their degree, kings and priests unto Him. In the Holy Eucharist, Christ Himself: His true Body and Blood, Soul and Divinity are verily and indeed present and He gives Himself to the faithful recipients.

Thus in contrast with those systems which looked upon Christ as a mere historic Person, whose Life we were to read about, words treasure, example follow, and death believe in, the Church's system brings us into union with a living and present Lord. He still abides with us, and, through the agencies of His Church, is in the world extending the loving acts of His visible ministry to the poor and needy; enlightening the blinded spirits; curing the fevered hearts; restoring the withered lives; cleansing the leprous souls; raising the dead in trespasses and sin. In contrast, then, with what we may call the sectarian system, which bids men look back to a dying Christ, the Church presents us with an abiding and living Lord enshrined in His Church and still going about doing good. He speaks through His priests and acts through His Sacraments. His Word faithfully preached has a convicting and converting power by the accompanying aid of the Holy Ghost. Would that all preachers were alive to the sacramental character of their preaching and so, subordinately to the Gospel and Holy Spirit, delivered the Word![32] So also the sacraments are the Word in action and communicate to the penitent and faithful Light and Life. Just as the believer in the supernatural believes in God and comes to find and know Him in himself, so the sacraments demonstrate to the faithful the reality of the Life and Presence of Christ they communicate. As the existence of God has no fuller proof than this double proof of testimony and experience,

---

32. "He who knows beforehand that the Personal Word is everywhere in the written Word, could we but discern Him, will feel it an awful thing to open the Bible" (Rev. John Keble, *Tract 89*)

"So if we lack Jesus Christ, that is to say, the Savior of our souls and bodies, we shall not find him in the marketplace, or in the guildhall, much less in the alehouse or tavern amongst good fellows... so soon as we shall find him in the temple, the Lord's house, amongst the teachers and preachers of his word, where indeed he is to be found." (*Homily on the Right Use of the Church*)

we must either, as believers in the supernatural, accept the testimony of the millions of Catholic Christians as to the efficiency of the sacraments, and the gifts they convey, or deny the supernatural and so God altogether. Miserable end to which rationalism within and without the Church invariably leads.

In this connection we must dwell on two prominent doctrines which, at the time and since, have provoked controversy. One was the Real Objective Presence of Christ in the Eucharist the other Confession. We should not be doing justice to the memory of these men or Dr. Pusey if we omitted to set forth their views on these subjects.

First, as to Christ's Presence in the Eucharist. The basic idea of this view is that our Blessed Lord, the God-Man, is ever present in the spiritual body which is His Church. He is the center of it just as the sun is the center of our solar system. By virtue of the union with the Divine Nature, which is everywhere, He can make His Humanity manifest, wherever He will. He does not have to move from one place to another in order to do this. St. Stephen saw the heaven opened and Jesus standing at the right hand of God. St. Paul saw and conversed with Him on the Damascus road. At the Consecration of the Sacred Elements, Christ, invisibly present with His people, does now through His Priests, who are His agents, what He did when visibly present with His Apostles at the Institution of the Sacrament. Then, taking the Elements into His hands. He said of one. "This is My Body," and of the other, "This is the New Testament in My Blood." He gathered them by that act of His out of the realm of the natural order into union with Himself. He did not, you notice, naming two things, contrast them, saying, "This bread is My Body: This wine is My Blood." If He had so spoken then we might have argued that the bread only represented the Body, and the wine represented the Blood. Again, He did not say "This is not Bread but is My Body." Then the Bread would have ceased to exist save to sense, and His Body taken its place. What He did was simply to name that which He took and held in His hands. He named it from that it became by His engifting. He said, "This," which he held, "is My Body, This is My Blood." Now when God names anything it is different from man's naming a thing. When man names a thing he simply pastes a label on it, he only puts it in a category of other like things. But when God names a thing, His naming is a creative act.

He makes it what His word declares it to be. Thus, the Church holds that the elements are not empty signs or symbols but, by virtue of Christ's word, are the Sacrament of His very Body and Blood.

What, it has been asked, is the difference between this teaching and that of the Roman Church? One and essential difference is this: The Roman Communion has defined, according to the terms of the Aristotelian philosophy, how the bread is changed into the Body of Christ, and how the wine is changed into His Blood, and makes this definition of the manner an essential of the faith, while the Catholic Church states the fact but leaves the manner a mystery.

But is not this Presence, it is sometimes asked, a spiritual Presence? Certainly it is. The whole transaction from first to last is one effected, not in the material universe, but in the spiritual universe, in the Mystical Body of Christ.[33] It is wrought, not by any known law of nature, but by the spiritual power of the Holy Ghost. In this sense, everything concerning the Sacrament is spiritual. The glorified Body of our Lord which is Present, true and real as it is, is a Spiritual Body; as He Himself declared when He said that the things that I have been talking to you about, namely, My Body and My Blood "they are spirit and they are life."[34] The sphere in which this Presence is manifested, being the Body of Christ, is a spiritual body. The power by which the Body of Christ is manifested in any part of the Church is a Divine or spiritual power. The persons to whom Christ is thus manifested are Christians who have been gathered out of the natural order into the spiritual order, and are in the mystical Body. While the Church thus declares that That which is present, and the sphere of His Presence, and the power by which the Presence is effected, and the persons to whom the Presence is made known are all spiritual, she does not thereby deny that the Body and Blood of our Lord present is a real body, and is not in consequence of the Consecration objectively present to the faithful.

Those who have grasped the idea that the Church is a spiritual organism, and Christ has not to move in order to present Himself in any portion of it, can then have no difficulty in believing that Christ may verily and indeed be present in the Eucharist. And those

---

33. "The Body of Christ is given, taken, and eaten, in the Supper, only after an heavenly and spiritual manner." (*Article XVIII*)

34. John 6:63

who take our Lord's words in their natural and literal significance have no question but they effect what they signify. The point the controversy has turned upon is whether Christ is simply present in the heart of the faithful recipient, or whether He is present by virtue of the act of Consecration. The two difficulties to man's reason, the one of His presence, the other, of that presence depending on a human agency, belong to both views. It is just as difficult to believe Him present in the heart of the believer as to believe Him present in the Sacrament. Just as difficult to believe Him present by the act of the believer's faith as by the priest's act of consecration. It would seem, however, more in accordance with His dignity that Christ's presence in the Eucharist should be dependent upon His own ordained action through His authorized agents, than upon the uncertain, varying degrees of faith of the receiver. It certainly is of more comfort and assurance to the humble or disturbed or distracted or faint-hearted. It is moreover as seemingly illogical to say that God is present in nature to those who believe Him to be there and not by His own act of immanence, as to say that Christ is present in the Eucharist by the faith of the receiver and not by the act of Consecration. These varying views of the Eucharist were prevalent in the English Church during the progress of her Reformation, but finally the Church solemnly pronounced between the conflicting schools by adding in 1604 to the Catechism the portion relating to this Sacrament. There she declared, in conformity with the universal teaching of the Catholic Church throughout the world, that, while there was "the outward visible sign," the inward part was "the Body and Blood of Christ" which was not only received but "taken and received by the faithful." She has thus put her seal upon the doctrine of the real objective presence of Christ in the Eucharist.

The other doctrinal question with which Dr. Pusey's name is so closely associated is that of Confession. This, probably, aroused more antagonism than even the doctrine of the Real Presence. It is a subject on which fanaticism and passion may easily be aroused, and they have been skilfully excited by opponents to the utmost degree.

What! it has been asked, can a man forgive sins? The idea is impious. God only can forgive. What! shall we put the human soul again under the bondage of designing priestcraft? Shall we run the risk of having the minds of our sons and daughters and relatives contaminated by evil suggestions of low-minded priests? Is it not far better for the soul's moral growth to be left free than to depend upon the direction of fallible, and it may be designing, directors? Denunciations, such as these and many other of like kind, the product of inflamed party spirit, were incessantly hurled at Dr. Pusey and those who sympathized with him. It is one thing, as our Lord found, to meet argument which appeals to reason and Scripture, another, to cope with passion and prejudice.

But in Christ's dear Name and for His sake, let us try. Confession is at times a bitter medicine. While the Roman Church has enforced it upon all her members as a matter of discipline, the Anglican Church has left it to the free, voluntary action of her children. Until one is a true penitent and possessed with a generous desire to make reparation to his Lord, he will not use it. There is little likelihood in our day that it will ever become widely prevalent. It is indifference not over-devotion we have to meet.

It is certainly beyond dispute that God only can forgive sins. It is equally beyond dispute that this power was committed to Jesus Christ and exercised by Him. For when His unbelieving opponents taunted Him with the question, "Who can forgive sins but God only?"[35] the Divine master, working a miracle that they might know it, declared that "the Son of Man hath power on earth to forgive sins."[36] He then gathered the Apostles into union with His own office and commanded them as His agents to act in His Name. Breathing upon them, with whom and their successors He promised to be to the end of the world, He said, "Whosoever sins ye remit, they are remitted unto them; and whosoever sins ye retain, they are retained."[37] True it is, then, no man or priest can by his own power forgive sins; but may he not be the commissioned agent of conveying Christ's pardon to penitents? It is our Lord and our Lord only who forgives, and the priest is but the telephonic instrument through whom His voice is transmitted. To the impenitent it conveys naught, to the penitent it conveys the assurance of forgiveness and healing and strength. After our Lord had forgiven the penitent He had healed, He gave a further blessing, saying: "Go in peace, thy faith hath made

---

35. Mark 2:7

36. Matthew 9:6, Mark 2:10

37. John 20:23

thee whole."[38]

There will always be those so satisfied with their own spiritual condition as not to feel the need, or have the desire, for the personal assurance of pardon which the priestly absolution brings, but there will always be those drawn now, as penitents were of old, to His feet, who long to have His word spoken individually to themselves: son or daughter, "Thy sins be forgiven thee; go in peace." True it is that it might be enfeebling to character to put oneself under the direction of another mind in the duties and business of life. But Dr. Pusey and those with him have pointed out the great difference between a confessor and a director of souls. What we are speaking of is confession, not direction. And concerning confession the Church of England has delivered us from those evils which may arise in a system which makes confession compulsory.

It has sometimes been asked, why does not it suffice for me to make my confession privately to God alone? Why do it in the presence of His priest? One reason is this, and it rests on the fact of the Incarnation; Before the Incarnation, my sins were acts done against the invisible God. Since the Incarnation and the gift of the Spirit, they are acts done against my Incarnate Lord. By our sins we now repeat the tragedy of Calvary, and crucify that Lord afresh. Men rightly feel that had they lived before the Incarnation, they might have made their act of acknowledgment privately and hiddenly. But now, since the Incarnation, that spirit of honor in men which demands that they make their acknowledgment according to the nature of their offense is not satisfied by a confession to the Invisible God. It is against the Man, Christ Jesus, they have sinned, and they must go to those who represent Him. Thus they fulfill the promptings of honor and love. They go also for strength. For the grace of Absolution not only seals pardon, but cleanses the soul, removes the stains of sin, repairs the injuries done, fills one with confidence and trust, fortifies the soul against future temptation. This is the testimony of those who have used this means of grace. In comparison with their testimony what are the criticisms and carpings and insinuations of those who have not tried it worth?

And yet a higher reason for its use is to be found in the Person of Christ. He loves to forgive. He is never tired of forgiving. He loves

---

38. Luke 17:19

to forgive more and more. He bought the right at the cost of His Passion. He rejoices in every exercise of it. Every act of new trust gladdens His heart. Every fresh Absolution more and more cleanses, beautifies, adorns the soul. While the world hates confession, and Satan fears it, the Divine heart rejoices with every fresh application of His absolving grace. It was this Pusey preached. It is the teaching of the Prayer Book. The teaching of our Church is this: The power of Absolution is inherent in every Priest; the privilege of using that gift is the right of every penitent soul.

IV

Having thus spoken of the theological principles of the Movement, let us conclude with treating of its spirit. These words will declare it to us: Union, Work, Holiness, Worship.

Pusey felt most deeply that Christianity's greatest weakness lay in a divided Christendom. It was this that laid needless burdens on the laity in support of Christianity. We can but feel this in our own country where, in small towns, are to be found a number of rival bodies, few capable of financially maintaining themselves. We can but feel it acutely when Christianity in its divided aspect presents itself to the heathen world. We all know that these rents in Christendom in-list be painful to the heart of Christ. We must know that the effective operation of the Holy Ghost is checked and baffled by Christian divisions.

While we all believe that every baptized person is a member of the Church, nevertheless we must grieve that this inward unity is not expressed in outward form. Oh, how the Church of God would go forward if we were united as one great army! How would not the Holy Ghost's power manifest itself through a body that was all of one heart and one mind! The great heart of Pusey long struggled and prayed for union. His object was to show how all could be gathered into an outer oneness and a united effort.

Surely it must be wrong for us to allow our prejudices, or party spirit, or contentedness, or personal opinions to hinder union. Why should anything more be required for Church membership than belief in the essentials expressed in the ancient Creeds? Why not accept such form of Church government, which, while preserving the ancient historical ministry, recognizes the priesthood and kingship of all members of the body and secures, in all diocesan and parish organizations, the rights of the laity? Under the impulse of this desire for re-union, the Anglican Church has made approaches both to the Roman and the great Greek and Russian Church on the one side; and to her children, the Congregationalists, Presbyterians, Baptists, and Methodists, who have gone out from her, on the other. She makes them with full recognition of her own shortcomings, and the acknowledgment that, while she has much to give, she has also much to receive from them.

O! Christian friends, whose hearts must have been sometimes touched with the melancholy aspect of our divided Christianity, shall we not hear the pleadings of our Divine Master, praying with agonized entreaty that all may be outwardly, as they are inwardly, one; and, laying aside prejudice and cultivating charity, endeavor with all our hearts to further the Divine purpose?

The next watchword of the Movement was Work. The old Evangelicals had chiefly been religious exhorters, bidding men to flee from the wrath to come. They sought to save men's souls and secure to them an eternal felicity. The Movement, of which Dr. Pusey was the center, sought the elevation of mankind and, filled with the love of God, it glowed with an enthusiasm for humanity. It declared that all men were equal before God, and strove to make the sittings in the churches free. It called upon the clergy to live higher and more self-sacrificing lives. Parish houses, workingmen's clubs, schools of all kinds night and industrial, Church homes, penitentiaries, refuges, guilds, religious orders, deaconesses, sisterhoods, all the machinery of the modern parish came into existence. More churches were restored and built during this century than since the time of Queen Elizabeth, lives, talents, position, wealth have been consecrated in home and foreign missionary work with such self-sacrifice and abandonment as recalls the fervor of Pentecostal days. The Church is all aglow with enterprises ameliorating the condition of labor, making all classes, rich and poor, feel their interdependence, and their duties one to another. This great Movement has been especially, not only a clerical, but a layman's work; and England's great statesmen like Gladstone and Northcote, her great lawyers like Selborne and Anderson, her noted merchants like Hubbard and Glenn, men of high social rank like the President of the English Church Union, and laymen of humbler position, heads of societies, guilds and workingmen's clubs, have all been filled with the enthusiasm of work. Let us go out of ourselves and live for other men.

O! Christian friends and brothers, as we read the lives of these great devoted Churchmen and servants of Christ, shall not our hearts be stirred afresh within us to do something more for the Master's sake, and press on the Kingdom?

The third element of the Tractarian spirit was the inculcation of Holiness. From the beginning, the Tractarians illustrated in their own lives the spirit of sanctity. They preached repentance, dedication to duty, consecration to the Master's service. They taught men by their own example how to lead more holy and interior lives. Men have been drawn under other systems to the Cross of Christ and by a penitential trust have found peace in Him. But there are higher gifts of the Gospel than those of acceptance, assurance of salvation, and its peace. There are other gifts of the Holy Ghost than those which accompany acceptance. There is a union with the Incarnate Lord and an extension within His members, of the very virtues which possessed His soul. Christian meekness, humility, spirit of prayer, fortitude, zeal, unselfishness, self-sacrifice may be the extension in us of the same activities which were in our lord. Transforming union, which, while we go about our daily tasks, sheds upon us the Light of Heaven, which lifts us into union with the Divine!

O, Christian friends and brothers and souls, dear to our Lord, shall we rest satisfied with our present attainments? Hungering and thirsting after righteousness, for the fuller, higher, richer Christian life, shall we fail to use any means of grace the Master has left us for our profit? Shall old-time associations keep us from entering into the full spiritual privileges which belong to us as Christians and which the Church enshrines?

O, if there be any noble feeling of dissatisfaction within any of you, if you feel that your present religious environment has done for you all it can, if, like followers of some teacher who like St. John Baptist, led yon to Christ, you feel you need something more for your soul's health, will you not make all Christ's gifts your own?

Lastly, Worship. Worship is the highest act of man's nature. It is no idle indulgence of feeling or emotion. It calls on all the energies of his being, his intellect, heart, and will; and in it is to be found man's greatest joy, for it is communion with God Himself. How bleak and desolate and barren was the worship of the Church as the Puritan and Protestant left it! He defaced God's Dwelling place, and in his iconoclastic zeal, broke down the images and sacred places with axes and hammers. Through fear of idolatry, he banished everything of beauty in the worship of God. He made the Sunday service consist chiefly in listening to a sermon or providing, when it became stale, some Sunday evening entertainment. But man, a religious being and formed for worship, requires some richer and nobler form to express his homage to the Almighty. All that God has endowed him with, skill of architecture, beauty of color and painting, carved work of figure and statue, the harmonies and glories of music, all must be brought into requisition that man may express His praise. For not alone does man enter into the sacred Temple, but with the eye of faith he realizes that the living and the dead make one communion. The Angels and Saints are round about him, and so with Angels and Archangels, he must utter his *Trisagion* and cry, "Holy, Holy, Holy, Lord God of Hosts."

Sometimes, one, drawn to love the stately dignity of the Church's worship, asks in a humble state of inquiry, "Where do you find the authority for it? True, God ordered such a worship in the Old Dispensation, and nothing has ever exceeded the glory of the Temple worship; but in the Gospels I only see the humble carpenter of Nazareth clothed in a garb of poverty, going about preaching from hillside or tossing boat, and so breaking the bread of life to the famishing multitude. Where do you find your authority for your vestments, and lights, and incense, and glorious music, and pomp, and splendor of your services?"

The answer the Church makes is simple and, to the humble and devout mind, a satisfactory one. As, after God had delivered Israel from Egypt, He took Moses up into the Mount and showed him the pattern of the Heavenly Worship, and it became the directory of the Jewish Church, so, after the True Moses had, as is recorded in the Gospel, prepared the way and led His people out from Judaism, then, after His Ascension, God took St. John up into Heaven and showed again the pattern of the Heavenly Worship and it became again the Church's directory for all time. There upon the Altar Throne filled with living light, arched by the protecting bow of the Covenant, radiant with all the colors of His Attributes, St. John beheld the lamb as It had been slain. He saw the High Priest standing in the midst of the golden candlesticks, clothed with His priestly vestments and girt about with a golden girdle. There, too, was the angel of the Covenant offering the golden censer with much incense in front of the Altar, before the great white Throne, where the seven lamps of sacred fire, even in the presence of the dazzling splendor issuing from the Incarnate God, burn in the eternal noonday. He saw the crowned elders of the Heavenly hierarchy prostrate themselves, and cast their crowns in mystic adoration, midst the harpings and hymnings of the white-robed choir, as, standing on the sea of mingled glass and flame, they antiphonally responded one to another, and accompanied the Divine liturgy with their hallelujah anthem and credo and thrice-holy hymn.

O dear Christian souls, let us in these days of struggle with the malefic forces of unbelief, close up our divided ranks. Let us return to the ancient ways of Church government and Catholic Faith. Let us live lives more wholly consecrated to the service of Jesus Christ, and by a worship formed after the pattern of the heavenly worship, offer to God something more worthy of His Divine Majesty, and become more fit to take part in that worship of heaven, where He is worshipped in Spirit and in Truth.

XVII

THE RELIGIOUS STATE
FOUNDED BY OUR LORD

T HERE is one other side of this subject often overlooked. The util-
ity of Sisterhoods is admitted, but clergy and parents often fail
to grasp the idea that it is a state of life established by Christ.

The Incarnation gave a new significance and dignity to marriage.
It revealed the purpose God had from the beginning in making human nature so different from the angelic. The duality of the sexes
and their union in marriage was to be a witness to the union of the
Incarnate Word and His bride, the Church. "I speak," St. Paul says,
when writing of this mystery, "concerning Christ and His Church."[1]

Hence we may see why Christian marriage was made permanent
and indissoluble. It was to testify to the indestructibility and eternity
of this union of God with human nature. In virtue of this high office
Christian marriage had a special dignity and grace bestowed upon
it, and for this reason under Christianity polygamy was abolished
and a Christian could have but one wife, even as Christ could have
but one Church.

But also the Incarnation, through the moral as well as physical
instrumentality of the Blessed Virgin, gave rise or value to the consecrated virgin state. Not that a dedicated virginity was unknown in
the old world's life. The Greeks had their virgin priestesses of Apollo,
and the Romans their vestal virgins, who kept alive the fire that symbolized the national life. The superstitious Scandinavian races of the
West had their virgin prophetesses, and in the East the followers of
Buddha adopted a celibate life. The virginity, however, upon which
Christ placed the seal of His divine sanction had a different origin
and a unique purpose. As Christian marriage was to bear witness to
the unity of Christ and His Church, so the virgin estate was to set
forth the idea of the self-consecration and sacrifice embodied in the
Incarnation. It was also to prophesy, by its sacrifice of the present, of
the coming kingdom of the Lord in Glory. It was further to declare
the power of the grace flowing from the Divine Humanity and to

---

1. Ephesians 5:32

extend its triumph. It would, moreover, ever tell the world of the love of Christ, for whom the suffering of the loss of all things was to His devoted followers a joy.

This consecrated estate, therefore, was not the product of human pride, nor did it spring from a gloomy and false asceticism. It was not the outcome of Indian ideas of deliverance of the spirit from the bondage of matter. Nor did it rise from that mistaken theology which supposes heaven is gained by man's own merits,[2] or that suffering and pain are in themselves things dear to God. The desire for this consecrated condition is born of the love of Christ, to whom, indeed, all Christian souls are united, but of a love so real, that as He is so would it be in this present world. With the keenness of love-begotten intuition it has fathomed the philosophy of Christ's own life, and seen how He made His life fruitful through the seeming sterility of death. Realizing how He endowed His Church with an unfailing energy of perpetual renewal, by letting the seed first fall into the ground and die, in the self-abandonment of love, it would go and die with Him. Through its mist of penitent tears it sees shining the love of God unable to express its fullness save by pouring out its life on Calvary, and so it must respond by an entire oblation of self and give back heart for heart, life for life, and love for love.

Christ knew there would be souls to whom such intense desire would be as daily hunger. He knew there would be some hearts so set on fire with divine love that they must steep them, as it were, in the blood of His own passion. He knew that some would so thirst to forward His work among men that they not in conscience hold back aught from could Him.

Do you, dear reader, in your comfortable home and surrounded by all He has given and blessed to you, blame Him that He has provided for the heart-wants of others? Can you find fault with Him because, having made for you life beautiful and your cup of blessing to run over, He has allowed others to share in His labours and given them out of His cup of suffering to drink? To you a saintly life is not denied, and you may grow in union with Him by all He has given you to love; do not hinder those who would be united to Him by

---

2. Abba Pambo asked St. Anthony the Great "what ought I to do?" The first thing Abba Anthony says in reply is "Do not trust in your own righteousness." (See *Sayings of the Desert Fathers*, 6)

ministering of their substance and following Him to His Cross. Your married estate has been ennobled by Christ and enriched by His grace; be diligent in corresponding with it and not troubled by the Master's different call to another. "If I will that he tarry till I come what is that to thee? Follow thou Me."[3]

"Each as they stand in their appointed lot
And seek to do His bidding, — here
Bravely set upon the right and noble duty
'Midst earthly struggle; or 'neath the sheltered roof-tree
Training with patient toil the children of His love;
Or in the cloistered home where prayers and service
Blending make continual praise, — each will of
The Master gain their blest reward."[4]

The higher or deeper life, call it what you will, is open to all, and according to the degree of our conformity to grace do we become more and more sanctified; and according to the measure of our sanctification will be the capacity of our future joy and our nearness to Christ on His throne. We should, however, recognize the teaching of Holy Scripture and of the Church that, as Christ created and blessed marriage, so He likewise established and blessed another estate. For the "devoted" or religious estate is not merely an unwedded condition, it is an estate of the Gospel, revealed by our Lord in the counsels given by Him of voluntary poverty, chastity, and obedience, as a special means of union with Himself, begun here to be perfected in eternity.

Let us consider how our Lord teaches this by His example and by His dealings with His disciples, and also the reasons for His choice of these three counsels as the counsels of perfection.

CONSIDER FIRST THE EXAMPLE OF OUR BLESSED LORD.

Among the principles of His own interior life was that of voluntary poverty. Christ was poor by His own choice and act. Born in poverty, leading for thirty years a hard and laborious life, yet on entering His ministry He voluntarily abandons what little He has and becomes a homeless, destitute wanderer on the face of the earth. "The foxes

---

3. John 21:22
4. Unattributed.

have holes and the birds of the air have nests, but the Son of Man hath not where to lay His head."[5] All the riches of heaven and earth are His, yet He will have nothing He can call His own save the dress His blessed Mother doubtless wove for Him, and for which by the Cross the soldiers cast lots.

There was a deep meaning of devoted love in this voluntarily adopted condition of abject poverty. Man, losing by his sin communion with the Voice which walked with him, the gates of Paradise are closed and he becomes an outcast. The Voice, to which man, by himself, cannot return, comes out to meet him. It comes to lead him back to God, and so identifies Itself with him. Thus it is that the Word comes not with the outward glory of the first Adam, but takes upon Him the likeness of our sinful flesh; is born, not in some garden shrine, but like an outcast in a stable cave; joins in contest with Satan, not in a paradise, but in the wilderness; takes His place among earth's penitents as they come to the baptism of John; as representing outcast and guilty humanity, kneels down in the garden where man has sinned, to repent there for man with tears of blood; is lifted up upon the Tree to replace there the fruit He never took. And as part and foundation of this blessed truth of His identification with us, He stripped Himself of every earthly possession, and for our sakes, "though He was rich became poor."[6]

Harder than the discipline of poverty, with its anxieties, its pains, and its scorn, was that of His affections. Never in this world has there been a truer or closer love than that which knit together the hearts of our Lord and His blessed Mother. The natural affection of maternity was increased by the grace-endowed love she bore for the Holy Child conceived in her by the Holy Ghost. It was a love returned by Him with divine tenderness and devotion to her, upon whose loving consent the mystery of the Incarnation had at one time hung. It was a love which had developed by every ordinary act of intercourse during thirty years, when every word of His was a hidden benediction, and every kiss a sacrament of grace. She had hung on every word and act, and treasured them in her heart, until that heart was melted into His and there seemed but one life between them, and that His own. She was by all Christian acclaim a type in

---

5. Matthew 8:20, Luke 9:58

6. 2 Corinthians 8:9

a singular degree of that Church which was to be His bride. Hence, in that mysterious first miracle where the marriage of the Incarnate Word to humanity is mystically set forth, the only names of persons mentioned are those of Jesus and Mary. Yet, dear as that intercourse was, at this feast the Lord takes leave of her, with the saying: "Woman, what have I to do with thee?"[7] Now the sword pierces her own heart, and what makes the pain to her so acute is the fact that He whom she loves best places it there. Whatever rewarding recognition He may lovingly grant her when the hour of His cross and triumph come, now He leaves her, trustfully abandoning her to the providential care of God. It is a revelation of her wondrous growth under His training that she discerns His purpose and without a moment's hesitation submits to His will. She immediately gives up what is so dear to her and, resigning her place of authority, says to the servants, "Whatsoever He saith unto you, do it."[8] By this voluntary detachment when leaving home, by this parting of hearts, this wounding of the most loved, by this subordination and triumph over the greatest of human affections at the call of God, our Lord manifested the glory of the counsel of chastity, or that choice of the love of God above all other love, which controlled His interior life. For chastity relates not merely to the government of the lower portion of our nature, but essentially to its higher, and is found in the single eye and purity of heart which has God ever in its embrace and lives in the perpetual subordination of the heart's affection to Him.

If voluntary poverty and self-sacrificing chastity are seen in our Blessed Lord's life, no less is the counsel of obedience. That which man most of all rebels against, namely, the dictation and control of another, was by Him most completely submitted to. It was more than submitted to, it was embraced as a law of His life. He was obedient from the first moment of His Incarnation. "Lo, I come to do Thy will, O my God,"[9] is His utterance while yet unborn. Obedient to the law, in infancy He is circumcised, and obedient to a divine command He receives His name. In childhood He goes down to Nazareth and is subject to Mary and Joseph, though they were wise only with imperfect wisdom. At twelve He is found in the Temple,

---

7. John 2:4

8. John 2:5

9. Psalm 40:8, Hebrews 10:7

obediently catechized according to the law by His servants. The one utterance of the thirty years, made so emphatic by the surrounding silence, is that of obedience: "Wist ye not that I must be about my Father's business?"[10] Later, He goes up to Jerusalem, keeping the prescribed feasts, and also He pays tribute to Cæsar; and thus, by His submission to His blessed Mother, and to St. Joseph, and to the lawful claims of the Church, and to the State, He gives to all men, in their common duties, filial, civic, and religious, a perfect example of obedience.

But beyond this, which was by way of precept, He voluntarily accepted a most searching and minute control over all His inner life. He did not come to save men, thinking His way out as He went along. He had a severely hard and most trying rule of conduct laid down for Him, on the perfect keeping of which the deliverance He sought to effect constantly hung. First, He was to be true to the terms and conditions of the human nature He had united to His own. He had to act out the divine life through it. He was to be true to all its conditions and at all times. True, for example, to the law of its infancy while He, the Eternal Word, lay as an infant on His mother's breast. Before Him were all the hosts of Heaven, and the secrets of all the universe were His. The marvelous panorama of all the orderly progression of nature lay before Him, and the forces of creation moved at His divine will. Yet not His mother's weakness, nor her oft-times fears or more enticing words or loving looks could draw Him to break that law of silence which made Him one with us in infancy, or exert that power for her succor or His own.

So also in the temptation. He had, when hunger gnawed within Him, the power to speak and the stones would have become bread; but He must not call upon the resources of His Divine Nature for His succor, for He must fight out the battle of humanity, and reverse its defeat by the powers of humanity alone. He was, moreover, not to act on His own judgment as to His course in life; it had all been laid down for Him in a written code. The types, the prophecies, the Jewish ceremonial which we read with curiosity, or for their evidential value, were to Him minute directions for His daily conduct. Every kind of sacrifice offered in the Temple had its special law to which He was continually to conform. It told Him, in its every detail, not

---

10. Luke 2:49

only what he was to be, in His outward life of suffering and death, but of the perpetual oblation of Himself in His interior life. Every prophecy and Messianic psalm gave Him direction concerning not only His every act and word, but moreover regulated His hopes, His desires, His fears, His aspirations, His every thought. God bound on the first Adam only one command; on the Second, the Scriptures, which were His constant guide, were filled with them. All were to be remembered and executed with an exactness perfect in its interior and outward expression. It is in reference to this law of His life that our Lord so frequently says, "So it must be,"[11] and "The Scripture must be fulfilled."[12] The will of Christ was surrendered to the will of God, and the mind of Christ was cast in the mold of Holy Scripture as the complete manifestation of that will. There was an absolute surrender of Himself to a revealed law, which tested every portion of His human nature, declaring what it must do, and, even in things otherwise lawful, what it must not do. The mysterious saying concerning the final coming at the last day shows how that in one thing this further discipline was planned for Him, namely, that His human mind might not gaze into the Divine Nature and know what so it might have learned, and which had for Him so intense an interest. His mind was to bear the mark of a humbled curiosity, a submission in this realm of knowledge to the sovereignty of God. So complete was this voluntary obedience that He did not speak of Himself, but "as He heard, so did He speak,"[13] for beyond the written rule, His humanity was under the control of a personal Master, and in all His actions and thoughts "He was led by the Spirit."[14]

Thus our Lord became the pattern Man through a perfect conformity to the will of God, wrought out by the practice of the three counsels of poverty, chastity, and obedience.

CONSIDER WE NOW OUR LORD'S DEALINGS WITH HIS DISCIPLES.

He first called them to leave all, as He had done, and follow Him. They were to leave their old religious teacher, St. John Baptist. They were to leave their father, their boats, their fishing, or their publican's

---

11. Matthew 3:15

12. Matthew 26:54

13. John 12:49

14. Matthew 4:1, Luke 4:1

table. His call had a constraining efficacy, and their hearts went out to Him and they left all, though they knew not all that following Him meant. They committed themselves to Him, and He made known to them the principles of His own life. They heard Him declare the counsel of poverty, when to the rich young ruler seeking perfection He said: "If thou wilt be perfect, go and sell all that thou hast and give to the poor, and come and follow Me."[15] When they disputed who should be greatest, He told them of that royal road of obedience He traveled, by putting the little child before them, and saying: He that would be greatest, let him become humble and docile as a little child. He revealed to them His own life of detachment of heart, in His saying, "He that loveth father or mother more than Me, is not worthy of Me."[16] He taught the same law when to one of His disciples who said, "Lord suffer me first to go and bury my father," He replied: "Follow Me; and let the dead bury their dead."[17] Further, when in answer to their question as to the advisability of marriage, He said, "All cannot receive this saying, save they to whom it is given. There be some who have made themselves eunuchs for the kingdom of Heaven's sake. He that is able to receive it, let him receive it."[18]

In what He by word made known to them as His own life, He trained them by a rigid and most exacting discipline. All portions of their triple being, body, soul, and spirit, were brought under the transforming power of His potent counsels. Trained already they were, for the most part, to endure bodily hardness, but the Master took them along with Him into His life of poverty. It belongs to the poor man to be despised, rejected, scorned. "If they have called the master of the house Beelzebub, how much more shall they call them of His household."[19] "If the world hate you, ye know it hated Me before it hated you."[20] He might at times enter the houses of the rich and sit at meat at the publican's table. St. Matthew might make a parting feast as he left all to follow Him. But the life of Christ was uniformly a severe one. He had entered on His ministry after so

---

15. Matthew 19:21

16. Matthew 10:37

17. Luke 9:60

18. Matthew 19:11–12

19. Matthew 10:25

20. John 15:18

terrible a fast that the marks of that discipline of hardness never left Him. In the hour of His crucifixion, when His wasted and lacerated body was exposed to view, the scoffing beholders stood staring and jeering at Him. Into His own life of days weary with labour and nights given to prayer Christ took the twelve. They must walk with Him even if the provision of bread fail. He who will work miracles to feed the hungry multitude will work no miracle to bring them food. They must eat at times of the raw corn as they rub it in their hands while walking through the field. Hardy, brave, and daring as they were, He will take them with Him into such a storm as makes their natural courage fail, that it may become supernatural by the supernatural strength of faith. They were to learn the poverty of all natural powers, that they might enter into the wealth of the power of God.

Comparatively easy was it to brace them for their future work by the outward trial of poverty; the more difficult task lay in the discipline of the mind and spirit. The breaking down of their Jewish prejudices was not to be effected by persuasion. Christ disciplines His disciples. He seems to act arbitrarily. He begins with little things. He makes them violate the lesser traditions of the elders and eat with unwashen hands. He purposely violates their rigid ideas concerning Sabbath observances. He utters parables they do not understand, which force them to come to Him for explanation. He questions them concerning their dispute for precedence; searches, as with fire, their consciences. He rebukes them when together for their want of spiritual discernment and their lack of faith. He humbles them before the people by sharp censures of their conduct. He warns one of them that he is a devil; tells others that they know not what spirit they are of; and says to St. Peter, "Get thee behind Me, Satan."[21] He sends them out on a trial mission of three months, giving them most precise rules respecting their conduct. They must go only into such places; they must not go as they please or where they will. They must not go singly, but two together. He gives rules concerning their coming into a town; where to abide; how to depart. He regulates their dress, their food, their silence, and their speech. His directions read like those of a Master of Novices dealing with his monks. The Apostles were so to come under obedience to Him as to believe and

---

21. Matthew 16:23

to obey without question what He said because He said it. To others the command might seem trivial, or impossible, or absurd. They were to go to a place where two roads met and find an ass tied and a colt with her, and to take them. They were to go into a city and would find a man bearing a pitcher of water, and they were to follow him, and take his large furnished upper room for their paschal feast. They obeyed because their Master's victory was complete and their minds and wills were His. Thus trained in the counsels of obedience, poverty, and detachment, their spiritual lives were formed upon the same interior principles as that of the Lord.

WE MAY NOW CONSIDER WHY THESE THREE PRINCIPLES WERE CHOSEN FOR HIS OWN GUIDANCE AND FOR THEIRS.

Threefold, according to the scriptural division, is man's being. "I pray that your whole body, soul, and spirit be preserved blameless."[22] Now in each portion of this triple unit there is a root of evil. Sensuality, or unruly appetite, has its seat in the body. Covetousness, or inordinate desire, lives in the soul. Pride, or independence, infects the spirit. These are the three roots of all our sins: the lust of the flesh, the lust of the eyes, and the pride of life.[23] And for these three primal germs of all sin there are three specific remedies. The discipline of the body, or chastity, whose lower function is to purify the body as in its higher it purifies the heart. The spirit of poverty, which is the cure for the unbridled desire for possession, whether it be of knowledge, or fame, or honors, or power, or wealth. Lastly, obedience, which casts out the pride and independence of the human spirit, and so makes man humble and docile toward His Heavenly Father, peaceful and at rest within himself, and kind-hearted toward others.

From their great excellence the Church has been wont to call these three counsels the counsels of perfection. Not that their profession makes one perfect. Not that their observance is exclusively confined to those called "Religious," for in a degree they enter into every Christian life. Not that they are in their highest degree of practice anything but the development of our Baptismal vows. Not that their practice, even with Apostolic heroism, makes them ends in themselves. But they are called counsels of perfection, first, because they

---

22. 1 Thessalonians 5:23

23. 1 John 2:16

are the principles of the inner life of the All-perfect One. And, secondly, because their practice makes us like Him, in perfect union with whom perfection consists.

It puts a new aspect on this matter of self-consecration when we realize that, for the better fulfilling of these three evangelical counsels, and thereby the more complete union with Himself, the Lord established the estate known as the Religious Life. He explicitly revealed this peculiar estate by His language, "All men cannot receive this saying, save they to whom it is given. For there are some eunuchs, which were so born from their mother's womb; and there are some eunuchs, which were made eunuchs of men; and there be eunuchs, which have made themselves eunuchs for the kingdom of heaven's sake."[24] In fairness it must be admitted that here Christ is counseling, not a temporary unmarried condition of life, but, by a carefully-selected term, describing a state having a permanent and unalterable character.

As having such a character He pronounced on it a special blessing both here, saying, "He shall receive an hundredfold now in this time... and in the world to come eternal life,"[25] "He that is able to receive it, let him receive it."[26]

In the presence of this solemn utterance of the Master, the question of duty as to a choice in life, whether on the part of the daughter weighing the thought of an entire self-dedication, or of a parent hesitating to permit it, becomes one of grave concern. The fact that the Religious estate has been created by the Lord as an institution of the Gospel, and that the Holy Spirit calls souls into it for their perfection, involves in serious responsibility both parent and child. "For God, who gives us," says England's not least-sainted teacher, Dr. Pusey, in discussing this matter, "the transcendent privilege to be workers together with Him, leaves us also the awful power of marring His work."[27]

---

24. Matthew 19:11–12

25. Mark 10:30

26. Matthew 19:12

27. The Rev. Dr. Pusey, *Report of the Proceedings of the Church Congress of 1862*, Afternoon Discussion, July 9th — Dr. Pusey's address having been by special permission allowed to be read to Congress, appeared as one of the papers. It did not, however, form part of the Program as originally arranged by the Committee,

It may be marred by refusing to obey His call; by choosing the pleasures of an Egyptian establishment rather than the hardness of the Christian wilderness; by casting some grains of disloyal incense on the altars of society and doing homage to the world's empire rather than sharing the ignominy and, it may be, persecution of the outcast Monarch; by letting the glittering baubles of ambition, clinking in the ear and deceiving the heart, drown the complaint that comes from the parched lips of the Crucified, asking the solace of our companionship and sacrificed lives; by an indulgent weakness which looks at the weight of the Cross rather than to the jewels of the Crown. Or, on the other hand, it may be marred by a parental selfishness which cannot give its best to Christ, or a hesitating faith which cannot trust the fullness of His promise, or worse, a blind worldliness, that wraps itself in an inveterate obstinacy and will not receive Christ's words.

Such a period of consideration of this question is a time fraught with grace and with peril. A time for the exercise of much patience and humility, and for much prayer. Here some soul is pressing forward, willing to respond to grace, and angel-hands are stretched out to direct her, and the blessed saints bend rejoicingly over her, and the great army of the martyrs, confessors, and virgins hope well for the promised accession to their ranks, and the heart of the great Monarch beats with the same love with which of old it moved toward those who sought perfection, and the assuring voice says to the child, "Come," and to the parent, "Let him."

Christ says to the one, "Come!" What subtle power is it that works within us to thwart Heaven's high purpose and turn our feet from off the narrow pathway shining with the safety of promised succors into the labyrinthine uncertainties and unsatisfactory pleasures of a worldly life? If duty bid thee remain at home, then remain. Duty first, and duty always. Duty is the voice of God. But if not duty, fear not to venture, for the "Come" of Christ is mightier than all the "Cannots" of our feeble hearts, and will sustain thee as it did one of old in his venture of faith upon the stormy waters to come to Christ. "And Peter said, Lord, if it be Thou, bid me come to Thee. And He said, Come!"[28]

---

and was therefore inserted in its place as part of the discussion.

28. Matthew 14:28

Christ says to the other, asking ofttimes the greater sacrifice on the part of the parent, yet with a pathetic tenderness that shrinks from giving pain, "Let him." Who is it that upon his own authority or upon the basis of his own experience, or through the following of the traditions of men, will venture to forbid what Christ approves? One limitation we know there is to all authority, namely, it must be "in the Lord." Christ says: Let him leave all as I left all; let him live after these counsels as I did; let him enter this estate I made My own; let him be so united to my interior life that I may reproduce it in him; let there be a wedded union of our hearts, and minds, and wills, that through him I may the better bless the Church; let him! What Christian parent, as he remembers at what a price he has been redeemed and thinks of what a true-hearted allegiance he owes his King, shall find it in his heart to deny his Lord's request and say to the Master, "No! He shall not!"

XVIII

HAVE I A VOCATION FOR A SISTER'S LIFE?

ONE and yet manifold are the calls of God. The voice of God sounds throughout the world, calling all men into fellowship with Himself. It fills the Church of Christ with a sanctifying power, calling all Christians into an active correspondence with the energies of Christ's life. Its vivifying power vibrates throughout the mystical body, calling all its members, by the thrilling impulses of its loving utterances, into unity of effort for the kingdom's sake. All the particular calls heard by the individual soul are but single notes recognized in the vastness of the one divine harmony, as articulate with some love-laden message to itself.

Such special calls being thus subordinate to the general one of Christ to His Church, do not assign duties or bestow gifts as private treasures for individual enjoyment, but that some new blessing may spread its luster throughout the City of God. In the intense unification of life which exists in the kingdom of Christ's Church, none can live for himself alone, and the spiritual gifts any one possesses are for the well-being of all. No one need look with envy on another's position in that kingdom, whatever it may be, and no one who has discerned his own call to any place or work may think: 'This is given me for my own personal possession or advantage.'

It is not, therefore, some few in the Church who have vocations, like the clergy or Sisters, but all are called of God. Each man has his vocation. It is that design for him which lay in the Eternal Mind ere he had being. He has been from all eternity the object of a divine choice. His Heavenly Father has created him for a special purpose, and has made him different from every other human being, and given him a special work to do, and loves him with a special love. Enfolding all in the embrace of His great love, yet no child of His creation but is especially dear to Him. It is a trite enough thought, but one tender with the freshness of God's never-withering youth, that "God loves me with an individual love, and is not merely the God of the universe, but my God, my own God, my own dear personal God;" and one's vocation is that line of life-duty or conduct, issuing out of God's predestinating love, along which He calls one, as along a road angel-watched and guarded by His providence, home to Himself.

It is not necessary for all persons to see what their vocation is. Some pass through life looking to God's direction taking the daily step before them, and only, it may be, as they reach the distant hills of age, can see, as they look back, how the Divine Will has chosen for them and shielded them from danger, and made them instruments of His merciful designs. But there are important crises in all lives, when decisions must be made, when the question must be faced: What is my present duty? — when we must consider the alternate course presented by the life of faith; — when we must solemnly seek the meaning of God's dealings with us, and to what they call; — when the truth forcibly presents itself, that one thing only is entirely worth the knowing, and that is God's will in our regard, and one thing only is entirely worth the doing, and that is obedience to that will.

For at times God allows some signal trial to come, and all the land, like "the land of Egypt as thou comest to Zoar,"[1] is spread out before our sight, bright with the sunshine of earth's honors and delights, and a choice for life has to be made, as by Abraham and Lot, between the right hand and the left. Until the eye has been schooled to discern the glories of the Cross, and the heart captured by its self-effacing sacrifice, it can but be attracted by the brave show of earth's royalties, or by the fair landscape where lies the sheltered home, embowered in flowers and childhood's laughter, and affection's living green. Until the holy will of God is recognized in its sovereignty, and the soul has trustingly yielded itself to its blessed-making control, it may seem that the peaceful rest of convent life is more to be desired than the harder and more homely task of caring for some aged and infirm parent, by which a loving Providence calls the soul into union with the Lord, in His own hidden but fruitful service to His foster-father St. Joseph. Until the magnificent vision of the City of God, with its many-crowned Monarch, and the saintly hierarchy of the Incarnation, and the Apostles and prophets on their thrones, and the innumerable multitude of the redeemed, shining with the internal glory of Eternal Righteousness, is in a measure participated in, the exciting politics of earthly empires, or the pursuit of scientific discovery, or the self-culture of the soul, or an elevating philanthropy,

---

1. Genesis 13:10

must command our obedient homage.

These and like cases tell of times in all earnest lives when the ways before us divide, and the soul is perplexed with doubt, or, it may be, assailed by fear; when thick darkness seems to blot out the sun at noonday, and the moon ceases to give her light; when we can only choose our way by the lantern of God's word, as it is swung about our feet, or catch the echo of some angel-voices to direct our course, or listen to the heart-beat silently responding to some inspiration of God.

As some are reading these pages, may not the question arise in the mind: Why should I not give myself to Christ in a Sister's life? May it not be my privilege and honour so to be united to Him?

Why may I not be of that band of devoted ones who through all the ages followed Him in this consecrated state and ministered to Him of their substance? If there be those who along Heaven's high pathway follow with a special nearness the Lamb whithersoever He goeth, why should I not be of that company? Is it for this that the direction of a kindly-guiding Providence has at last revealed such a life-purpose for me? Why does this thought of waiting on Him in His poor, sick, and needy ones, of giving myself to a life of prayer, attract my heart, unless God has placed it there?

Possibly the question presents itself as a somewhat unwelcome one. It has been partially heard before and put aside as beneath one's social position, or as involving too much sacrifice, or as too exacting in its discipline, or as unsuited to our natural disposition, or as repugnant to our love of freedom. Perchance one may have seriously considered it once, but now, grown wise with worldly wisdom, the desire has faded. When the Voice spoke to us we delayed, and when we arose to open to Him, "Lo, He was gone."[2] It may be the call never came in so pronounced a way as to satisfy us of its divine origin, and so we were content to go on in our comfortably devotional way without placing ourselves under rule. Perhaps we heard stories of the failure of aspirants, or criticisms on the conduct of some Religious, and have deemed it safer not to strive "to wind one's self so high," or we have never had the courage to think seriously of the matter, and with mistaken humility have said, as we dwelt on its privileged and wedded nearness to Jesus, "It is not for me."

---

2. Psalm 37:37

Now, to all these classes, however they may finally answer the great question of their vocation, we would address two general considerations; one, respecting the call to the Religious Life, and the other, the place and time in the Church's history in which it comes to us.

First, you are not to conclude you have no vocation because you have no natural liking for the Life, as some of the best of Religious have become so by the very violence by which they gained victory over self. Nor is it clear that the Life is not for you because your gifts look small — as small as the widow's two mites — or because you can but gather up the fragments that remain.

Neither are you to decide that you have no vocation because as yet you have experienced no self-demonstrating and controlling call. It is true that God may in some cases excite the soul by such an abundance of grace and force of desire as to exclude all doubt as to His call. But in a large number of cases, without producing so powerful an impression, the longings of the heart in all its better moods may be such as to make it dangerous to neglect the obvious drawings of the Holy Spirit. If these are faithfully listened to, they will increase. We cannot stand still and continue to hear God's call. For God's calls draw us, as the cry of her child the mother's heart; and He allures us into the solitude of the wilderness that we may the better hear. God speaks to persons according to their temperament. He that draws the affections can enlighten the understanding. He that speaks to the hearts of watching shepherds by the angelic hymn draws the wise men across the desert by the leading of a star.

Secondly, consider the time and place in which God addresses us. We are living in times and in a Church in which it is given to persons to do more for God by embracing the Religious state than in any other period. The millennial days, when the Church was united by its faith and discipline, and Satan was bound, are over. The worldly-minded darkness of the age of Hildebrand and the darkness of the fleshly-minded age of the Renaissance have been succeeded by the brightness of this latter Satanic age, in which either the existence of any personal spiritual energy is denied altogether or a counterfeit supernaturalism is substituted for the true. Is the Christian dispensation, called "the last time"[3] by St. John, drawing to a close? At the end, along with the prophesied falling away, will there be a heroic

---

3. 1 John 2:18

correspondence to Divine Grace? The gates of hell will indeed never prevail against the kingdom and destroy it. Yet there will come a time when the light of the moon will suffer eclipse and the stars will fall and the powers of Heaven be shaken. The convulsions in every national Church are but forewarning preludes of the catastrophe which ends with the victory-bringing advent of the King of Kings. All times of peril are good to live in, for they are glorious with splendid opportunities of saintly service.

As from the agonies of the French Revolution came Religious Orders filled with souls more noble in their devotion than even by their high birth, so it may be with England's Church. If she is fully to recover her lost heritage, and her daily Sacrifice, and her penitential discipline, and extend her borders, it must be by a large number of able, refined, devoted persons, men and women, giving themselves up to the Religious Life. A few thousand such will effect more than Bishops and parochial clergy alone can do to catholicize the Church and raise the standard of Christian holiness, and more than all the opponents of the faith within and without the Church can do to overthrow it. Does it not seem as if now, in the last hours of His contest with evil, and from the Cross itself, Christ were plaintively asking for some alleviation of His sore distress? And strange it is that any Christian should not welcome love's high privilege of waiting round that death-bed and holding up the hyssop of a devoted life to slake a dying Master's thirst for the consummation of the kingdom and the salvation of souls.

Is it not, then, the urgent and imperative duty of every Christian woman whose path in life is not already determined, to consider, What does God desire my life should be? How shall I best consecrate it to Him? And yet, if the answer to this question is to be the service of a consecrated life, it is a most consoling assurance to know that such a choice is not wholly dependent on our own purpose. For the Religious Life is not something we are to seek or to select to please ourselves. We cannot give ourselves a vocation or make ourselves Religious. Our being such depends on the calling of Christ Himself. He chooses the person, He seeks the opportunity, He bestows the needed gifts, He inspires the thought, He orders the events, He enlightens the soul, He makes the voice to be heard, He removes the obstacles, He offers Himself in so definite a way that we cannot, with reasonable care, mistake it. The voice, which pleads with the agonized earnestness of His Passion for our union with Himself, becomes articulate through His providence and inspirations, and is made audible in the loving heart by the Holy Ghost.

Let us, then, see what it is to be thus specially called, and how we are to know it.

To be called to the Religious Life is to receive a summons from a Person. In the performance of ordinary duty we acknowledge our obligation to law, but vocation is the voice of God to the individual soul. It is a direct message from Him, and it calls for a response. It is addressed to an individual, and the proposed duty cannot be assigned to another of Christ's servants. "The Master has come and calleth for thee."[4] It is a manifestation of God Himself, for it reveals God in the heart. Not by learned studies or high speculations do we know God, but only in proportion as we hear His voice within. It is none other than the voice of the Incarnate Word, calling us, not to the performance of some service, but into union with Jesus. Enlightened by His indwelling wisdom, difficulties disappear, and in union with the will of Jesus the soul finds entire satisfaction. It is a call into the heart of Jesus, not as into a mere resting-place, but into its life. United to Him, He puts forth His own power and reproduces Himself in us. It is a call which, as we surrender ourselves to it, goes on continuously, progressively unfolding the graces of His life. The Religious is not a person who has once been called. The voice of an earthly master once heard dies away. The call of the Divine Master to Discipleship is a single act, but vocation is an abiding gift of the overshadowing Spirit. The Life that is born in thee is of God. It is not like some jewel possessed only of a limited value, or like an earthly treasure that may be exhausted by use. It is a living Gift, a living Utterance, a sound that swells out more and more distinctly within the soul as the years go on, ever fresh with the love of Jesus, ever drawing the soul into a more wedded union with His desires, and enriching the life with endless revelations of His Goodness and Beauty.

Has the first cadence of that divine call wakened an echo of desire within thy heart? Not in its final fullness, tested by time and experience, certified by the Church's acceptance, and authoritatively sealed with its blessing, canst thou now possess it; yet if truly called it

---

4. John 11:28

may even now be discerned to be God's message to thee!

Now, in order to answer to yourself the question, am I called, you must observe that God's will is manifested in two ways: externally and interiorly. Externally by His providences, interiorly by His inspirations.

The external signs are these: First, the possession of those natural and physical gifts which are necessary to keep the Rule and be of service in the proposed Sisterhood. Of these something has already been mentioned. It is sufficient here to say that a convent is not for the reformation of the indolent, the undisciplined, or the hysterical, nor a field for the self-opinionated, the morbid, or the designing; nor a home for the feeble, weak-minded, or destitute. It is the court of the Lord, and the maidens there gathered are as to Shushan, the palace. A mind well cultivated, good common sense, a cheerful and contented disposition, a teachable and docile will, and some natural greatness and generosity of soul, are the qualities which most fit one to be a maid of honour to the Great King.

The second sign is such a freedom from family duties as will allow of one's rightly leaving home. Where there is an aged or infirm parent or relative dependent upon a single daughter for pecuniary support or personal care, the case is plain. The daughter should remain at home. There is a middle class of cases which can only be decided by a knowledge of all the facts, and in which much forbearance should be exercised by all parties, and particular and wise counsel sought. There are other cases also quite plain. Where there are other daughters in a family, then ordinarily no reason exists why one should not be spared to the Master's service. It may be here noted that the call comes not only to the one drawn to be a sister, but to all the members of the family, and although all may keenly feel the separation, yet in some degree the sacrifice is to be participated in by all. It is a helpful, but not universal, rule that where a young person would not feel it her duty to remain at home, but might be married, she might leave it to be espoused to her Lord. True, there are other opportunities of Christian service, and duties other than those of home, which must be left. This is but God's usual way of dealing with us. He does not promote idlers to honour, but the faithful. He calls from duties to duties. In our self-importance we are apt, in regard to our work, to estimate ourselves as necessary to Divine Providence. God often calls His servants from most productive service to a most seemingly barren field in order to train us to trust to His providence what we leave, as well as to His love in what He calls us to. In this matter of vocation duties need not be weighed against duties. We need not try to balance our supposed usefulness in one state with that in another. To be a perfect Religious is to become the most perfect instrument for service in God's hands, and so to do the highest and most effective work it is possible for man to do for God. As there is no parish work of sufficient importance to hold back any young clergyman from being a Religious, much less should the parish or social duties hold back any woman. Save, therefore, in rare cases where high or State interests are concerned, no other than important home-duty need prevent any daughter from becoming a Religious. What we leave for God, God will bless.

The third external sign, although not so held by all writers on the subject, is the Christian father's consent. The Scriptures regard the father as the head and mouth-piece of the sacramental entity formed by marriage. He is the natural priest of the family. So that properly the privilege belongs to him of giving his daughter to the Lord. To this reference is made, in the judgment of many wise commentators, in I Corinthians 7:38–39. If he cannot give his consent, and so approve, he may assent, and so put no hindrance in the way. God has indeed the first and highest claim, and the father should learn by his own love to trust that of the Heavenly Father. He loves our children better than we do, and He expresses His love for us in promoting them to honour. He, who has a right to take your child away by death though you must shed tears over her grave, asks you now to trust her with Him to be His bride, that you may rejoice over her espousals. And as in the call of the patriarch and child, of old, each took part in the sacrifice and shared in a common blessing, so now will God most richly bless and unite more closely in the end parent and child. The God for whom together they labored, and in whom together they rejoiced, will knit their hearts together in an eternal jubilation of love and praise.

The interior signs of a vocation are discerned in the desires of the soul. All good desires come from God, and are His voice speaking in us. These signs of a call to religion may be tested by the questions: Do you desire the Life? What in it do you desire? And why?

God, who knows best how to plant the seed of grace, and how best to awaken the heart to respond, in some instances grants this desire at an early age. It is not unusual for a person to say: "I have always wanted to be a Sister. I do not know how the wish came or when;" or, "I remember, when quite a little child, it came into my heart." Thus, in old time, into the youthful hearts of Joseph, Samuel, and Timothy, and John Baptist, and pre-eminently the Blessed Virgin, the grace of vocation fell silently as light from an angel-hand. In other instances it comes later in life. God creates the germ in some by disappointment, by humiliation; the heart is empty, and it must seek rest in God. In others He brings it by fervors and aspirations; the heart is full and it must empty itself back into Him. It grows with an increasing gratitude for sins forgiven or for some signal succors in distress, when, with the Magdalen's courage and the Magdalen's devotion, it cries out, What shall I render unto the Lord for all the benefits He hath done unto me? It is developed into life by some text of Scripture, by some word of grace, or by the pleading cry of the Master in His Church's hour of need. It gradually takes shape in a desire to do what it can for His service, becomes more ardent with a longing to make some reparation for the neglect His love has received, craves at last a fuller sense of His nearness and a life closer to Him. It lacks now but little for its perfection. How is this to be obtained? The heart must catch sight of the inner life of Jesus and desire to be united to it. God loves souls with large desires, and loves to aid the formation of such desires. And so it may be that by some book or merciful providence the soul on its life-journey gains a view of the Religious Life, stretching out its arms and revealing God's eternal purpose for His chosen ones, just as, in Alpine passes, at some sudden turn, the traveler unexpectedly comes in sight of the Cross, and is forced to forget nature in presence of that symbol of surpassing love. Blessed are they who come to this knowledge of the Life. It is a knowledge hidden from many Christian souls. It is given to those who are called. They see that the essence of the Religious Life is not a dedication merely to works of charity. It is an entire surrender of themselves to Jesus. It is a new covenanted estate. It is a special and consecrated union to the Lord. He is bound to them as well as they are bound to Him. It is a wedded union to His inner life, a transformation of body, soul, and spirit by the practice of the same three principles which governed His Humanity.

Do you desire, for the sake of this union, to adopt these principles? This is the real interior test.

It may happen that persons may be able to say that they have heard an interior voice speaking to them, or have had some singularly confirmed dream, or have beheld some magnificent vision of Christ or His Saints, or that some remarkable and concurring providences, like converging lines, have declared their duty. No one should desire or seek any such signs. It was the wise prayer of a great saint: "Lead me, O Lord, by the common way." And no one should act upon any such extraordinary manifestation. God may use such means for warning or directing His servants. They are liable, however, to be misunderstood, or not to be from Him. They may be regarded as confirming and encouraging us, but should not otherwise be taken into account. Consider the Life: its end, union with Jesus: its principles, the means to the end. Is this end your desire? Are these means your resolve?

If this is your spirit and you are not governed by the desire to escape from an unpleasant home, or to exchange a laborious life for one seemingly less so, or by a wish to improve your social position, or by an affection to live with some particular Sister, but are willing to leave all for the love of Christ and give yourself up to be moulded according to the principles of His life, you have the interior sign of a vocation. He has given you the mind and will to desire what He would have you to be. You are called of God. Christ offers Himself to you, and by a humble recitation of either the *Te Deum* or *Magnificat* you should give thanks to Him.

Greatly now will you stand in need of discretion, patience, and courage. "My Son, when thou comest to serve the Lord, prepare thyself for temptations."[5] Be careful not to make your concerns a matter of common conversation. If you are influenced by the vanity that seeks to make one's self an object of interest, you will not do for a sister. In the Apostolic sense: "Consult not with flesh and blood."[6] "Winnow not with every wind, and go not into every way."[7] "Let your complaints be made known unto God."[8] Wait upon the Lord and put your trust in Him.

If possible, go to some Retreat, or arrange a partial one by your-

---

5. Ecclesiasticus 2:1

6. Galatians 1:16

7. Ecclesiasticus 5:9

8. Philippians 4:6

self. It would be well at this time to review your life, not in reference to your sins but to God's providential guiding and blessings. Eat, like the prophet, the scroll of life. Give thanks to God for all He has given you and all He has withheld. Make your Communions with special care, and for conformity to God's will.

Consult with some priest; yet not necessarily a Religious, but one who knows what the Life is, and is not opposed to it. The different kinds of clergy have their own peculiarities, which need to be guarded against. Saints may be found everywhere, but perfection in the world is formed on different lines from that in Religion. The member of a Religious Order is apt to force his own Rule into the lives of others. We who are Religious are wont also to be over-eager in the matter of vocations. Always distrust those who would persuade or try to frighten you in any way into a Sisterhood. Vocation cannot be made by man. "No man can come to Me, unless the Father draw him."[9] Parochial clergy, on the other hand, are apt to underrate the value of the Religious Life. They are often unwilling to lose good workers from their parishes, and so are prejudiced. Or perhaps they do not wish to go against the wishes of parents who may be their parishioners. They are also in danger of overestimating the importance of the family obligations. The family is indeed of divine origin, but there are other institutions equally sacred. The Religious Life is one of these. When one said to Christ, "Suffer me first to go and bury my father," the Master declared a primary and higher duty in His reply: "Follow Me, and let the dead bury their dead."[10]

Two general cautions may here be given. Be open and straightforward with your parents. Never act in an underhand way. Do not be advised to do anything which is only to be told afterward. Such counsel is not of God. God does not need man's deceitfulness to help Him to accomplish His plans. And also do not allow yourself to be drawn into making indiscreet promises. The Apostles did not reply to Christ's invitation that they would follow Him when their parents were dead.

If God shows you that it is His will you should remain at home, He will perfect you there. Where He places you, there He will bless you. The Law of the Kingdom is now, as of old, they that tarried at

---

9. John 6:44

10. Luke 9:59–60

home divided the spoil. If reasonable grounds exist for believing you have a vocation, and the external signs do not prevent, act at once. To defer responding to God's offer is to run the risk of losing it. It is a serious truth that, though we may be eventually saved, yet we may, by neglecting a distinct call, miss the special crown proffered us. We may go on piling up a large amount of "wood, hay, and stubble" which will have to be burned up, and we "saved as by fire," instead of doing our appointed task and building the "gold, silver, and precious stones" Christ had designed for us.[11]

It may be you will have to wait. If so, wait so as not to lose. Patience is one of the best signs of a vocation. Tarry thou the Lord's leisure, be strong and He shall comfort thine heart.

Be loving in all your intercourse with others, but decided, because He has called you and you are not your own. Do not go over old matters in perpetual debate with self or with others. "God spake and it was done."[12] If tempted to give up, look to Christ crucified saying, "This I have done for thee, what hast thou done for Me?"[13] Listen to the blessed saints, weak once as you, but made courageous through the blood of the Lamb, saying, as you ask them how they triumphed, "Grace did it all."

If you are allowed to go to the Sisterhood, go as soon as you conveniently can. Arise and trim your lamp and go you out to meet Him. Acting under the guidance of the Holy Spirit, in the strength of the Blessed Body and Blood, with the counsel of the Church, with a single eye to Christ, you cannot go wrong. If you really have not a vocation by reason of want of health, or of the needed capacity, or from failure of Community spirit, or other latent cause, it will be shown you in the Sisterhood. Act then courageously, as you would wish to have done when the short term of life is over, and its honors and delights and charms are fading, when the darkness of earth, with its troubles and sorrows and cares, is passing away, and Christ with His welcome of reward is seen standing on the eternal shore.

Blessed are they who, in whatever outward lot, are with virgin souls espoused unto Christ, in faith entire, and grounded hope and

---

11. 1 Corinthians 3:12–14

12. Psalm 33:9

13. Frances R. Havergal's famous Hymn *I Gave my Life for Thee*, 1st stanza.

fervent charity.[14] Blessed, whether married or unmarried, are the pure in heart, who seek to make their souls a bridal chamber for Christ, fitted by His grace for His indwelling by His spirit.

"Blessed, thrice blessed, they whom Christ alone sufficeth, the one aim of whose being is to live to Him and for Him. For Him they adorn themselves; His eyes alone they desire to please through His graces in them; Him they long to serve without distraction; at His feet they ever sit; to Him they speak in their inmost souls, to Him they hearken; He is their light, their love, their holy joy; to Him they ever approach with trustfulness; Him they consult in all things, on Him they wait; Him they love, even because they love Him, and desire from Him but His love, desire no love but only His. Blessed foretaste of life eternal, to desire nothing on earth but the life of angels and the new song; to be wholly His, whom her soul loveth, and He, the Lord of Angels, to be wholly hers, as He says, "I am my beloved's and my beloved is mine."[15]

---

14. "No, the life of a true sister of mercy must needs be a blessed one. To have companions altogether of one heart and one mind — to have so much of the distractions of the world cut off — to lie at peace for the future, having no further solicitudes for the present life — to have opportunities of usefulness which may be desired, but in vain sought for elsewhere — to have our time divided between prayer and praise and such labors of love as best mold the heart for the home of perfect love, whither we trust we are tending. Oh! can Christian women, free to choose, see no beauty in such a life, that they should desire it?" (Rev. Dr. William Augustus Muhlenberg, *Two Letters on Protestant Sisterhoods.*)

15. Song of Solomon 6:3

XIX

A Religious Order for Men

There has been a growing desire in our Church for an order of laymen devoted to the service of Christ in Community life. There are many reasons for an adoption of the Benedictine Rule. It has been established now for thirteen hundred years. It was formed in the early times to which we Anglican Churchmen appeal. The Benedictine Rule was written before Roman errors had arisen and is consequently free from every trace of them, whether modern or mediaeval. The new Community which has been formed under this Rule professes sincere loyalty to the true Catholic position and teaching of the Anglican Communion. It recognizes Episcopal authority and conducts all its work under Episcopal direction.

St. Benedict gave a Rule based on family life. The Abbot was the Father of the family. The members lived together under a common Rule of life adapted to the age and country in which they lived. In the comprehensive spirit of our Church there is room for such an order. We are in the midst of a forward movement among men. The Church is feeling the impetus of a great spiritual movement. The revival of the consecrated Religious Life in our Community is due to Dr. Pusey. He laid the foundation of the first Sisterhood in 1844. The members at first were few, but they had the prayers and guidance of a great saint. There are now, according to a statement made in the English Church Quarterly, 5000 Religious women in different societies and a hundred, and perhaps more, men. Many laymen among us are intensely desirous that our Church should regain its full Catholic heritage in doctrine and worship and be better known by the American people. A lay order can do very much to forward this glorious cause. The Church needs lay missionary helpers. There are not a few who, from a lack of trained scholarship, are not adapted to the Ministry but can do effectual missionary work. Sometimes a word from a layman goes farther than from the professional lips of a priest. Moreover, the life of a Religious gives a special emphasis to his words, and the consecrated Religious life has a great effect, not only within the Church but on those outside of her. We live in a money-making and pleasure-seeking age, with vast numbers whose intellectual horizon is bounded by the world. Worldliness, and the indifference to God, rule in the market place, exchange, in business and politics, and in all professions. The Religious Life, with its simple living, spirit of poverty, and self-sacrifice, testifies with tremendous force against the world and bears an effective witness to an unseen spiritual one. It preaches more effectively than any sermon can do. Over against the world, with its honors, pleasures, and delights, it bears witness to the blessedness of simplicity, self-denial, the following of Christ, and the Eternal reward.

Again: what our Church needs in clergy and laity is a real deepening of the spiritual life. We become so intermingled with the world as to lose the fresh enthusiasm of the early martyrs and confessors. We are lacking in that zeal and self-sacrifice which won, in early times, England and Europe to the Faith. Many of our Clergy perform their duties in a perfunctory way, and their families naturally demand their chief interest and care for their support. To preach Christ effectually the minister must preach of the Cross from the pulpit of the cross. We would say not a word against married clergy. But their work can well be supplemented by a Religious dedicated to a celibate life, and helped on also by a lay order.[1]

Moreover, our age has risen to the importance of specializing different departments of work, making a special study of bodily diseases and social problems by scientific investigation. We need Communities whose life enables them to study and practice the mysteries of the spiritual life. How far below most of us come from the standard of that "fullness of God"[2] revealed in the New Testament! How comparatively little is known of the science of prayer, as developed by the great teachers and saints! Laymen say a morning or evening prayer and some clergy make meditation, but in a Religious House its members would practice the life of devotion and their prayers would bring a blessing upon the Church and thus especially enrich it.

These are some of the reasons for a need of Religious Orders. It is the highest life a man can live. By it a great work for God can be

---

1. "I believe, sir, that in the case of heresy or error of any kind creeping into the Church, these Institutions, once founded, will be the powerful barrier against their progress. I begin to feel this to be the working of our own system already: CATHOLIC TRUTH without party" (The Rev. Dr. James Lloyd Breck, *Letter to Bp. Kemper*, 1846)

2. Ephesians 3:19

done, and it has the promise of a special reward.[3]

The Rule of St. Benedict allows for Priests. It is well that in every House there should be one or possibly more brothers in Priest's Order who can say Mass for the Community. This saves them from being dependent on the charity of outside secular clergy. But by the Rule, Priests belonging to the Community have by virtue of their holy orders no preference or standing over the lay members. They are not allowed to be called "Father," but simply "Brother," like the others. So, in my judgment, if Priests want to enter the Religious Life, they had better enter some other Order, as there are two excellent ones in our country the *Society of the Holy Cross* and the *Society of St. John the Evangelist*. There does not appear to be need of any other.

Laymen can join either of these orders, but on becoming lay brothers, they have no vote in Chapter, and they do the work of house servants. In the Benedictine House, they are full professed choir members, and can hold any office and are the governing body.

---

3. "Why may we not hope that even within this generation Christian Brotherhoods as well as Sisterhoods of Mercy may be found taking their place in the work of Christ among us? seeing that there is no more palpable fact in all Church history, than that Almighty God has ever been pleased to make use of such communities—devoted men severing themselves more or less from the ordinary ties and affections of earth—when His time was come for converting, not here and there one, but whole nations, to the obedience of His Son." (Rev. John Keble, *Women Labouring in the Lord*)

XX

The Second Adam

"For as in Adam all die, even so in Christ shall all be made alive." —*1 Cor. xv. 22*

THE text gives us two points for our consideration: 1. Our death in Adam; 2. The new life in Christ.

I. Let us consider our death in Adam. We turn to the opening chapters of Genesis to learn of God's creation, and first revelation to man, and in our study here, let us be reverent and not critical. The hand of God seems like some fair river, rising from among the hills, winding along in its course, developing here and there into a calm, still lake, and then hiding itself and going on. The very source is bright in the morning sun, though enveloped in mist and cloud of mystery, but these very clouds are aflame with the glory and majesty of the rising sun, and at the end, in Revelation, there are still the clouds, for there is always mystery attending the Word of God, but their glory is like the clouds at sunset, beautiful by the setting sun. Let us take our shoes from off our feet, for the ground whereon we stand is holy.

Though this river comes and goes in mists, yet there are facts, which stand out clearly, reflecting the truth of God, as those quiet lakes reflect the sky above them. It matters not to the Christian what science may say, theology will not complain. It matters not how many millions of years there may have been in those early ages, or what contests there may have been on this earth before the existence of man, or what races may have existed before our own primogeniture; it matters not to the Christian. In the mist and glory of the first Creation of God, we see, not science, nor those things which as men we must learn, but the things revealed for our moral and spiritual development and advancement. We see there man, created in the very Image of God, crowned with glory, and the gift of supernatural grace.

II. As we look at human nature, we can but mark certain differences between it and other natures, — angelic, for instance. Certainly, it seems an impertinence for us to think we crowned creation, or, in ourselves, exhausted the wisdom and power and ingenuity of the good God. No! We believe in those nine great orders, or tiers of

Angelic beings leading up step by step to God. But we make a great difference between them; and human nature. The Ever-Blessed Being of God created the Angels as an artist does some special work, on canvas, or in stone. He thinks of some fair form of beauty, and gives it expression in his work, and it was thus with the Angels, — Michael, Raphael, Gabriel, Cherubim and Seraphim, Angels and Archangels, Thrones, Principalities, Dominations, Virtues, Powers — are manifestations of some special beauty, which had its existence in the Heart of God. They are distinctly before Him, each one by himself, but it was not so with man. He was intended to combine in himself, as it were, or to be, the uniting point between material and spiritual natures.

Human nature was created at once as an entity. God made it as one beautiful thing, and it stood in perfection before Him. He gave it the law of perfection and development, in order to manifest it in the law of His own Being, for His Own Life was in it. He gave it a work to do, to conquer the earth, and unite in itself the two natures, and He crowned it with supernatural grace, and all that followed or happened to Adam and Eve happened to human nature as a whole, and so, "in Adam all sinned and died."[1]

III. But your ask me, 'Was there not death in the world before Adam sinned?' Surely, long before. You who read the history of this little world as it is found in the record of geologists see death's traces before human nature was created. We learn of the long struggle and contest going on in the animal kingdom, the higher orders preying on the lower; everywhere we see the battling for life. Now, God for His own purposes, made this to be so. There was war on earth as well as in Heaven.

The story of those long ages, as we trace it back by the aid of science, is a great parable left for us to read on those stone registers. And one great truth God meant man to learn from it, i.e. that death must precede final life.

IV. How then do we say that "By Adam came death?" When Adam sinned, he died spiritually. We must remember that there are three kinds of death:

1.   Physical death, the cessation of animal life, the separation of the soul from the body.

---

1. Romans 5:12

2. Spiritual death, the separation of the soul and spirit from God.

3. Eternal death, which comes to human nature, which was made for glory: when it misses its end, it sinks back into a state of eternal loss.

V. Now what was it that happened to Adam? We must consider what he did not do, as well as what he did do. He had been created in the very Image of God, and had received this gift of supernatural grace. By his sin, he did not separate himself from the power of God. The whole subject of our creation and consequent union with God is a great mystery, but one thing is clear. Once created, the creature cannot separate itself from the Power of God, for, if he could do this, he would exist independently of God, and become, in fact, another God. It is impossible: we cannot do it by any means, — "In Him we live and move and have our being."[2] He is "creation's secret force,"[3] and in every step and thought He is with us and in us. We can never break away from Him. "If I climb up into Heaven, Thou art there; if I go down into hell, Thou art there also."[4] No sin, however great the shame and guilt, can separate us from the power of the Creator. We cannot annihilate ourselves, 'tis as great an act as to create. God alone can do it.

But there was one thing which Adam was able to do. By his disobedience, he could separate himself from God's favor, and the grace flowing from it. Man, made so glorious and beautiful, perfect and flooded with the wondrous gift of grace, but Adam separated himself from it by his sin.

VI. What does the supernatural grace do for Adam? We know what man has more than body and soul: he has a spiritual nature. In this spiritual nature rested the gift of grace, enabling him to see God, and know Him, to discern right from wrong, and by sin, Adam lost this gift, this grace.

Now God had made a special gift of immortality to man's spiritual and material being. There seems to have been some special protection afforded his body, and when by sin he lost grace, his soul

---

2. Acts 17:28

3. The Rev. Dr. J.M. Neal's Hymn *O God, Creation's Secret Force.*

4. Psalm 139:8

became darkened, his will and conscience weakened, and his body had no longer that protection, but fell under the laws of chemistry — (which is nothing more than the expression of the Will of God) — the law of physical death. Thus we see that, in parting from the grace of God, the soul of Adam fell under the law of spiritual death, and even his body (under physical death) suffered temporal loss.

VII. We must understand the difference between temporal and eternal loss or punishment.

Temporal punishment is like that inflicted by the state for crime, or by a parent for disobedience, but there is no logical connection between the wrongdoing, and the going to State's prison for it, or between the disobedience, and the parent's punishment. But there is a logical connection, which all can see, between the taking poison, or walking off a precipice, and the consequences, and this is like eternal or consequential punishment. These only illustrate God's work in our souls. Our temporal punishments He gives us in love, in order to win us back to Himself. His dealing with Adam is still another parable for us. He thus inflicted temporal punishment upon him, for He took His child out of the Garden of Eden to teach him how his sin had separated his soul from God, and He caused his body to come under the law of physical death to teach him the state of his soul when separated from God. The temporal was to teach him of his spiritual state or loss.

Of course, the creature could not, by his own self, get back to God or restore the relations previously existing between himself and his Creator: it had been a gift of God originally, and God must give it back again. Adam stood there with death in his soul and body, and must finally come under the condition of eternal loss or death, unless his condition should be relieved. Physical death was to teach him this truth, but the grace by which he was to win eternal life was gone.

God, in His dear love, may punish us with death, or take away His grace from us, but it is to show us our sin, and here let us remember the power Adam had given him to do something, a terrible power. He had the power of choice, and if he would, he could choose his own eternal loss.

God, though omnipotent, yet cannot sin, nor can He make $2 + 2 = 5$, nor can He make a man holy against his will. Man must love the end for which he was created — his life in God, if he wills, but the temporal punishments which do come to us are granted in love to bring back to us the grace by which we may attain to Eternal Life. Adam had lost that grace, and could not regain it of himself, and thus, "in Adam all die." God cannot prevent consequential or eternal punishment when merited. God had warned Adam in love, "in the day . . . thou shalt surely die."[5]

VIII. But in Christ all may be made alive. God sent His own Son, Who came to the world, wrapping the same human nature about Him. Our failures were not to baffle the Divine Work. He had always meant to become Incarnate.[6] By the loss of grace, humanity was in despair and needed light, and the light streamed from the Eternal Truth Who comes to lighten the world. It had been the cry from long ages, "Give us Light." It was the cry rising from the altars in Athens, and all the old philosophies, "Give us light." And in Christ God's Light was embodied in the Sun of Righteousness. He took our nature, and uttered His Word.

But we need more than light and truth. If that would have been enough, the Angels might have shown us. If a belief in a future state was enough, such a truth might have been written in the sky, and taught by Angels. We could have learned in that way that good would be rewarded and evil punished, but No! Truth, to be effectual, must be embodied, for this our Lord became Incarnate, and so acted out the Divine Life before us, that He could take our hand and say, "Follow Me."

IX. He became an Example. But in Adam we had lost grace, and we needed something more than an Example. There must be reconciliation, restoration, and this was wrought on Calvary but it is always God in Love we are to see. There was on the Cross no opposition between Father and Son. The Cross was the manifestation of the Love of God. On the Cross, the creature of God (who had lost the supernatural grave given, and thus became separated from God) by the "atonement," became united to Him again.

If an Example were all we needed, God might have made another man like Adam, and created him in perfection, or, if the At-one-ment were all, our Lord might have suffered on Calvary, and then laid our nature aside, but No! — He took it, wears it now, and will wear it forever — a continual source of union between us and God.

---

5. Genesis 2:17

6. See the footnote on page 57.

This becomes a new source of grave, so that "in Christ all are made alive," by the gift of grace, "as in Adam all died" by the loss of the grace.

X. But we want not only truth, or the power of Example, for forgiveness. —No! We want life, for body, soul, and spirit. Now, "As in Adam all die, even so in Christ shall all be made alive." Then, how, in Adam, do we all die? for it is in that same way, that in Christ we live. Do we die in Adam by thinking of him? by believing in him? by any mental act or emotion? by trusting in him? No! But we are actually descended from Adam, and our death is the result of our actual contact with him. It is thus we die in Adam, — his very blood is in our veins. "Even so In Christ" are we made alive. It is not by any emotion or mental act, or by trusting or believing merely, but as we are in Adam, so we are in Christ; by actual contact we are descended from Him. We have been inoculated with His Life, and in this way, the body, soul, and spirit have received eternal life; the God-Man infuses the Divine Life into us. His invitation to all men is to be re-created in Him.

But, if by this communication of Christ's Nature, we receive the gift of grace whereby we may attain Eternal Life, what shall we say of those who died before Christ came to us?

Our Bible and our Creed teach us that, after the Crucifixion, Christ bearing His Five Wounds went and spoke to the spirits that were in prison. That same life which he now communicates to us by material agencies in the Sacraments, He then communicated to them by His Own Word. Adam, Abraham, all the Patriarchs, received the same gift given us, because they became communicants with Christ. They received His Nature into themselves, and thus became the "spirits of just men made perfect,"[7] — and perfect, they had not been before.

XI. This work He is still carrying on, for Saints and the heathen who are walking according to their light.

We then must remember our responsibilities. Before us is Eternal Life, but there is no way to perfect our nature, but by the communication of the Incarnate Son of God. If we are baptized, we are members of Him, and may claim our rights, i.e. the gift of the Holy Spirit in Confirmation, and the feeding upon Christ Himself in the

7. Hebrews 12:23

Blessed Sacrament.

And let no one think we claim these gifts as being worthy of them. Only as desiring by them to become more worthy, for in them He gives us His own dear Life and Strength. "As in Adam all die, even so in Christ shall all be made alive."

XXI

RESURRECTION LESSONS

Fear not ye: for I know that ye seek Jesus, which was crucified. He is not here; for He is risen, as He said. —St. Matt, xxviii, 5, 6.

THE resurrection of Christ is the hard adamantine fact upon which Christianity rests. It is the great credential of Christ's mission. It is the foundation of our Christian hope, "for if Christ be not risen we are yet in our sins."[1] The difference between Christ's death and His resurrection is this: by the sacrifice of Himself, Christ made an atonement for mankind, by His resurrection He became the source of our justification. "He died for our sins," we read, "He rose again for our justification."[2] As crucified He is our propitiation, as the conqueror of death He is the source of our new life.

One of the many, certainly one of the dearest, proofs to the Christian of His resurrection is our Lord's own prophecy that He would rise. "He is not here," said the angel, "for He is risen, as He said." "As He said!" How the loving heart trusts itself to, and rests on, our Lord's promises. Believing in Him she knows all He said must be true. He made many prophecies, all of which came to pass. He prophesied as no philosopher or religious teacher ever did, that His word should go throughout the world, and so it has come to pass. He prophesied that ere that generation should pass away Jerusalem would be destroyed, and it came to pass. He prophesied that the simple act of a loving soul, breaking a box of alabaster over His feet should be told in all the world as a memorial of her. We know that this prophecy also has been fulfilled. He prophesied that St. Peter would deny Him; that one of the Apostles should betray Him; that all of them would desert Him. He prophesied that He would be delivered into the hands of wicked men and crucified. It all came to pass, "as He said." He declared how that on the third day after His crucifixion He would rise. The prophecy was made known both to His friends and His enemies. And so it came to pass "as He said." The loving heart that believes in Jesus believes in His power,

---

1. 1 Corinthians 15:17

2. Romans 4:25

and trusts His word. The body of the crucified Jesus, that very body which was taken down from the cross and laid in the tomb, rose from out it. "I know," said the angel, "that ye seek Jesus which was crucified. He is not here, for He is risen, as He said."

To understand this act of our Lord we must remember that His death, or the separation of His human soul from His body, was accomplished by His own act. "I have power," he said, "to lay down my life, and I have power to take it again."[3] It was not the pain of the crucifixion that brought about the separation, but His own act, by which the spirit was loosed from His body. To certify it to us He uttered the loud cry, and by His own word commended His spirit to the Father. But though the soul and body were thus temporarily separated, neither was parted from His divine nature. To use an old patristic illustration, they were like the warrior's sheath and sword, separated from each other as the soldier draws the latter from its scabbard. He holds the sword in his hand while the sheath hangs by his side. Neither are separated from his person. So it was with the body and soul of Christ. Though separated from each other, neither was parted from His divine nature. Consequently His body could not, like our bodies, die. His body could not see corruption. Our bodies being disjoined from the soul, their life principle comes under the disintegrating forces of nature. This is necessary in our case, in order that in our new spiritual body derived from Christ we may rise. But our Lord's body being connected with His divine nature, which was the further and supreme source of its life, was indestructible. As it lay in the tomb it was not only guarded by angels, but, as connected with His divine nature and person, an object of their adoration.

Our Lord's soul being separated from His body, went, as we know, into Hades, and there "preached," as St. Peter tells us, "to the spirits in prison."[4] All departed souls up to that time were detained, for as yet, no one, as we read, "had ascended into heaven."[5] Heaven, or the soul's union with God in the beatific vision, could not be attained until the Incarnation. It was attained first of all by the humanity of Christ, through union with the divine nature, and mankind can only attain this proffered end through union with the humanity of Christ.

---

3. John 10:18

4. 1 Peter 3:19

5. John 3:13

Until our Lord came this end could not be reached by man. He has provided the means for our attainment of it through His church and sacraments. He provided for those who had preceded Him by going into the place of departed spirits, and there communicating to them that same life He communicates to us in the sacramental system. The holy souls who were detained had received from the forerunner, John the Baptist, knowledge of His advent. When our Lord came to them, by communicating Himself through His loving utterances, those good and holy patriarchs and prophets became "the spirits of just men," or men justified by faith, "made perfect."[6] When our Lord had completed this work in the under world, His soul reunited itself to His body, and then He rose. It was not, however, like a coming back to His former condition. It was not like the resurrection of Jairus' daughter, or that of Lazarus. They returned to their former natural life. They would still have to die, but by the reunion of Christ's body and soul, human nature in His person passed through death. Death could have no more dominion over Him. Creation passed on in His person to a new stage of development. He became the completed new head of a new race; a new race of human beings, who by their union with His nature could pass on to a higher stage of existence. Man is by nature immortal, but eternal life or resurrection to glory is only secured through union with the risen God-man, Jesus Christ. Jesus Christ is the head of this new race, made capable of attaining to future union with God in glory. In Jesus Christ, those who are one with Him are elevated to a permanently divinized condition with its vouchsafed security of eternal bliss. Consequently we can see why Christ did not appear to Pilate, and Caiaphas or His other enemies. One reason was He had done His work with and for them. The works of God in the spiritual order proceed as in the natural order, from stage to stage, with ordered and fixed regularity. One geological period succeeds another and never returns to a past condition, so too, Christ had in His public life done His work for humanity. He had completed one portion of His work. His work for the world was now over and done. "I pray not," He now said, "for the world, but for those Thou hast given me out of it."[7] So in this new stage of creation into which humanity had passed, Christ gath-

---

6. Hebrews 12:23

7. John 17:9

ered about Him those and those only who were His, and who were becoming participants of His nature. Imperfect as yet, weak as they had been, nevertheless they were those God had given Him. They were His sheep, the lambs of His own fold, the sinners of His own redeeming. He appeared thus to them and to them only. They were His dear children. He called them by the most endearing terms. He comforted, restored, reestablished them in Himself. The work of the new or developed creation thus advanced a stage to its completion. It is founded in union with Himself and His risen person.

Let us consider now some lessons from His various appearances to those He loved. He first appears in the garden to Blessed Mary Magdalene. As the Holy Virgin is a type of the Church in its purity, so Mary Magdalene is a type of the Church pardoned and restored. As in the garden, man, tempted by woman, fell, so in the garden is woman made the apostle to the Apostles, and brings the knowledge of the resurrection. There in the garden God had withdrawn the super-added manifestation of His presence with its gift of grace, here by the manifestation of Himself He gives knowledge of its restoration. There he had punished woman's inconstancy, here He rewards her fidelity and devotion. At the cross our Lord spoke not to her as she heroically waited beside Him; now He makes up for that silence which she so humbly accepted, by speaking first to her.

His resurrection is not only an object lesson and proof of the future to all those who are re-created in Him, but also a pledge of our future recognition and union with those we love. Natural ties and relationships have only a natural endurance, but ties formed in grace have on them the seal of eternity. The love of the Magdalene for her Lord was to be permanent, and her recognition of Him and His word to her were to be a pledge to us. "Touch me not," He said, "for I have not yet ascended."[8] It was not to forbid her loving embrace, but to spiritualize and elevate it. She must come to realize the higher and more spiritual union between them. "Touch me not," He says not now in the old human way, "for I am not yet ascended." His word contained, however, the promise that when He had ascended He would not be separated from her. He said the same, indeed, to His disciples. Not only would the Holy Spirit be with

---

8. John 20:17

them, but "I will come unto you."[9] Abiding in His Church He would provide the means by which those who loved Him might not only kiss His holy feet, but receive Him into themselves. He would make Himself known unto them in the breaking of bread. He would feed them with the spiritual food of His most precious body and blood. He would gather their hearts and wills, their bodies and souls, into union with His own. His life would flow into their life; His virtues into them, transforming them, as they corresponded by faith and hope and love with His gift of grace. This transformation and future elevation into glory and secured condition of sinlessness and bliss no other system so fully as that of the Catholic Church and its faith and sacraments secures and makes known.

Again, consider how our Lord sought out the two wandering disciples, on the Emmaus Road. If He first appeared to the great, generous, courageous, intensely loving penitent, He next would shepherd-like seek for the straying sheep. These two disciples were in their depression wandering away from Jerusalem. They, in great distress of mind, were losing their faith. They had received a great shock. Like unto persons in our own time, they had set before them the work Christ was to accomplish.

They had conceived the kind of Kingdom He was to establish. It was to revive the ancient splendor of David and Solomon. The Roman yoke was to be broken, and in all their magnificence the ancient prophecies of a temporal kingdom would be fulfilled. So too, now, many are looking for some outward triumph of Christianity, when the world will acknowledge its supremacy, and submit itself to its rule. But as the world rose up against Christ, so finally it will rise against His representative, the Church. "When the Son of Man cometh will He find faith on the earth?"[10]

To the wandering disciples the glory that once surrounded Christ had faded away. They were disconsolate and sad at heart, and the light of faith was flickering in its socket. Then Christ puts Himself beside them. He lovingly stoops to their condition. His object is to aid them in the recovery of their faith. Little by little He opens their minds to the inner and true meaning of the Scriptures. The Messiah they looked for was not to come in the pomp and glory of an earthly

---

9. John 14:18

10. Luke 18:8

King, He was to conquer by suffering. He was to be afflicted for His brethren's sake. By his stripes we were to be healed. He was to be the priest and victim, the Lamb of God, and of His atoning death, the law, the prophets, and the psalms bore concurring witness. And as He spoke, their hearts burned within them and their faith revived and finally their eyes were opened and they knew Him, as He made Himself known in the breaking of bread.

How common is that experience of the soul's recovery of faith. It is the work of Christ and the Holy Ghost. Restored faith is the result of an acceptance of the Church's traditional interpretation of the Scriptures, and our cooperation with the grace. For we Christians live in two worlds: in the natural and material world, and that new order or world Christ has established. The natural world is upheld by God, Who is immanent in it. All its activities, and we ourselves, are upheld by the Divine power. In this world we see and know by our natural powers of reason and conscience. But the other or spiritual world, the new spiritual organism, is upheld by the God-man, Jesus Christ. What Almighty God is to the natural world, that the incarnate God is to the new spiritual world. The first is sustained by God's power, for all power comes from God; the second is sustained by grace, and grace comes forth from the humanity of Christ. In the first or natural order we walk by reason, experiment, and sight; in the other we walk by our natural powers illuminated by faith. We are in a new environment. We have the Holy Spirit in us. We have also the gift of illuminating grace, so we walk by the light, not of mere reason, but of faith.

This explains to you, beloved, why not many mighty or wise in their own conceits are Christian believers. In our time we find many intellectual persons, some of whom call themselves higher critics, who disbelieving in the supernatural, or minimizing it, are denying the miracles of the Old and New Testament, and such fundamental facts of the Christian faith as our Lord's birth of the Blessed Virgin, and the resurrection of His crucified body. They are either persons like most of the German critics, who are yet in the natural order, and not being members of the Holy Catholic Church, are not in the reception of all the sacramental means of grace Christ has left, and so are living without the sphere of the divine illumination. They are mostly moral persons, leading good useful lives, for it is in the interest of the great enemy of souls to leave such without special temptations. There are others, some in our own communion, who not corresponding with that environment as members of the divine organism of the Catholic Church, and walking chiefly by the light of natural reason, have fallen into like errors. It is impossible to convert such by argument. It can only be done by the grace of God, leading them to give up their own opinions, and to submit like little children to the decisions of the Catholic Church, in which Christ and the Holy Spirit dwell, and through whose united voice They speak. Faith, dearly beloved, is the gift of God, and real faith, as Dr. Pusey wrote, is entire. It accepts all that Christ says because He says it, and it listens to the teachings of the Holy Church as to a spiritual mother.

Again, take our Lord's appearance to Blessed Peter. Christ first seeks the wanderers, then sends His word of welcome to the broken-hearted Apostle. He had prayed for Peter especially. He did not pray that Peter should not deny the faith, for he did so. He made no prayer or promise of his infallibility. We know this by the result, for Peter who confessed our Lord to be the Son of God denied the faith when he implied He was but a man. But Christ prayed that denying the dogmatic faith, Peter's faith in Himself should not fail. And though he did thus fall, nevertheless our Lord by His look won Peter to true though bitter repentance. And now we behold our Lord in the day of His resurrection restoring Peter to the Apostleship and the place in it he had forfeited. He was the first of the Apostolic College; he was the foundation layer of the new kingdom; to him were given the keys to open it to Jew and Gentile; he was to guide the sheep and feed the lambs; he was to bring in the sheep of the old dispensation and feed the lambs of the new. This duty did not involve his having any authority over other shepherds or imply that there were other shepherds to be under him. Such an idea is rendered impossible by our Lord's saying, when St. Peter asked what his brother Apostle John should do, "What is that to thee?"[11]

We joy in St. Peter's restoration and find in it also a promise and pledge of our own; no matter how far we have gone astray, or however we may have lost our gifts of grace, Christ can restore them to us. Man says the past cannot be recalled. God says it can. "I can blot

---

11. John 21:22

out thy iniquities."[12] He can re-create the soul, He can give back all the graces we have wasted. He can restore the soul to the fullness of its lost heritage. And we see how, in the days of His resurrection, He established the means for this rehabilitation. It was at this time He established the sacrament of Baptism, and also gave to His Apostles the power of absolution. The order, we perceive, of the administration of the sacraments is different from the order of their institution. For we find Baptism and Absolution instituted after that of the Blessed Sacrament. Why is this? Because it belongs to our Lord's kingship, to make subjects of His kingdom by Baptism, or restore them by His royal power of pardon. The sacraments of Baptism and formal Reconciliation were therefore established in the days of His resurrection. He breathed on the Apostles and said, "Whosesoever sins ye remit, they are remitted,"[13] and thus left in His Church the power of restoration to penitents. It is a wonderful gift, for by the sacerdotal absolution not only is forgiveness sealed, but the stains of sin are removed and a gift of grace is given to fortify the soul against future temptation. Do not, however, suppose that our public absolutions, in our public prayer or communion office, are the exercise of this sacerdotal power. They may avail for the removal of the dust of infirmities which settle upon our souls, but they are not the exercise or communication of that gift of absolution. For that is a judicial act, and so necessitates the confession of sin to God made in the presence of the priest. In the early church confession was public, and penances were severe. So severe was the penitential discipline that it led many, in the third and fourth centuries, who believed in Christianity, nevertheless to refuse to be baptized. So the church under her spiritual guidance wisely altered her discipline. What a blessing this is to humble and loving souls. Ask any who use this means of grace what are its results. The largely concurrent opinion and the lives of the saints bear witness to its efficacy and power.

Lastly, let us consider the appearance of our Lord in the upper chamber. The terrified disciples have closed and barred the doors for fear of the Jews, when suddenly the thin air seems to yield before them and our Lord appears in the midst. He comes not only to forgive and restore, but to be in the midst of His Church, its abiding

---

12. Isaiah 43:25

13. John 20:23

strength. Thus the true church of Christ has within it a resurrection power. Nothing can destroy it. The Roman Empire plotted its destruction and sought by persecution to stamp it out. The great flood of barbaric invasions swept over Europe, but failed to sweep it away. The rise of Mohammedan fanaticism which once seemed to threaten its destruction, met finally its own defeat. Heresy after heresy rose within the church, but the Holy Spirit speaking through the church's ecumenical councils, preserved, by new definitions, the faith which had been received from the beginning. The worldliness and sensuality, which invaded the church from within and presented so ghastly a spectacle at Rome in the tenth and other centuries, passed away conquered by religious orders and the lives of the saints.

The modern spirit of rationalism can no more overthrow the Catholic faith than that of former attacks. As the discoveries of Copernicus and Galileo only made more clear the faith they seemed at first to contradict, so the discoveries of modern science are only strengthening the Catholic position respecting God and Christ. The disintegrations of Protestantism are showing to thoughtful men the necessity of having some more solid basis of belief than that of "the Bible and the Bible only." Attacked again and again as the Church has been by the winds and waves which have seemed almost to engulf her, nevertheless the earnest cry of the ship-men has caused Christ to rise and at His rebuke there has been a great calm.

Of all portions of Christianity perhaps none have gone through greater trials than that of the Anglican Church. For more than a century she was struggling with Protestantism on the one hand, and Papalism on the other. She was almost crushed out of existence under the iron heel of Cromwell. The secession of the non-Jurors drained her episcopate of its learning and its spiritual life. The Erastianism of the eighteenth century and its cold legality scarce left her alive. The bitter and ignorant opposition of the nineteenth century to the revival of the Church's life, drove many of her devoted sons to Rome. Yet in spite of all opposition, the validity of her orders and efficacy of her sacraments have demonstrated themselves by their results. The body that was thought to be dead has arisen. The Church has vindicated her Apostolic descent and catholicity.

The Religious life for men and women has been revived. The Holy Sacrifice is being offered daily on many altars. The ceremonial and ornaments that mark the Real Presence of Christ in the Eucharist are being restored. The Church, filled with a fresh love for her Lord and zeal for humanity, is going forth to a world-wide mission. Angels are guarding her. The saints are interceding for her. The Holy Ghost is inspiring her. Her sons and daughters are being found in every part of the world among the heathen, and the worse heathen in our great city slums; yielding up their lives in the Master's service. It is a glorious and blessed cause.

What part have we in this work? How do we stand towards it. Are we letting it pass by unheeding the call for help? Are we too absorbed in pleasure, or gain, or the world's interests to recognize it? Are we missing the day of our visitation and its eternal reward? Are we doing what we can and all we can for the great cause? There is none greater on earth; none dearer to God, none more profitable for our own and other souls. Upon the Catholization of the Anglican Church hangs the destiny of Christendom. What shall we personally do toward it? What reply shall we make to Christ's call? One thing is there, and one thing only, in this world entirely worth knowing, and that is God's will in our regard.

One thing is there in this world, and one thing only, entirely worth the doing, and that is conformation to His will.

XXII

AN AMERICAN RELIGIOUS COMMUNITY

August 15th, 1885

I T is because some who have authority to speak in the Church have asked me to write something on the formation of an American Community of clergy and laymen, dedicated in the Religious Life, which will aid their brethren having parochial charges, that I send this letter to you. Though having now more than twenty years' experience in this country and in England in connection with Religious Communities of both men and women, I yet feel that one's views on such a subject should be put forth submissively to the greater wisdom of the Church, and as liable to be corrected by it.

It is noticeable that, in any portion of Christendom blest with a priesthood and Sacraments, and thus fully organized for its work, great religious movements are usually accompanied by the formation of societies of persons associated together under various rules of Christian living. The Life of Christ manifests its power in an increased desire of conformity to itself. Souls, as by a heavenly illumination, catch sight of the inner principles of that Divine Life of self-sacrifice and are brought by a divine call together in order the better to make those principles their own. This has been the case in both the Latin and Anglican Churches at various epochs of their history. The freedom allowed to individual action in the Anglican Communion has led to a large number of separate efforts, which, as organizations, have met with various degrees of success. Some, because they neglected the Church's order, or through the mistakes attending all new efforts, or because they were not needed for the Church's present work, have failed to attain permanence. Nevertheless, at no time has the presence of the Holy Spirit more certainly manifested itself than in our own day by the revival of the Religious Life in our midst.

It is said that Cardinal Newman has in the Birmingham oratory a picture of Oxford, crowded as it is with the towers and spires of its numerous churches, and underneath this symbolized representation of the Anglican Communion has written the words: "Can these dry bones live?" Lacordaire declared that the Religious Life was the fairest fruit of the Catholic Church, and only where there was a true priesthood and Sacraments could it be found. And now, after these many years, the answer comes from a hundred houses and a thousand "Religious" that the English Church is indeed a true branch of the Church of Christ, and that the highest developments of Christ's Power and Life are seen within her.

Much has been done in America; the Sisterhoods of St. Mary, St. John Baptist, St. Margaret, St. Barnabas and others, filled as they are with many bright examples of the Life, show how the American women have responded to their Master's call.[1]

As regards orders of men, while something has already been accomplished (for which God be thanked) yet, as the aspirations and counsels of many devout persons show, there is room for a society different from any now working in the Church and one not engaged, save temporarily, in parochial work. In such a society there would be a place for clergy of various talents and also for highly educated and devout laymen. These latter would not occupy the place of lay brothers in the society, but would have on profession the same privileges as the clergy. Such an association wisely formed could do a great work for God by its life of study and prayer and by aiding the bishops and clergy in their missionary and parochial labors. Its life of sacrifice and entire self-consecration would witness to the Church's belief in the unseen world and the power of her Sacramental gifts enabling her sons to reject honors and wealth, and live above nature. It would help to dissipate the spirit of worldliness and self-satisfied respectability which hangs over the Church like a miasma poisoning her life. It would, by its constant intercession, ceasing not day nor night, bring a blessing on many a lonely worker in his

---

1. "In every age of the Church's history we find in time of trial woman standing by the side of man, and vying with him in his work for Christ. Though the Priesthood was, for reasons, to be filled exclusively by men, yet Our Blessed Lord did not by this lower woman's privilege or woman's position, for 'He was incarnate by the Holy Ghost of the Virgin Mary,' and ever since the days of that Virgin Mother woman has repeated her words, 'Behold the handmaid of the Lord.' Early was her work organized, and made a powerful auxiliary for the propagation of the faith, by means of those quiet and gentle ministries, which are often the mightiest. And it is an indication, not a slight one, that we are getting back more and more toward primitive and Catholic methods, that we are reviving the Order of Deaconesses and instituting Sisterhoods to aid the Church's work of love and mercy. . ." (Sister Mary Hilary, CSM, *Ten Decades of Praise*, Ch. 9)

labors and make the whole heart of the Church beat quicker with the answered gifts of grace. It would throw open to all the clergy a place for short periods of retirement and prayer for their own spiritual refreshment, and aid them in their parishes by supplying preachers for the Church's seasons of Advent and Lent, by giving retreats, quiet days and missions, and by taking charge temporarily of vacant parishes or missions which the bishops might wish to assist.

And not only within the Church could the influence be felt. In our country the contest between Christianity and unbelief, righteousness and evil, is obviously deepening; and the realization of this makes the spiritually minded of all Christian bodies look somewhat anxiously towards each other. As the net breaks, the toilers beckon to their partners to come and help them. If our Church has anything of value to contribute she must show it, not on paper, but embodied as a life. A Church on paper, like a Christ on paper, will as little affect the world as the surpassing beauty of "that countenance which is fading on the walls of the refectory at Milan." If the Church is possessed, as she claims, with special Sacramental gifts of grace, the Life of the Incarnate Lord within her must show itself in lives specially conformed to His own. A society of sincere, unselfish, humble-minded men, unostentatious in their piety, seeking no honors, giving up all for Christ and laboring for Him alone, would effectually aid the Church to manifest this Life.

Never in any age or country was there a greater opportunity to serve Christ. Never a portion of the Church where a few, even without great natural gifts, could do greater things for Him. More clergy are indeed needed everywhere and nothing here said must be taken in disparagement of the Church's wisdom in giving us an Order of married parochial clergy adorned as it is with devoted and noble lives. But the Religious Life is no revival of medievalism. It has always existed in the Christian Church. It is an integral portion of her life. The Church is not fully equipped for her work without it; wherever in any portion of Christendom it has been wanting the Church has suffered. It was instituted by the Lord Himself. Like the work of God, it has been at times greatly perverted and misused, but its perversion is no disproof of its divine origin.

The Master Himself gave the counsels of perfection and said: "He that is able to receive, let him receive it."[2] The counsels unite the soul in a special way to Christ, and the Religious Life becomes an instrumentality for the extension of the divine energy latent in the Life of Christ. It has a power, when in a community form, different from that which comes from organization. The world can make organizations and is ever, in and out of the Church, weaving and unweaving them. A Religious Community is a special work of the Holy Spirit manifesting the Incarnate Lord's triumph over nature, testifying against worldliness, witnessing of the unseen glories of man's coming union with God. Preaching the cross from the cross, it draws men to the Master with an efficacy all its own.

And if ever the constraining force of redeeming love called men to this Life, surely it does so now by the unparalleled splendor of the opportunity for effective service and by the agonies of the Church as she gathers her energies for her last great conflict with evil. Shall we not see a fuller development of this Life in our Church? Will not the prayers and the sufferings and the sacrifices of so many who have waited and labored for this consolation of our Israel find a response?

It is not the hardness of the Life, though far less than that of many of our western missionaries, that will deter Americans from entering into it. The American clergy are not cowards, they are as patient of discipline for any recognized good end as any nation, and are not wanting in devotion to their Lord. What others, what Americans in the Roman Church are doing, what women in our Church are doing, they can do. The sacraments are as full of grace to us as they were to the saints of old. It is an infidelity to our Blessed Lord to say His grace cannot make, or but rarely, Americans "religious," and that they can succeed only when mixed in with a predominating number of another race.

The reasons why those, not held back by worldly-minded considerations or whose position has not been already determined, do not seek this Life are for the most part such as these; men do not realize the importance and value of this Life to the Church, or they have become engaged in some Church work and think they are necessary to it, or they do not know whether they are adapted to the Life and feel they cannot trust themselves, or they have not seen the Life presented in a form which attracts them or commands their confidence.

---

2. Matthew 19:12

It may help any really seeking to know God's will, to meditate on the fact that this Life, like that of the priesthood, is the product of a divine call. "Ye have not chosen me, but I have chosen you."[3] This call to 'Religion' is the exercise of our Lord's sovereignty calling whom He will, however weak or feeble they may seem to themselves, away from any work in which they may be engaged, however important. The call is at once a warrant and a pledge. A warrant for one to come, and a pledge of help. It is an assurance that God will provide for all He calls us to leave, and that He will give all needed grace to sustain us in the Life. He betroths the soul to Himself in an espousal, taking it "for better, for worse," and will never leave or forsake it even if it should stray from Him, but will seek it out and recover it, and claim it for His own.

As to the character of a society which shall win the confidence of the Church and attract members by its wisdom and unselfishness and by reflecting the love and beauty of Christ's crucified and risen Life, in an article like this only some general principles can be stated.

I. Such a society must not be an imitation or attempted reproduction of anything in the past.

This has been a source of failure in some cases. One clergyman in England tried to revive the Franciscan Order; another has tried to reproduce the Benedictine. In neither case did any of the clergy unite themselves to them. It was suggested by an able writer in your paper not long since that a type would be better found in the Oratorians. This was Dr. Pusey's advice to the writer some twenty years ago. There is much to be said in favor of such an idea as relates to the interior life and discipline; but, so far as the general government is concerned, it is a bad model for us to follow. A society formed of independent houses, without a central novitiate, would among us soon develop great diversities of practice and life. No! To succeed in the America of our day the foundation of a society must be the work of the Holy Spirit working in our Church and producing that which is needed for our own times. It will not be an imitation but an original work. It will not be the work of good men enthusiastically experimenting with holy things and so sure to fail, but of those called of God to the work of founding a society, and through whom He will speak. He will speak and His word will endure. For

---

3. John 15:16

"His word shall not return unto Him void but shall accomplish that whereto he sends it."[4]

II. The society must be an American one.

The Religious Life does indeed lift us above all nationalities unto Oneness in Christ. In any society there might therefore be found men of all countries and kindreds working harmoniously together. But the Religious Life does not lift any above the Church's order or make any superior to its law of jurisdiction. It has been said that the religious vows are superior to a priest's ordination vows; but such a theory would, I hope, be almost universally rejected. A society in our Church, therefore, cannot legitimately have its head in another Church, whether Greek, English, or Roman; if it does, the inherent disregard of the Church's order will eventually show itself in some disaster.

III. Again, if a society is to succeed, it must grow out of the real wants of the Church and be able to meet them.

Now there are several departments of service requiring associated clerical labor. Such a work is needed in our large towns in attacking the sin and destitution found therein in certain localities. It is needed in certain missionary districts in the country for the extension and planting of the Church. It is perhaps needed in the special work our Church is now being called to do among the colored people at the South. These useful labors do not, however, necessarily require that the workers should be organized or dedicated as "Religious." The work can be done as well by clergy simply associated temporarily together in clergy houses. This fact, so far as city needs are concerned, is clearly seen by the efficient work done in London, at All Saints', St. Alban's, St. Peter's in the East, and many other places. It would be a help for all such clergy to be under some rule of life as the associates of some Religious Order, but not to be full or professed members. For it may seriously be questioned whether the experiment of trying to combine the needed discipline, hours, study, poverty, recitation of the many Offices, etc., of a Religious house, with the care of modern parishes or with city missionary work is not a mistake. But let this be as it may, there is a clearly recognized need of a society removed from the daily care of parochial charges, whose members

---

4. Isaiah 55:11

shall give themselves to study and prayer and to the assistance of
their brother clergy. Some of the ways in which such a society could
afford assistance have been previously stated. The point here we
would insist upon is, that such work needs an Order of "Religious"
and can be well done by them alone. It needs men unharassed with
parochial care, and so able to live in their own house undistractedly
their life with God and free to go out at the call of others.

IV. A society formed for such work should have Episcopal
approval.

When clergy combine under rule and obedience, and form a society, they become a power in the Church, and the Church has a
right, if it sees fit, to legislate concerning such societies. Apart, however, from the question of legislation, if such a society wishes to be
established in a Churchly way it must seek Episcopal approval. In
the Roman Church, as is well known, any tentative effort may be
begun with the approval of the diocesan authorities; but to obtain
further recognition it must receive the approval of the Holy See,
which is only obtained after a long and patient examination of its
proposed constitution and rules by a body of clergy whose special
business it is to have charge of all matters relating to Religious Orders. If approved, the society is first allowed the rights pertaining
to a "congregation," and is so-called. After many years it may obtain the further privileges of an "Order." In the first case, though
approved by the Church, yet any Bishop may decline to allow its
entrance into his diocese. Without being in some way established by
the Church, the society is a merely human one, and the authority of
its Superiors is such only as may be granted them by election. In our
own communion there has been, to speak with loving plainness, an
unwillingness on the part of some of the advanced school to trust
the Bishops. This arose partly from a feeling that the Bishops were
out of sympathy with everything Catholic and would persistently
confound it with Romanism; and partly from the natural self-will
of the reforming spirit that wants to give a lesson to its brethren in
poverty, chastity and obedience, but does not propose to begin the
lesson by giving up its own will. So the difficulty of a Superior not
having any Churchly-derived authority has sometimes been met by
saying that he is directly called by God and so should be obeyed, in
all things not obviously sinful, as God's voice. There is involved in

this, the danger pointed out by our Lord of following some man and calling him Master; and which led to the rise under ascetic and devout men of Arianism, Calvinism, Wesleyanism, Irvingism, Swedenborgianism, etc.

Now the Episcopate is a divine order, and to it especially the government of the Church has been entrusted. The divisions of Christendom do not make the voice of any Bishop of less authority who honestly seeks to express the faith and practice of the United States and the law of his own communion. If God trusts the government of His Church to the Bishops, we also ought to trust them, and a society in its various stages of formation should seek their counsel and approval. Until the latter has formally been obtained the society is not formed and established. The answer to the question what should be submitted for such approval and what such approval is to cover, is: all that by virtue of the rules and practices of the society is of obligation on its members. No Bishop can give his official sanction to a society simply because he approves generally of its life, purpose, and work. His recognition must mean more than this to be of value, and all that it covers should be submitted to him.

V. It is not for the sake of gaining any, the least, favor from those who are opposed to the Religious Life as such and the doctrines of Sacramental grace connected with it, but because an open and honest avowal of felt dangers is the best way for their removal, that I would state the next principle to be that the society in its teaching should be loyal to the Church.

There should be no other standards of doctrine than those of our own communion, and these should be recognized as such in the constitution of the society. This is necessary, not only to command the confidence of the Church, but for the protection of the society itself. The Church should feel assured that the society has no occult objects, political or ecclesiastical; is not seeking to bring in a foreign theology or to undo, if that were possible, the work of the Reformation. The priests of the society should feel that they were not to be committed by the extravagant utterances of individual members, and also were free from the dangers of being moulded by some one powerful mind to peculiar views and so become the vehicle of a new theology. Seeking to present Christ as the power of God unto salvation, delivering the sinner from condemnation by the merits of His precious blood, and saving him from his sins and raising him to holiness by His life, the doctrinal statements of the Book of Common Prayer and the Sacraments are sufficient for the purpose. To such a society, loyal to the Church, broad in its sympathies, true in its life, practical in its teaching, the doors of churches of various schools would be thrown open, because their Rectors would feel that their parishes would not be upset by peculiarities, or galvanized into spasmodic activity by sensationalism, but the presence of such missioners could not but bring a permanent blessing.

VI. IF THEY ARE TO BE MEN OF SUCH A CHARACTER, IT IS OBVIOUS THAT THE SOCIETY SHOULD HAVE ITS OWN DEFINITE SPIRIT.

A Religious Society is not an agglomeration of Christians, each pursuing his own spiritual fancies, but one having, as part of its own divine call and foundation, its own religious spirit. For societies differ from societies, and Orders from Orders, and in nothing more are they seen to differ than this: their vows and the spirit of devotion they embody. In the Roman Church some societies have only simple, and under certain conditions, terminable vows; others allow of vows of a mixed character, vows of profession intentionally for life on the part of the offerer, but without agreed permanent acceptance on the part of the society; in others, the vows are solemn with a stipulated power of dispensation reserved to the authorities of the society, or remaining with such stipulation of power only in the Pope.

In some a further vow "of stability" is taken, which binds the member not only to the Life, but to the Life in that society only. In some the support of the interests of the Holy See forms another vow. They differ also greatly in the emphasis put on the separate vows one making poverty the chief feature, like the Franciscans; another, like the Jesuits, emphasizing obedience. Now as to vows in our own Church, without stating here more fully the provisions and conditions under which they might be taken, yet, as in every case in the Roman communion, it should be under the implied condition of a power lodged somewhere whereby for grave cause one might be wholly or partially relieved from his obligations.

The societies of the Roman Church, especially the modern Orders, differ still more in their devotions. One Order will be devoted to the cultus of the Sacred Heart; another, to the Passion; another, to the Blessed Virgin, and they are named after these devotions. In the

English Church some of this tendency may be seen. Now in respect to the spirit of devotion, what it comes to me to submit to the kindly judgment of those Bishops and clergy who may sympathize with any effort for the establishment of a community, is this: it seems fitting that the spirit of a society which, like our Lord's Life, would be in its labors both contemplative and active, and which should go out not only to win souls to Christ, but to build them up in Him, should take as its special devotion, and seek a special conformity to, the interior Life of our Lord. Not to any one portion of His Life, but the whole Life, hidden, public, suffering, and risen. It seems wiser and safer to look to Jesus alone, to Jesus only, to Jesus entirely, to Jesus wholly, to let the loving and divine Heart be the source of all our grace, the inspiration of our actions, and the model of our own. This will give an interpretation to those counsels, upon which the life of all Religious Communities is based, peculiarly its own. We are called not only to follow Christ laboring and suffering and winning His way to the establishment of His Kingdom, but have by the Holy Spirit been incorporated into union with a risen and triumphant Lord, whose victories participating in we extend. The society in every part of its rule will not only have the cross inwrought into it as a principle of life, but will be possessed with the gladness and peace of the Resurrection and the brightness and joy reflected from the Glorified Lord. The Life will not be one of that depressing asceticism which seeks to attain Heaven by its own holiness, or its members be trained to become corpses, dead to everything but the will of a Superior.

If the Life unites us to His Spirit of chastity, Who on the Cross cared for His Blessed Mother, it cannot be such a spirit as would make us dead to all human affection. We cannot learn to love God more by loving man, for whom He died, less. The purity God delights in subdues nature by grace, casts out selfishness, purifies the motives, makes the inward eye single, inflames the heart with a supreme, obedient, effectual love to Himself. It binds the "Religious" in a wedded bond of union to the Lord as her spouse.

If the Life joins us to the Master's poverty, Who not only was born in the poverty of the manger and the carpenter's low estate, but Who voluntarily abandoned home and family and had no place whereon to lay His Head, yet the poverty need not array itself in dirt or neglect the laws of health, or be any more ostentatious than His own. The practice of Religious poverty must indeed be true and real though different from that that was practicable in simpler and ruder times. There will also be a real hatred of worldliness in all its forms; the seeking to gain its wealth or influence by the accommodations of Christian conduct to its standards, or that transplanted worldliness which gives up personal ownerships but seeks to acquire wealth and power for one's society. If poverty is true, its motive will be the love of Jesus. Jesus poor, Jesus scorned, Jesus destitute of earthly power, Jesus rejecting an earthly kingdom, Jesus triumphed over by His enemies. It will be a love which will bind us to His self-abandoning repose on His Father's care and protection. It will be an extension of the victory of His choice of the cross over all the proffered glories of the kingdoms of the world.

If the Religious Life binds us to Christ, Who, from infancy to His cross, was bound by the swaddling bands of the Father's will revealed through human instruments and the written Word and the Spirit's leadings, it is not such an obedience as will on principle seek to crush the inward mind and judgment. Wherever a Superior orders that which is obviously morally wrong or is against the Church's law, he thereby terminates his own authority. The Superior should represent the Church, and govern by a rule She has approved. He should be aided in the determination in all the important matters by the advice of a council chosen by the brethren, and he, whose lot it is to bear rule, should be among them "as he that serveth."[5] When the heart is emptied of self, Jesus will be recognized as standing in the midst, and in His heart as in their true Center all wills will be as one.

CHARLES C. GRAFTON.

---

5. Luke 22:27

XXIII

To Candidates for Holy Order

Lent 1892

MY DEAR SON IN CHRIST,
It was my expectation to have seen you and all my Candidates and Postulants this Lent, but I have been unable to do so, and in place, send to you all this circular letter.

Naturally, you will at this time, by special prayers and meditations, be striving to deepen your own spiritual life and get a more vigorous perception of your vocation.

It is a special act of love for God to call us out, not only from the world, but from the ranks of ordinary Christians, to become associated with Himself in the awful dignity of His Priesthood, and to become living examples, by the transformation of our characters, of the reality and power of Divine Grace. You are hereafter as Priests, to be associated with Him in His tremendous work of saving souls from the power of sin and delivering them from its thraldom. You are to take part, as soldiers of Christ, in the great conflict which enlists on one side or the other, all the powers of good and evil in heaven and earth. In union with Jesus Christ and through the power of His spirit, you are to save souls from being eternally lost, and to train them in holiness for union with God in glory.

There is no dignity so high, no responsibility so great, no work so noble, no reward so blessed, no life more full of beatitude, than that of a faithful Priest. It is a singular mark of God's predestinating love that He calls any of us into this association with Himself.

What I want you to make as the very fiber of your whole moral and intellectual nature, and to become stamped in on your mind and burnt into your will, that you will at all times be governed by it, is this fact, that your success as a minister of Christ depends on the conformity of your life to His.

We are not merely teachers of truths, who perform our office chiefly by preaching. We are not like men of other professions, whose success may not be affected by their lives. Our success in delivering men from sin and making them holy, depends on the extent of our own self-victory and our own increasing sanctification. Natural abilities, learning, powers of speech or administration, make men popular. They help men to get on. They bring the reward that will perish. But they are not the sources of the Priest's real strength. To draw others to Christ, the Priest must be a spiritual magnet filled with divine energy. To deliver others, he must have fought a terrible fight with the world, the flesh, and the devil in himself. To win others to a real self-surrender, to a life separated from the world, he must himself be separated in life, aims, and conduct from it. To make men willing to submit to the mortification of true penitence, the Priest must preach the Cross from the Cross. His whole life must be united to Christ, not only as the Priest and advocate, but to Him as the Victim and the Lamb slain. He must become a Man of God and bear in every part of his life the brand of the Cross, if he is to compel others by the spiritual power in him, to be separated from the world and bear the Cross. You must put, my sons, nothing less than this before you, if you want the "well-done" at last and the eternal reward.

There are a number of clergy in our day, who do not put this high standard before them or seek to conform their lives to the life of Christ crucified. There are those who go in, as they say, for what they can get, whose lives are governed by secondary motives, who are popular, successful, and will probably be well spoken of when they die, but who will wake up to find the Master saying, "You lived for yourself, not for me, and you have had your reward."[1] They will say, "Lord, Lord, have we not prophesied in Thy Name, and in Thy Name done many wondrous works; built churches, presented large classes for confirmation, aided many charitable enterprises, preached the Gospel?" He will say, "I know you not,"[2] for it is true now, as it was in the days of St. Chrysostom and other fathers who declared that a large number of the clergy would certainly be lost, a larger proportion probably than of any other profession.[3]

This is in itself very terrible to think of, but it applies to those who have no high aim concerning the Priesthood, no real purpose of self-consecration, who look away from the Cross and not to it, who

---

1. Matthew 6:2

2. Matthew 7:21–23

3. There is a saying commonly attributed to St. Chrysostom that goes: "The road to hell is paved with the skulls of bishops." What he really wrote was: "I do not think there are many among Bishops that will be saved, but many more that perish" (*3rd Homily on the Acts of the Apostles*)

do not realize to what Christ calls them and trust in His grace. For to aim high, to take the stricter line, to make sacrifice for Christ's service, is the way of safety. Christ's grace will never be wanting to those who have abandoned themselves to His protection. He loves men of great desires and aspirations as he did Daniel, and will provide all things necessary for their fulfillment. The only difficult and dangerous clerical line is that of half-hearted service and worldly conformity and prudential reserve. If our hearts are wholly with Him, His grace will be sufficient for us. His word "come" will sustain us in our venture on the water. The only thing you need fear, is the listening to some old and deceitful prophet, who bids you take a more comfortable and lower standard, or, if with generous devotion to our blessed Lord, you are determined to seek for nothing less than sanctity, dependence in any way upon yourself. The foundation of the saint is, distrust self. Grow in this distrust. Trust God. The sacraments are as full of grace now as when they made the heroes and the martyrs and the saints of old.

Another matter I wish to speak to you about is your life as seminarians. There is a danger, especially among men who have never been in any institution before, to look upon the seminary as if it were a college. Now, the spirit of a theological seminary should be very different from that of a college, not only in its discipline, good order, devotion, its sobriety in manners, its edifying conversation, and in the spirit of piety which should pervade it, but in the relation of seminarians one to another. We stand in very different and in closer relations to one another than the members of a college. The relation between college students is a temporary one. They are independent one of another. Each has come with his own ulterior aim in life, each is to use or waste by his choice, the provided equipment for his future life. The collegian is not therefore bound to feel concerned in the success of his fellow-student, or in any way to exercise supervision of his conduct. The latter he would rather regard as a dishonorable thing. But it is very different in a seminary. We are united together by a divine call to be trained as officers in the army of Christ. We are to form, thus, one body. As the success of an army depends upon the fidelity of all its different members, so any unfaithfulness to Christ on the part of any one works an injury to all. We are bound therefore by every principle of honor, by the trust Christ reposes in us, by our allegiance to Him and His interest to guard the discipline, the spirit, the devotion, the spiritual life, of the seminary. As in the army, an officer would deem it disgraceful not to report neglect of duty of which he was cognizant on the march or in the field, so that same spirit of honor should animate you when any one is known, as the Apostle says, to be walking disorderly. Let no mistaken sense of fellowship or good-nature or indifference blind you to your duty as an officer of the army, to your loyalty to Christ. By your own diligence and faithfulness, try to increase the spirit of devotion in your comrades, and with that high sense of honor which marks the military profession protest against everything in others which mars the effectiveness of the service. You are in training to be men of God. You are to be spiritual athletes. You are to be men of high moral character, men of firm resolve in matters of duty, men watchful over your own conduct, lest a world hateful of religion should be able in you to find any cause of offense. You are Christ-bearers. Christ trusts Himself to you by giving you the Blessed Sacrament; He trusts His Sacred Presence to your care. He relies on your honor to guard himself against insult. Guard His Presence in you. Like true Knights, determine to die, rather than do what is wrong. If thy hand or thy foot offend thee, cut it off, for it is better for thee to enter life maimed than, having both hands and feet, to be cast into hell-fire.

There is a third matter about which I want to speak to you. You are my Candidates for Holy Orders. In admitting you to the Sacred Ministry, I take a grave responsibility. It is a responsibility which weighs upon my heart when I think of the number who have been unpreparedly admitted to Holy Orders. It is not because I do not trust you all, but because I love you, and earnestly desire you may be most useful here and reach the highest rewards hereafter that I write this. When you came to me, I had not formulated the rules for my candidates, which I now must do. If any of you feel you cannot accept them, I will transfer you without blame, to any other Bishop you may choose. But we are living at a time when the Church's faith and practice is assaulted within and without, when men are denying the inspiration of Scripture, the reality of our Lord's Resurrection in the flesh, the vicarious character of His offering on Calvary, and the oil and wine of the Priesthood and the Sacraments. The Church needs trained men, devoted men, faithful men, who will live and die for her faith, men who are willing to cast their lives at the feet of Christ, men who will answer back the love of Christ who died for them by the responsive love which gives themselves and all they are to Him. Only by such a spirit can this Church of ours be saved. If you have anything of this spirit, I ask you to follow me. I ask no man to do what I am not willing to do myself. I ask no man to make sacrifices in which I do not lead and share. I believe with my whole heart this Church of ours can be saved and the dead bones as in Elijah's vision come together and be filled with life. And I believe an outpouring of the Holy Ghost throughout the whole Church of Christ has already begun, and that men and women are giving themselves up to a consecrated life with such enthusiastic devotion to the interests of Jesus as to recall the Pentecostal days. It is a blessed privilege to fight for Jesus in such days as these. Fear nothing. Hope for everything. With God nothing is impossible. This is my motto and I pray it may be yours, "Jesus our All, and our all for Jesus."

Now, without asking you to consecrate your lives entirely to Christ's service as celibate priests, I do ask you to pray over it and ask God to give you the grace for the state of life which He Himself instituted, and to which He has given a special blessing.[4] It is now as when "The ark, and Israel and Judah abide in tents; and the servants of my Lord are encamped in the open field;"[5] and it is to a self-denying priesthood, and the offering of the Daily Sacrifice that the conquest of the world is given. While a celibate consecration is what I want you to think and pray about, there are some other minor matters of sacrifice which I must insist upon. If you wish to continue my candidates, during your candidateship I must ask you to promise to abstain from the use of all intoxicating beverages, save as used medicinally and under direction; to give up the use of tobacco, not to dance, play cards, nor to visit saloons or theaters. At the seminary I wish you to wear your cassocks at Church, in the refectory, and at recitations. I also request you, as it is more clerical, to remain shaven, if you do not wear full beards. Respecting these things I am only laying down rules for you while in training for the Priesthood.

If you will remember how the Disciples were trained by Christ for

---

4. Though less common than at other points in our history, clerical celibacy has remained a virtue within the Anglican Tradition. The Saintly Richard Baxter writes: "If he that marrieth not doth better than he that doth marry, surely ministers should labor to do that which is best. And if he that can 'receive this saying,' must receive it, we should endeavor after it. This is one of the highest points of the Romish policy... It is a pity that for a better cause we can no more imitate them in self-denial, where it might be done." (*The Reformed Pastor*, Ch. 3 §1)

5. 2 Samuel 11:11

their work, how minute His rules were,[6] and consider that your work is no different from theirs, viz. the advancement of a Kingdom upon which the eternity of souls depends, you will not deem these things either unwise or harsh. You will rejoice at every act of discipline which binds you closer to the Apostles and to the hero Saints of the Church. The Kingdom of Heaven suffereth violence, and the violent take it by force. The good soldier of Jesus Christ must learn to endure hardness. If St. Paul found it necessary to beat his body with blows in order to bring it into subjection, we cannot afford to miss any discipline which may advance us in sanctity. In this present time of distress, when the gates of hell are pressing against the Church, and she is calling for better-trained and more devoted warriors, let us not be cowards. As we realize how the heart agony of Christ is being prolonged and the Spirit's converting and convicting power hindered by the inefficiency of the Priesthood, let us try to mitigate that agony and further the Spirit's work, by casting ourselves and our little all of this present brief time on earth into the furnace fire of the Sacred Heart of our Blessed Lord.

With my love, prayers, and blessing,
YOUR FRIEND AND BISHOP.

---

6. Matthew 10